Gender and Home-Based Employment

Gender and Home-Based Employment

Edited by
Charles B. Hennon
Suzanne Loker
Rosemary Walker

AUBURN HOUSE
Westport, Connecticut • London

Library of Congress Cataloging-in-Publication Data

Gender and home-based employment / edited by Charles B. Hennon, Suzanne Loker,
  Rosemary Walker.
     p. cm.
  Includes bibliographical references and index.
  ISBN 0–86569–271–8 (alk. paper)
  1. Home-base businesses.   2. Home labor.   3. Sex role in the work environment.
  4. Women—Employment.   5. Men—Employment.   I. Hennon, Charles B.   II. Loker,
  Suzanne.   III. Walker, Rosemary Adams, 1931–
  HD2333.G46   2000
  331.25—dc21   99–054266

British Library Cataloguing in Publication Data is available.

Library of Congress Catalog Card Number: 99–054266
ISBN: 0–86569–271–8

First published in 2000

Auburn House, 88 Post Road West, Westport, CT 06881
An imprint of Greenwood Publishing Group, Inc.
www.greenwood.com

Printed in the United States of America

The paper used in this book complies with the
Permanent Paper Standard issued by the National
Information Standards Organization (Z39.48–1984).

10 9 8 7 6 5 4 3 2 1

This book is dedicated to

Deanna, the love of my life and the reason I try to work at home.
cbh

Tom, an explorer of home-based employment.
sl

The original NE-167 researchers, especially Ramona Heck and Mary Winter.
rw

And to home-workers everywhere and the professionals who are interested in
home-based employment

Contents

Illustrations

Acknowledgments

Many people have helped in making this book a reality. Chuck Hennon, Suzanne Loker, and Rosemary Walker would like to thank Jane Garry of Auburn House for making the publication of this book possible and for her patience in seeing the process through to the end. We also want to thank Marcia Goldstein and Susan Thornton for all they did to get this book into shape. Especially, we want to say how grateful we are to Rebecca Ardwin for her helpful advice and assistance as the production editor for this project. The members of the Cooperative Regional Research Project, NE-167, entitled *At-Home Income Generation: Impact on Management, Productivity and Stability in Rural and Urban Families*, supported and encouraged the creation of this book. We also acknowledge the contributions made by each chapter author and all the people who assisted in the production of these chapters.

Chapter 1

Home-Based Employment: Considering Issues of Gender

Charles B. Hennon, Suzanne Loker, and Rosemary Walker

INTRODUCTION

This is a book about men and women engaged in home-based employment for pay or profit. The focus is on gender and its influence on the type of work individuals do as well as their work processes and outcomes. Because of the spatial link between these workers and their families' living activities, a study of home-workers provides a unique opportunity to study paid-work and family interaction with a special emphasis on gender differences and similarities.

Traditionally, women dominated the home front as the so-called bread-makers with major responsibilities for child care and household chores; men were mainly considered to be breadwinners, providing the money income for the family. Increasingly, however, men and women engage in similar patterns of paid employment activity. Home-based employment seems an ideal situation to explore whether or not the traditional gender division of labor still influences what men and women do for pay and family as well as the outcomes of their efforts. For example, do home-workers take on different types of employment than on-site workers, or do they tend to follow the same gender conventions when choosing jobs? How do the motivations for choosing home-based employment differ from the motivations for choosing on-site employment? Do home-workers manage their work in the same way as on-site workers? Is being a home-worker associated with a different division of family and household labor, or different home-management practices, from the patterns associated with on-site workers? Are outcomes, such as economic rewards, human capital development, or "psychic income," different for home-workers? And, importantly, what are the differences and similarities associated with the gender of the worker both among home-workers and in comparison to on-site workers in all of these areas just mentioned? In a sense, the question becomes, does gender make a difference? Is home-based employment an arena where conventional gender ideologies are challenged, contested, negotiated, and changed? Or, given the linkages of family, household, and employment to other social spheres, are the prevailing patterns and gender ideologies of a society or culture reproduced in home-based employment? Another way to frame the question might be, how is gender constructed in home-based employment and what are the implications for all the people and all the levels of society concerned?

WHAT IS HOME-BASED EMPLOYMENT?

In this book home-based employment is defined as the work done for income in one's home, on one's premises, or emanating from the home/premises, with the worker's having no office or consistent workspace elsewhere. A home-worker might be a plumber who schedules appointments from the home phone and stores tools and supplies in the garage, or a home knitter who seldom leaves the house. A home-worker could be a Tupperware salesperson, a person running a food preparation microenterprise through an incentive provided to help empower people to rise above poverty, or a telecommuter for a large corporation. Likewise, a home-worker could be a person assembling parts for an automobile firm, an owner of a large landscaping or gardening enterprise, a person who has turned a crafts hobby into a modest income generating activity, or a person stuffing envelopes with discount coupons and mailing them for a company. In some households there is more than one home-worker or a home-worker working more than one home-based occupation.

What is not home-based employment, as the authors of this book define it? Unpaid household production and "bringing work home from the office" are not included in the definition. Although numerous unpaid productive activities that take place at home—nurturing children, preparing meals, scheduling doctor appointments—are valuable and necessary to the maintenance and development of individuals and their families, these are not considered to make a person a home-worker. In a similar mode, occasional paid-work can contribute to household income and an enhanced standard of living, but in many research investigations such activities would be outside the parameters set for defining and operationalizing the activities that constitute home-based employment. Many investigators make distinctions between "casual" home-based employment (short-term and perhaps low paid activities) and other activities that seem to fulfill a definition of "regular" employment. A person who works only a few hours a year selling surplus vegetables from the garden, a person who occasionally repairs small motors or appliances for friends and neighbors, or a person who takes a time-limited job delivering phone books or advertisements would not be considered a home-worker in many studies.

Individuals can choose to engage in home-based employment for a number of reasons. In some cases, people become home-workers as a result of perceived lack of other employment options. Perhaps these are people living in economically marginal locations but wishing to stay there. Others choose home-based employment to fulfill entrepreneurial or other creative dreams, including being their "own boss." Some people might do their paid-work at or from the home because they see this as a better way of life, allowing more freedom and time for personal or family activities. There are likely many other reasons for being a home-worker.

GENDER AND HOME-BASED EMPLOYMENT

An empirical question is whether this type of employment and the motivations for choosing to be a home-worker vary in some patterned way by gender. That is, do women and men systematically engage in different types of home-based employment and for different reasons? If so, then gender and the way it shapes one's life would appear to be important conceptual tools for gaining better insight into home-based employment as a social phenomenon. As home-workers, do men and women manage their time and activities differently? If this were true, then gender would be a force shaping the processes associated with home-based employment. Do family dynamics, including interruptions to paid-work and family life, division of household labor, work-family conflict, and child supervision or care, differ, depending upon whether the home-worker is a man or a woman? If there are consistently different patterns for male and female home-workers related to these activities, then once again gender is to be regarded as an important force. Likewise, if the outcomes of home-based employment, the rewards and costs, vary systematically by the gender of the workers, then once again the concept of gender and its social construction are important analytical tools for gaining understanding of this widespread employment life-style.

THE NUMBER OF HOME-WORKERS

The popular press would have the public believe that a significant and expanding number of people are working at home for a variety of reasons. Among reasons frequently mentioned are that people increasingly choose home-based employment to gain flexibility in balancing paid-work and family responsibilities, that corporations are increasingly contracting with at-home telecommuters to reduce costs and increase efficiency, and that many "down-sized" workers are starting their own home-based businesses in response to economic restructuring. Chapter 2 of this book points out the widespread nature of home-based employment worldwide and indicates that in some societies significant proportions of the populations are home-workers.

Disagreement among researchers as to the definition of home-based employment results in widely varying estimates of the numbers of these workers, disparities in estimates of their growth as an employment sub-population, and conflicting descriptions of their demographic characteristics. In the United

States, for example, Deming (1994) analyzed the Current Population Survey using responses to a question about hours worked at home. He found that 67% of the home-workers were women, with jobs mainly in the service industry. He did not include in his count those who worked from their homes with no other permanent work location. This exclusion eliminated many men such as electricians and plumbers whom others would consider to be home-workers.

Edwards and Field-Hendrey (1996), basing their description of home-workers on 1990 census data, included only those who worked at home, had earnings, and were between the ages of 25 and 55. They included farmers. Compared to traditional on-site workers, the home-workers sample was disproportionately female and these women were more likely to have pre-school children. Comparing average earnings of home-workers to those of traditional on-site workers, the researchers found that at-home men earned 85% and at-home women earned 75% of the pay of on-site workers by gender.

The U.S. Department of Labor reported that the number of nonagricultural wage and salary workers doing paid-work at home grew between 1991 and 1997 (U.S. Department of Labor, 1998). However, not until May 1997 were self-employed home-based business owners counted by the Department of Labor; there were 4,134,786, consisting of 47.7% women and 52.3% men. In contrast, the representative sample that is used for most of the analysis reported in this book contains more men (58.1%) than women (Heck, Owen, & Rowe, 1995).

In Canada, a national child-care survey was conducted as a supplement to the September 1988 monthly Canadian Labour Force Survey. In this survey a total of 2,198 respondents, or 9.1% of the employed parents with primary child-care responsibilities surveyed (of whom over 90% were women), were home-workers (Lero, Pence, Shields, Brockman, & Goelman, 1992). Of these home-workers (defined as answering "none, works at home" to the question "What is the approximate distance from your home to your [main] place of work?"), 63.7% were self-employed and 36.3% were paid-workers.

ORGANIZATION OF *GENDER AND HOME-BASED EMPLOYMENT* AND AN OVERVIEW OF FINDINGS

The authors in the chapters that follow present the results of several studies, showing how home-based employment, its causes, context, and consequences, is often gender-linked. A variety of theoretical approaches are described and applied to the study of gender and home-based employment. The empirical studies focus on the United States and Canada; one chapter is a review of literature with a more global perspective. Each empirical study presents a well-developed literature review that sets the analysis in context. All of the analyses shed light on what is acknowledged worldwide as an important means for many workers to contribute to household income. Each chapter concludes with a discussion of what the findings imply for further research on home-based employment as well as interventions such as policy or education.

In Chapter 2, Charles Hennon and Suzanne Loker consider home-based employment from a worldwide perspective. They discuss the important contributions of these work activities in both the formal and informal economic sectors across the globe. For many families, women or other "secondary" workers conduct these activities, providing supplemental income for their families. This additional income can make the difference between a poverty level existence and a somewhat better subsistence level of living. These authors note that home-based employment can provide wages or salary additions to family income as well as make unpaid contributions to family enterprises. Furthermore, the home-based businesses range from microenterprises to rather large corporations. The types of activities, the economic sector in which they are conducted, the amount of income produced, and the relationship of the work activities to human capital and family dynamics are often tightly interwoven with gender. The authors, using a gender framework, provide a critical analysis of current employment patterns and their consequences for women, men, and their families worldwide. They note that home-based employment, or specific types of such employment, and why it is undertaken, are often aspects of en-gendering (i.e., categorizing certain behavior, attitudes, objects, places, and emotions as separate and unique for women, and others as separate and unique for men) and doing gender (everyday interaction that fabricates differences between women and men as well as using these differences to create a female–male polarity that devalues women).

Chapters 3, 4, 5, and 7 extend the analyses of the data from a U.S. nine-state study conducted in 1989 and described in a number of journal articles and the book *Home-Based Employment and Family Life* (Heck et al., 1995). The authors ground the analyses in theoretical and conceptual frameworks related to gender and pay special attention to gender effects. At least one stereotype of home-based employment portrays a mother of a young child who works at home in order to combine earning income with child care and performance of household duties. Suzanne Loker's study (Chapter 8) demonstrates this vision might typify one segment of the home-based employment population. However, the nine-state study informed the reader that the majority of home-based workers were men (58.1%) and that 44.1% of them had no children living at home.

The nine-state study, *At-Home Income Generation: Impact on Management, Productivity, and Stability in Rural/Urban Families*, is unique in that it was designed to examine specific interactions of employment and family activities among households with a home-worker. Utilizing a household sample, a two-stage process provided a random sample, stratified by rural/urban location, of 899 respondents from the participating states. The respondents lived in households with a home-worker who had been in home-based employment for at least 1 year, for a minimum of 312 hours per year, and whose work was not production agriculture. A 30-minute telephone survey with the household manager was the information source (Stafford, Winter, Duncan, & Genalo, 1992).

Chapter 3 highlights the economic outcomes for home-based business owners. Barbara Rowe, Kathryn Stafford, Rosemary Walker, George Haynes, and

Jeanette Arbuthnot use human capital theory, occupational segregation, discrimination by employers, and the gender ideology of housework to provide the conceptual foundation for their empirical work. Using a business owner sub-sample of the nine-state data, the investigators find that on average, women home-business owners work fewer hours, reap considerably less income, and do different kinds of work than men owners. Being in a female-dominated occupation reduces the amount of annual earnings of both men and women home-based business owners. Although the statistical analysis shows that the determinants of women's earnings are different from those of men, having more education is associated with greater annual earnings for both men and women. Working more hours increases earnings, although the effect of an additional hour of work on annual earnings is different for women and men. The finding that the presence of young children in the household has a negative effect on women's annual earnings in contrast to a positive effect on the earnings of men implies that traditional gender expectations are operational even among these business owners.

These authors additionally show that male home-based business owners on average have more employees who are relatives and more paid workers or independent contractors, compared to female home-based business owners. Men are also more likely to have another job in addition to their home-based business than are women. The female home-workers are mostly in service and crafts/artisan occupations, and male home-workers are mostly in mechanical/transportation trades and contracting. Within their businesses, men are more likely to use practices indicating a greater degree of "professionalism" than are women.

Different factors combine to predict the log of women's and men's gross business earnings. Five variables are significant for both genders: the number of professional practices and the number of paid workers, which are positively related to gross business income, and the categories of professional/technical, mechanical/transportation, and crafts/artisans-related businesses, which are negatively related to gross business earnings. Being married and having employment in addition to the business lower women's business incomes, whereas living in an urban county increases it. Average earnings for women in all of the occupation categories are lower than the average earnings for men. Age of the owner and the number of years of education both have positive effects, whereas having multiple workers in the household has a negative effect for men's gross business earnings.

The significant occupation variables in this analysis indicate higher earnings for men than women home-based business owners. There is one exception, contracting, in which the few women in the sample earn more income than do men. These authors also report the answer to an interesting question—What would their average wage be if female home-based business owners kept their own characteristics (e.g., age, education, and marital status) but owned businesses in male-dominated occupations? The answer is that their average wage would be greater than men's would. Likewise, if men were in female-dominated occupations their predicted hourly earnings would be less than their current earnings.

Holly Hunts, Sharon Danes, Deborah Haynes, and Ramona Heck (Chapter 4) report on their study of the interface between home-based employment and family systems. The authors are interested in the intersection of gender and household structure with household management and child-care decisions. These authors consider the simultaneous roles an individual can assume as he/she combines family management, management of the home-based employment activities, income provision, and child care. The investigation combines the variables of gender and household structure (non-family, single-parent, full-nest, and adult-only) as the authors delineate and investigate the 899 respondents in the nine-state study. Household management practices of the male and female household managers are followed by a gender–household structure comparison of household management practices for the sub-sample of dual-role holders (individuals holding the dual-roles of managing family work and performing home-based employment).

After showing that there are some demographic characteristics of the sample that vary by gender (such as that households with female home-workers have more children and more children under 6 years of age, and male home-workers earn on average about three times more income than do female home-workers), Hunts and her colleagues find that male household managers are more efficient as managers than are women. This same general pattern is observed among dual-role holders. The analysis of management practices within different household structures also shows that in some cases women appear to manage differently than men, with men more often being the more effective managers. The authors raise some questions about the measurement of household management and consider that the instrument used might have a male-bias that does not well describe the way women manage households.

These authors consider yet another role combination—that of home-worker and child-care provider, asking the question, "Is gender of the home-worker a factor in deciding whether or not to purchase child care?" The authors find a particularly large gender effect in households having two children under 5 years of age, with a much higher percentage of households with male rather than female home-workers purchasing child care.

Logistic regression analysis helps the investigators determine that the variables predicting the likelihood that a household with a female home-worker will purchase child care is quite different from the variables predicting the likelihood that a household with a male home-worker will purchase child care. For example, being a female home-based business owner decreases the likelihood of hiring child care, whereas business ownership is not a significant factor in decisions about purchasing child care in those households with male home-workers. Other factors having a negative effect on purchasing child care when the home-worker is a woman are living in Iowa, New York, Pennsylvania, and Utah. When men are the home-workers, three factors are associated with not purchasing outside child care. These factors are the number of children under the age of 5 years, other employment, and the amount of income earned from the home-based employment (the higher the income, the lower the probability of hiring child care).

The analysis also shows factors that increase the likelihood of purchasing child care. For households with female home-workers, having at least a bachelor's degree, having other employment in addition to the home-based employment, spending more of the home-based employment hours away from the home, and living in a town of less that 2,500 population all are associated with the purchase of child care. For households with either female or male home-workers, having a management, professional, or technical occupation is related to purchasing child care. Additionally, for households with male home-workers, having other household income and living in either Missouri or Vermont are associated with hiring child care.

The authors speculate why differences are found in the factors that predict the purchase of child care depending upon whether the home-worker is a man or a woman. They conclude that household management and child care choices are linked to the gender of the home-workers. They offer some consideration of why (such that women are more likely not to have other employment and spend less time working at their home-based employment than do men) and what this might mean for the motivations behind home-based employment that are different for men and women.

In Chapter 5, Cynthia Jasper, Karen Goebel, Kathryn Stafford, and Ramona Heck report on the gender differences and similarities in management strategies used by home-based business owners, utilizing the data from the nine-state study of home-workers. Focusing on styles of management in the business and in the family domain, the authors report that both men and women use managing and leading styles in their businesses as well as in their family lives. Women, however, utilize sensing as a third style in business and family management; a third style of business management practiced by men is evaluating, which is in contrast to their doing/action style of family management. These authors also speculate upon the adequacy of the instrument used to measure management practices. They suggest that as women are consistently dovetailing employment and family responsibilities, they likely function differently than do men when it comes to home-based employment.

These authors also relate the business services used by female and male home-based business owners in addition to the owners' promotional strategies and distribution methods. The authors discuss why there might be differences in the choice of services and strategies related to gender-linked differences in how women and men start up and maintain home-based businesses.

Rosemary Mills, Karen Duncan, and Jill Amyot (Chapter 6) present the results of a study of work-family conflict experienced by mothers of young children in dual-earner families. The data for their study are from the household survey component of the 1988 Canadian National Child Care Study. Specifically, a sub-sample is used in which respondents were employed at least 30 hours per week and hired child care. The data provide an opportunity to test hypotheses related to work-family conflict and workplace location (home-based employment versus an away-from-home job site). These authors provide a review of the effect of traditional gender ideologies on employment attitudes and household division of labor, leading to the expectation that gender differences in views of employment and family roles would be associated with different levels of work-family conflict in relation to workplace location.

Using regression analysis, Mills and her colleagues relate variables that predict the amount of work-family conflict. The authors find no significant statistical associations between work-family conflict and workplace location, thus providing no evidence for the assumption that being a home-worker is associated with lower levels of work-family conflict, nor that the husband's being a home-worker is associated with the work-family conflict experienced by wives. They do discover, however, that the total hours worked, the age of the youngest child, and the total family income are related to the level of work-family conflict. Longer hours in employment, lower age of children in the home, and higher family income are associated with more work-family conflict. The authors discuss why these findings prevail, including information concerning the different types of occupations that female home-workers choose and how this might relate to gender role ideologies.

Elizabeth Trent (Chapter 7) adds a different dimension to the categorical investigation of home-based employment and the concomitant gender effects. Utilizing an industrial classification system for the home-based employment of the respondents of the nine-state study, this author reports findings that are consistent with the results reported in Chapter 3 regarding gender and occupation. Male (compared to female) home-workers have higher total family incomes that might be related to their having worked more years and working at second jobs. A relationship between gender and industry class is reported. Women's jobs are much more likely than men's jobs to be in the health and education services industry; men in this sample are more likely to be in the construction industry. Women are less likely to be in jobs in which they work from the home than they are to work in the home.

Using multivariate analysis, the author answers two major questions. First, are there demographic and employment characteristics (including industry class) which predict that a home-worker will be male? Second, what demographic and employment variables (including gender) predict that a home-worker will be self-employed? The analysis finds that the home-worker's being a man is predicted by being older, earning higher home-based employment income, and holding other full-time employment, as well as being in the consumer services, construction, and transportation industries. The home-worker's being a woman is predicted by having a household size greater than three.

Factors related to being self-employed are age, other full-time employment, and work in construction (which all are positive predictors) and employment in seasonal work and in the wholesale trade, retail trade, or finance, insurance, or real estate industries (which are all negative predictors). However, gender is not a predictor of self-employment among home-workers.

Trent also investigates interruptions to the family that are associated with home-based employment. She finds that women who are home-workers report more interruptions to their family life than do men who are home-workers. Although levels of interruptions do not differ when being self-employed or working for wages, the industry in which the home-based employment is classified does relate to differences in interruptions. Home-workers in retail trade and health and education services report more interruptions that do home-workers in wholesale trade and construction. The author notes that these types of jobs are linked to the gender of the home-worker.

Chapter 8 by Suzanne Loker presents a qualitative study of one particular type and location of home-based worker—Vermont knitters. The study incorporates interviews with and observations of six women and one man. Some of the public policy issues surrounding home-based employment serve as a background. The author includes rich narratives and descriptions providing the reader with a greater understanding of the knitters' psychological motivations for doing this work in addition to the psychic income they accrue. The chapter ties to a public policy controversy by drawing on the views of the knitters. The author also indicates that policy can both support home-based employment as well as act as a barrier to such work.

Loker points out that those women who are home-workers have two jobs in the home—one paid and one unpaid. The people in the sample made a conscious decision to do paid-work in the home, partially to be able to accomplish their two jobs. This study emphasizes the importance of the knitters' family roles to their satisfaction with their jobs and the income they earn, as well as the interaction of those roles with gender. In the framework used, three types of production by the individual home-worker create different outputs: knitting provides income; child care, laundry, and other necessary outputs result from household production; and family members develop socially and spiritually as a result of propinquous production and the relationships it embodies.

A male knitter indicated that many think knitting is women's work, lending a gender bias to the choice of employment. Other knitters identify other disadvantages of knitting at home for pay. However, the author's conclusion is that, at least for the persons interviewed, home knitting provides the flexibility to fulfill economic and emotional needs for the knitters and their families. While working for pay, the knitters had the flexibility to do household chores and child care. They were in control of their lives, making a decent income and feeling positive about their family roles, in most cases with traditional gender roles.

IMPLICATIONS AND NEW QUESTIONS RAISED

The findings, theoretical discussions, and policy issues reported in this book about gender and home-based employment provide the basis for additional investigations, educational and clinical interventions, and helpful policy and legal frameworks. General contributions made by the authors as well as the gaps in theoretical and empirical knowledge are synthesized briefly, and additional work that can contribute to descriptive, conceptual, and theoretical explanations is described. The totality of findings provides themes that can be helpful for home-workers and those studying or providing support to home-workers. Implications for policy and other legal frameworks that can promote a higher quality of life are noted, especially as they relate to possible differential outcomes for male and female home-workers. It is important to keep in mind that the empirical results come from studies conducted in the United States and Canada. Chapter 2 sets home-based employment in a more global context, but does not report new empirical findings.

Gender and Cultural Expectations

The studies show that there are inputs, processes, and outputs of home-based employment that are linked to gender. For example, the number and age of children in the home and the gender of the home-worker are related to the decision to purchase child care. In general, unless the woman spends time away from the home that is related to her home-based employment, child care is not purchased. When the home-worker is a man, it is more likely that child care will be purchased, especially if there are two or more children under the age of 5 years. This pattern might reflect a gender distinction in "who watches the children," or perhaps a difference in the types of jobs that male and female home-workers perform. A clearer answer could be obtained by investigating men and women performing the same paid jobs at home who also had the same ages and numbers of children. Controlling in this manner could make it clearer whether the gender of the home-worker was the operative variable related to hiring outside child care.

Some people, both men and women, opt for home-based employment in order to fulfill desires to be at home, to be around family, to have more flexibility. Family life can be of utmost importance, and home-based employment can be an effective means to furthering this end. But home-based employment might be a choice that is not equally available to men and women, or, if available, not equally chosen by both. Perhaps women, in greater proportion than men, do opt for home-based employment in order to be better able to fulfill other duties to their families. What makes men who choose to work at home for family reasons different from other men? Are male home-workers who choose this life-style because of the primacy of their families more akin to female home-workers than to other male home-workers in other regards? More study is necessary to find out the influence gender plays and under what conditions.

As gender is contested and negotiated in a specific locale, gender expectations can and do change. Home-based employment might be one of those settings in which what it means to "do gender" can be different from that in other settings. Although families are embedded in societies and reproduce culture more locally, families are also the settings in which people confront daily the notions each member has of what is proper behavior. Maybe male home-workers are more likely to define what it means to be a man in ways that are different from those other male workers use. Conversely, female home-workers, given their relative isolation from other peers in a work environment, might be more traditional or conventional in gender terms than their employed women peers working elsewhere. Investigating which aspects of gender are causes of home-based employment and which are consequences will add to the literature. Said differently, investigation can illuminate whether the act of home-working creates important gender effects or whether discovered gender differences are a result of the actors involved. Perhaps women's (or men's) self-selected employment types and the outcomes are more a factor of characteristics of these people than of gender alone.

General themes of cultural expectations for women such as those regarding child care and other unpaid household production activities have seemed to assign these tasks to women, but many women also have reaped great satisfaction from performing these tasks. Classes for men on parenting and popular books are contributing to a societal change in the United States in which men are being held more responsible for equitable family approaches to unpaid household production. However, this is not true worldwide. Educational programs and public policy need to be developed with consideration of current cultural expectations and of future directions appropriate to each cultural context. The rewards of child care and propinquous production activities should be emphasized to give them acknowledged societal value when performed by women or by men.

Gender Influencing Type of Home-Based Employment

The jobs that home-workers do raise another important question. Why do men and women seem to have different types of home-based employment? It appears that although gender is not necessarily linked to being self-employed or owning one's own business, the types of businesses and the income earned do vary by gender. Thus certain occupations and job types are en-gendered. As en-gendering occurs, it erects barriers to the type of employment options that are potentially available to all people.

Qualitative investigations could help explain why people choose home-based employment and how this could be gender-related. When home-workers are lumped together into broad categories of occupations or industries, such distinctions concerning the meaning of the work to the individual and her or his family are covert. Home-workers within similar occupations or industries, regardless of whether they are women or men, could have quite different motivations, plans, and commitments to their work and its relation to other aspects of their lives such as children, household chores, marriage, or other personal relationships.

The social construction of gender might be different within homes where home-based work for pay is conducted and those where it is not. Elucidating these differences for use in educational programs will help current and potential families to understand the consequences of home-based employment to each of its family members. All family members can find satisfaction in economic, social, and psychological terms more easily if they understand and discuss the underlying nature of home-based employment. Men and women can modify their attitudes and behavior when open discussion clarifies the issues.

Economic Gender Inequity

Gender effects on income are similar in home-based employment and employment away from the home—men earn more than do women. Further investigation into gender linked issues such as motivations for home-based employment in general and choice of specific types of jobs in particular might clarify whether biases are operating in obtaining of capital, in training, or in other areas that determine occupational opportunities. That is, do women and men have different types of home-based employment because of gender biases in the society, or do women and men choose their type of home-based employment for other reasons? One of these other reasons might be gender ideology. Given the culture of the time and place, do women and men have free choice in their employment? Are some avenues of income earning closed off to members of one gender or the other? Or, do men and women have differing interests in working at or owning particular types of home-based businesses?

There is a caution however—the extend to which there is gender inequality in one culture when considered from the viewpoint of a different culture can be hegemonic. What some outsiders perceive as serious gender inequity might be acceptable to those people directly involved. In other cases, gender inequity cries out for policy intervention to protect rights and provide economic subsistence. In all situations it is advisable that serious attention be given to the social construction of gender and its relationship to home-based employment and the effect it has on human worth, dignity, social justice, and meaningful employment

Given the findings that men earn more than women in both home-based employment and traditionally located employment, educational and career development efforts focused on choosing an economically viable occupation should include both employment options. Moreover, the economic facts resulting from occupational choice perhaps need to be presented to women in special forums or with unique methods that focus on the consequences of choice rather than on their current interests and inclinations toward particular occupations.

Intersecting Employment and Family

Studying home-based employment provides a unique view at the intersection of the social and economic roles of employment and family life. Interdisciplinary approaches using social and economic theories for the development of educational programs and public policies are essential. Integrated perspectives will enhance the dialogue among family members, community organizations, and governments to consider family and local economies as well as individual and family well-being. Home-based employment brought to communities will be evaluated both for its consequences for individuals and families as well as for its infusion of dollars into the local economy. Perhaps these strategies will then be applied to choosing new firms for away-from-home employment in the community as well. Home-based employment is just a special case of employment. Home and employment issues will always be better understood with interdisciplinary approaches integrating social and economic issues of the reported research.

LIMITATIONS

One limitation of the work presented here is the lack of distinction between home-workers who work *at* home and those who work *from* their home (with no other office or consistent work site). Differences between the two groups of home-workers obscure significant gender influences on either group. First, it is important to ascertain whether gender plays a role in who works at home or from home, and the types of jobs that people do in either situation. In societies where women are typically confined to domestic roles and "staying at home," distinct gender expectations would likely be present in employment conducted either at or from home. But even in other societies, gender could be a determining factor in who works at or from the home. Second, if there are differences in work at or from home by gender, or in the amount of time spent out of the home when fulfilling home-based employment activities (making service calls, buying supplies, delivering products, and so on), then some research findings attributing differences between home-work and work at a more traditional location might be confounding gender with work site. Third, if gender is a determining factor in working at, compared to working from, home, then not considering this might further muddle research findings. Real estate agents or truck drivers who work a great deal of the time away from their home are not likely to be able to take their children along. Likewise, they are not going to be interspersing home chores with paid-work. In these ways, working from home might be more like having conventional employment than working at home. Without considering in a more systematic fashion the way gender is linked to such decisions, important gender differences in processes and consequences can be overlooked.

A second limitation of the research presented here is the relationship between gender and the length of time employed at home for pay. It seems fundamental to know whether home-based employment is seen as a short-term option that is fulfilling a need for income earning while the children are of a certain age, in contrast to a lifetime career. Do both women and men employed in the home tend to move in and out of the traditional work force? Also, in how many cases does the home-based employment precede the need to fulfill household duties? That is, does being a home-worker allow certain decisions to be made about having children or dividing household labor that would perhaps not be made if the person were working at a more traditional work site? Investigating more closely who works at home, why, and how the decision is made can shed more clarity on how home-based employment and gender are linked. Careful studies of the etiology of home-based employment as well as the internal family processes over time can help bring understanding to what being a home-worker means to the women and men involved as well as to their families.

Another point that must be considered is that each study and its findings in this book are bound by a particular cultural context—modern and industrialized societies with an emphasis on individualism and achievement—and each context studied here has some sense of gender equality. It is important to consider what the gender effects discovered mean within a particular society and how these findings fit into larger considerations of home-based employment as a global phenomenon. Whereas home-based employment might be seen and promoted in the United States or Canada as an effective way for women to combine child care and employment, it might not be so readily apparent that such beliefs are consistent with a more globally woven pattern of export-oriented business production that serves to perpetuate the image of women as secondary workers, more fit for home-based duties than those required in the public spheres of employment. Cross-country comparative analysis, either in primary research or in an integration and critique of findings from various locations, can further pinpoint the roles that gender plays in these contexts of home-based employment.

A final caution is in order. Gender is certainly an organizing factor in how societies are structured and in how people live their daily lives. In each society and subculture there is a gender ideology that gets played out in lived reality. Being a woman is different from being a man. The differences are reflected in choices about family division of labor, including income earning, household management and production, and propinquous production. But people are actors on their own behalf, having agency and making choices. Not all women home-workers are alike; nor are all men home-workers. When looking for gender difference, there is some danger in seeing and reifying more differences than might otherwise be important. So, although gender is certainly important, researchers and others must keep in mind that there are differences within genders and that not all members of one gender or the other will be similar.

REFERENCES

Deming, W. G. (1994, February). Work at home: Data from the CPS. *Monthly Labor Review, 117* (2), 14–20.

Edwards, L., & Field-Hendrey, E. (1996, November). Home-based workers: Data from the 1990 Census of Population. *Monthly Labor Review, 119* (11), 26–34.

Heck, R. K. Z., Owen, A. J., & Rowe, B. R. (1995). *Home-based employment and family life*. Westport, CT: Auburn House.

Lero, D. S., Pence, A. R., Shields, M., Brockman, L. M., & Goelman, H. (1992, February). *Canadian National Child Care Study: Introductory report* (Catalogue 89-526E). Ottawa: Statistics Canada.

Stafford, K., Winter, M., Duncan, K. A., & Genalo, M. A. (1992). Studying at-home income generation: Issues and methods. *Journal of Family and Economic Issues, 13,* 139–158.

U.S. Department of Labor, Bureau of Labor Statistics. (1998). *Work at home in 1997* (USDL 98-93). Washington, DC: Author.

Chapter 2

Gender and Home-Based Employment in a Global Economy

Charles B. Hennon and Suzanne Loker

INTRODUCTION

Home-based employment can be found worldwide.[1] In some regions it is institutionalized and common, in others more novel. Some regions have experienced recent growth in this employment pattern, for a variety of not yet fully explained reasons. This type of work arrangement, including the actual work undertaken for pay or profit, either as wage laborer or business owner, as well as factors such as amount of earnings and influences on other aspects of one's or one's family's life, appear to be tied to gender. Some activities or occupations are considered more masculine in nature, some more feminine. What is considered as an appropriate job for women in one region might be more appropriate for men in another region, or in another historical period in the same region. The impact of this employment on use of time, family relationship quality, quality of life, and standard of living also appears to vary by gender within and across different cultural regions, and within different households.

Theoretical and empirical understanding of home-based employment has been attempted through use of several conceptual frameworks, including household adjustment and adaptation (Wieling, Winter, Morris, & Murphy, 1997), occupational segregation (Bergmann, 1980), rural economic development (Gringeri, 1996), household strategies (Clay & Schwarzweller, 1991), systems (Hennon, Jones, Roth, & Popescu, 1998; Weigel & Ballard-Reisch, 1996), family management/ecology (Heck, 1992; Heck, Owen, & Rowe, 1995; Winter, 1992), and feminism or gender (Boris, 1994; Boris & Prügl, 1996; Hsiung, 1996). However, a great deal of the research on this subject appears to be descriptive or conceptual in terms of its explanatory mechanisms, answering questions concerning the type, frequency, and people of home-based employment. Theoretical explanations offering "because" answers to "why" questions (Sprey,

1995) concerning home-based employment phenomena are relatively lacking. Consequently, more appears to be known worldwide about the "whats, whens, and whos" of home-based employment than about theoretical explanations of gender and the dynamics of home-based employment. It also appears that many studies of home-workers outside the United States take a more critical approach, whereas many studies of home-based employment in the United States are of a "scientific, detached" variety.

This chapter integrates some of the extant literature on home-based employment as a global phenomenon, especially as it relates to gender. Its purpose is to introduce the relationships between gender and home-based employment in the global society as a foundation for the research-based papers presented in Chapters 3 to 8. The chapter's focus is on (a) who participates in home-based employment and why, the types of jobs they perform, the interrelationships this employment has with family and other responsibilities and activities, and (b) the relationship between participation in home-based employment and the construction of gender.[2] Thus, the approach here is critical and inquiring, considering home-based employment in general and certain aspects of such employment in particular as being part of a larger system of gendered relationships and conceptions of gender. Such an analysis, by taking the perspective of gender as a social construction, also considers issues of power, opportunity, and division of labor, as well as labor for love and/or duty, and money for one's self, one's family, and one's community. Using home-based employment as a socioeconomic development tool for the enhancement of families, communities, and societies is also explored as it might relate to disproportional rewards or costs falling to members of one gender or the other.

EMPLOYMENT WITHIN FAMILY SPACE— CONSTRUCTING GENDER

Home-based employment takes place in what is often considered family space. When employment activities take place in one's dwelling, it brings paid work into the space where duty, need, and love motivate labor. Home-based employment helps to construct gender at the household level.

Gender and its influence on family and household activities are rooted in the more general conceptions of gender within larger sociohistorical settings (West & Zimmerman, 1991). The historically structured conceptions of gender within a particular cultural system (the gender order) influence the beliefs and expectations about the appropriate activities of men and women within a family or home setting (a gender regime). To understand the effects of gender on and from home-based employment, then, one must be mindful of the intersections of culture, society, economy, and family at both the more macro-process and micro-process levels. The more micro-process level are face-to-face daily processes of negotiation and doing gender and are the lived reality of home-worker households.

Gender is a general category of social relations, like race or social class, which can have a variety of specific forms (Whatmore, 1991). Patriarchal gender relations are one such form. This form empowers men and subordinates women and is contested with a range of social practices and institutions (Cockburn, 1986). Feminist scholarship uses gender as an organizing concept involving two interrelated facets (Osmond & Thorne, 1993): (a) the social construction of gender, especially through the emphasis of differences between men and women, and (b) the uses of these distinctions to legitimize and to perpetuate the relations (especially seen as power) between men and women. Gender relations in most forms are basically power relations (Stølen, 1991; Whatmore, 1991). Women as a group are subordinated (legally, economically, politically, and socially) to men (Chafetz, 1991; Ferree, 1990; Loscocco & Leicht, 1993; Stølen, 1991; Whatmore, 1991). Although this contention is expressed by many feminist scholars, it is also recognized that women are not just passive victims. Women are agents and creators of culture—participating in the making of history as well as their own personal biographies. In other words, their gender relationships are constructed.

Feminists argue that the dichotomy between public and private, for example, the economy or society versus the household or family, is a false one. Such dualistic thinking contributes to the canard that logically men are the actors in the public spheres and women are the actors in the private spheres. It also hides the way gender in the home is connected to gender in the greater domains of culture and society.

How does feminist theorizing shape the consideration of home-based employment? As Osmond and Thorne (1993) determined:

Feminist scholarship on the historical development of the public-private dichotomy offers scholars a wealth of theorizing and research on the complex interrelationships between family and economy. In the process, feminists redefine social scientists' concepts both of work (traditionally defined in terms of men's occupations and organizations) and of family (traditionally defined in terms of "the" nuclear, middle-class, American model and "sex roles"). In summary: feminist scholarship (1) focuses on the organization of work within and outside of families as shaped both by a patriarchal gender system and by a capitalist economic system; (2) refutes the family-linked stereotypes of the man as sole provider and breadwinner and the woman as dependent and economically unproductive (this is neither a useful ideal—it embeds women's subordination—nor a description of the actual lives of most people); (3) demonstrates that the locus of women's subordination is not just in the economy nor just in the family, that is, "separate spheres" do not exist in women's (or men's) daily experiences; and (4) recognizes a societal gender system that is autonomous with regard to any specific institution yet links all major institutions. (p. 612)

Given the many overlapping spheres or institutions that influence home-based employment (especially for family businesses [Hennon et al., 1998]), it seems that the home is a prime location to find how gender shapes all aspects of labor, both paid and unpaid, more visible and less visible.

Gender is not absolutely tied to biological sex. Rather, femininity and masculinity (what it means to be a woman or a man, or of one gender or the other) are understood within feminist scholarship as contested, negotiated, and constructed via a magnitude of face-to-face transactions and more macro-dynamics (e.g., policies, laws, media, religions) within specific sociohistorical locations (West & Zimmerman, 1991). Biological sex (e.g., chromosomes, anatomical and reproductive physiological characteristics) is distinguished from cultural gender, which can be defined as all the cultural phenomena associated with biological sex (Osmond & Thorne, 1993; Stølen, 1991; West & Zimmerman, 1991; Wood, 1999). Gender is understood as a social construction that organizes one's life and the people in it. Gender is also understood as something people do in their daily lives. " 'Doing gender' is the everyday interactional process of constructing and reconstructing differences between women and men, girls and boys, and using these differences to create a male–female polarity that devalues women" (Osmond & Thorne, 1993, p. 593). Gender and the associated expectations for appropriate behavior acutely influence both men and women.

Individuals' experiences with gender encompass a core gender identity, or awareness—of being a boy or girl, masculine or feminine, man or woman—and the extent of phenomena circumscribed by masculinity and femininity (Osmond & Thorne, 1993; Potuchek, 1992; Wood, 1999). Begun in childhood, the procedure is lifelong, one of constructing and reconstructing a gendered sense of selfhood. Family interactions as well as those within employment, religion, leisure, and other settings all add to this process. Personal gender is central to emotional conflict, trust, jealousy, dependency, and their opposites, as well as other interpersonal actions including child rearing and employment.[3]

Furthermore, gender is a property of collectivities and organizations. Some argue that "gender divisions of labor and the separation of 'men's work' from 'women's work' are basic to the economy" (Osmond & Thorne, 1993, p. 605). Gender is also axiomatic to the structuring of other institutions such as religion, medicine, and education. Symbolic notions of gender (including by media in news reporting, entertainment, and advertisements) influence the meaning people hold of what it is to be a woman compared to what it is to be a man in a particular sociocultural context.

CHOOSING HOME-BASED EMPLOYMENT

What are some of the reasons that explain why people choose home-based employment? In some cases it could be due to the lack of other employment opportunities (Owen, Carsky, & Dolan, 1992). This can especially be so in rural areas, or where social customs and norms constrain or encourage women to focus on home and family as their primary role. In such cases, working at home for pay or profit is an acceptable alternative to gainful employment outside the home. For example, in Iran some women do home-based work for pay in order to save money for their retirement, often in a secretive fashion (Aghajanian, in press). In Taiwan, married women can earn income in the "satellite factory system" and "frontroom factories" (Hsiung, 1996). The satellite factory system concept casts light on a hierarchical subcontracting system of manufacturing composed of many small-scale, family-centered, export-oriented factories. The majority of these factories are located either in urban residential neighborhoods, at urban-rural conjunctions, or in the front yards of peasants. Within the factories, as mothers polish, assemble, pack, and package, their children play. These factories also contract work to home-workers who have converted their living rooms for factory production. In some areas there are government schemes to help individuals or families start microbusinesses (Barrantes, 1997; Hennon et al., 1998). These businesses are often home-based. Choosing to participate in this type of home-based employment might provide for a better standard of living, perhaps even an eventual route from poverty, welfare, or social assistance dependency.

Other reasons for home-based employment include

- the lower costs involved (transportation, start-up, rental and other overhead, child care or dependent care, etc.),
- the ability to use other family members as fill-ins or as low cost or free labor as necessary,
- a disability that might limit other employment,
- ability of a family or individual to live in a given location (rural or other economically peripheral areas),
- participation in the informal economy as a result of the structure of global economies or the lack of education or other job skills, and
- ability to join livelihood activities more closely to family or other activities.

Home is also where many economically successful businesses begin. For example, Julie Sautter launched her $10 million a year Curves business from her home in California while raising two children under 5 years of age (Foglino, 1998). In the United States the majority of people with home-based employment are self-employed, numbering over 5 million business owners in the early 1990s with over 2 million of these owners women (Pratt, 1993). People begin home-based businesses as a result of entrepreneurial motives, un- or underemployment, and lack of career advancement.

The role gender might play in why home-based employment is undertaken in specific occupations in specific regions and the exact consequences of home-based employment for both the shorter and longer terms are not clearly known. Critics have argued that women could be choosing this option because of social notions about appropriate activities for women. In some cases the situation can be framed not as women's freely choosing home-based employment so much as their being constrained and limited in their options. Some home-based employment can permit women to contribute to household income while attending to their main functions—child care and household production. But taking low pay for these activities also perpetuates the "reality" of women's deserving and accepting lower economic remuneration than do men. Participation in such activities can thus be a consequence of gender construction while contributing to furthering these conventions about appropriate behavior for women and men.

There is also some evidence that women in the United States are more likely to start a home-based business based on a "hobby," such as gardening or crafts, and men are more likely to begin home-based businesses that are based on previous experience or training (Clark & James, 1992; Pratt, 1993; Rowe, Stafford, Walker, Haynes, & Arbuthnot, 2000). Women more than men might also charge lower prices for their products or services as well as earn less profit from their home-based businesses than do men (Rowe et al., 2000). Gender can play a role in occupations chosen and profits earned.

GENDER IN THE CONTEXT OF HOME-BASED EMPLOYMENT

Home-based remunerated labor, like housework, tends to be invisible (Prügl & Boris, 1996). Home-based work for income, unpaid labor for a home-based family business, and unpaid housework are part of a larger ideological system of gender. This larger ideological system shapes labor such that some occupations, some tasks, some processes, and some places become identified as either feminine and thus for women, or masculine and thus for men. For example, the image of the typical wage worker is often a man whose wife takes care of the family responsibilities (see for example the discussion in Hennon & Brubaker, in press). Women, especially mothers, are seen as having primary responsibilities for family, and thus in some cases are considered less reliable employees. When employment scripts are written with the idealized man as worker in mind, women (or men) who have family and household responsibilities can find it difficult to earn good wages (de Vaus, in press; Hildenbrand, in press).

Worldwide, employers have used this gender ideology (Greenstein, 1995) to their advantage. Women are paid less because women belong in the home. As women accept low pay for doing home-based employment, the economic structure as well as the gender ideology that rewards men with higher pay are perpetuated. In essence, women working in their homes for pay help to create and reinforce barriers that women often face when seeking out-of-the home employment (Boris, 1994; Prügl & Boris, 1996). On the other hand, defining home-based employment as women's work closes off to men some avenues for earning a livelihood.

How does this often held perception that the home or dwelling is a "woman's place" and thus work done there for pay is women's work influence employment choices? Regionally and more locally, certain patterns can result. For example, if "home" grounded work is invisible or not highly or publicly regarded, it might well be en-gendered as "women's."[4] Wives in Baggara households in the Sudan, for example, buy food supplements for the herds cared for by their husbands and market the milk. This is considered "women's" work and is an important source of household income (Michael, 1997). Nevertheless, women's role in maintaining herd health is not publicly acknowledged as animal husbandry as this is "men's" work. Women in Eastern Turkey work for their husband's families as unpaid laborers. This work is invisible and not socially acknowledged (Cindoglu, in press).

In Australia, women are particularly attracted to home-based employment. Women with home-based employment made up 6% of all employed women in 1995 compared to men with home-based employment who constituted 2% of all employed men. In numbers, women (230,700) also surpassed men (112,600) in pursuing home-based employment (McLennan, 1996).

Pratt (1993) noted that the U.S. Census Bureau reported there were 5.6 million home-based businesses in the United States in 1991. Over 2 million of these were owned by women. The U.S. Department of Labor reported that more than 4.1 million self-employed persons were working in home-based businesses in May 1997. Managers and professionals accounted for more that 1.7 million of those working in home-based businesses. About 2.1 million persons with home-based businesses were working in services, about 726,000 in construction, and 532,000 in retail trade. Workers in home-based businesses worked on average 23 hours per week (U.S. Bureau of Labor Statistics, 1998). Edwards and Field-Hendrey (1996) indicated that on the basis of 1990 U.S. census data, 59% of all home-workers were women. In the early 1990s approximately 15% of women over the age of 16 years were home-based self-employed, working at least 8 hours a week (Deming, 1994). However, many of those recently working at or from the home for pay in the United States are men (Heck, 1992; Heck et al., 1995; Winter, 1992); the samples for these studies indicated that almost 60% of home-workers were men. Inconsistencies in figures reported on the number of home-workers in the United States are due to the definitions of home-worker or home-based employment used in each study. Some of the variables that cause these inconsistencies are full- or part-time employment; inclusion or exclusion of agricultural related work; the ages of those included in the sample; inclusion of work away from as well as at home; inclusion of work taken home from another employment site with the home not necessarily the main work site; and the definition of self-employment.

It seems clear that some occupations and activities done at home are perceived in the U.S. culture as masculine and the domain of men, such as construction or plumbing. But some women also run these types of home-based businesses. Other home-based occupations in the United States are feminine to the extent that large proportions of those with such employment are women (e.g., food service, beautician) (Rowe et al., 2000). Men in such occupations tend to earn less income than do men in other home-based employment occupations (Rowe et al., 2000). Although "home" space is often considered the province of women, in some cases men are in control of home-based businesses or wage labor that takes place in this space. Power and control of space and activities are often ascribed or achieved attributes of men. Women, and children, are often low or unpaid participants with limited power and control in these family businesses or other employment activities in the home (Hennon et al., 1998).

In rural China since the mid 1980s, household-run private businesses as well as other forms of economic enterprises have emerged (Entwisle, Henderson, Short, Bouma, & Fengying, 1995). Women participate in and benefit directly and indirectly from these opportunities, especially those home-based. However, as home-based paid-work opportunities increase, women's opportunities in rural China are often "determined and constrained by the male household head" (p. 38). If a household operates a business, men more than women are likely to work in the business. Men are leading the development and expansion of home-based businesses while women are increasingly specializing in agricultural work. But, in many cases, the work done by women in home-based family run businesses is invisible, considered as incidental and "helping out." One speculation of why this pattern is developing, especially given the long Chinese tradition of households' being involved in sideline economic activities mainly conducted by women, is that women are regarded as "filler-ins." That is, more junior women (i.e., not the mother-in-law) are perceived in the rural Chinese culture as having no well defined economic roles. Yet, these women do a large share of any household or economic activity. They "simply did the work that needed to be done—they 'filled-in'" (Entwisle et al., 1995, p. 53).

In some regions the role of women in economic development, including through home-based employment, is more explicit (Espinal & Grasmuck, 1997; Hennon et al., 1998; Stølen & Vaa, 1991). Women's household income production and industrial productivity can be braided with the cultural values concerning the moral responsibilities of women—their roles in social reproduction as caring wives and mothers. In Taiwan the "economic miracle" is sustained by policies that promote employment, including home-based, and the participation of married women. Hsiung (1996, p. 1) indicated that the government slogan "Living Rooms as Factories" revealed the "particularity of Taiwan's economic development, the special roles played in it by the state, and married women's significant contribution to it."

The Living Rooms as Factories proposal was developed by the government (along with Mothers' Workshops—programs to educate mothers to assist their husbands and instruct their children) as part of a social development initiative. Designed as a method "to incorporate women into productive labor while instructing them to fulfill their moral obligation to promote Taiwan's economic development through their traditional roles in the family as wives, mothers, and caretakers" (Hsiung, 1996, p. 49), the community development project partly occurred as a reaction to the fact that there were many "idle women" in the community. Survey research indicated that the Living Rooms as Factories program has helped two-thirds of the respondents to improve their families' welfare. In rural areas, more than 50% of respondents indicated the project has had a significant or notable impact on their lives. However, Hsiung argued that at the same time the state became an agent of capitalist production, its role was sometimes in direct conflict with the interests of women. Basically, the state failed to protect women against exploitation by capitalists. Hsiung (1996) noted:

From a broader perspective, families whose female members did homework in their living rooms were not the only beneficiaries of these programs. Capitalists were relieved of a labor shortage in the factories and spared an upward pressure on wages. To the extent that living rooms were converted into "factories," the capitalists were able to spend less on factory facilities, energy, dormitories, and management. The society as a whole was able to benefit from productivity increases, consumer price stabilization, economic growth, and the reduction of conflict between capitalists and workers. (p. 53)

Scholars interested in the role of women in relation to development have shown the extent to which women contribute in a variety of paid and unpaid ways to social development of nations. This scholarship also enlightens scholars and other professionals as to how such contributions are related to conceptions of gender and contribute to gender construction. It includes income earning activities that are often invisible, uncounted, and undocumented because they take place in the informal economy and often in or from the home (Bennholdt-Thomsen, 1988; Cindoglu, in press; Espinal & Grasmuck, 1997; Mies, 1988; Stølen & Vaa, 1991). These activities include producing items as well as selling goods and foodstuffs on the street. Although much of this is home-based activity for pay or profit, it is often not recognized in a formal way as contributing to gross domestic production or to the quality of family life. In many cases, this income adds significantly to the standard of living for the household and is produced in addition to the other home-based work that women do.

The other home-based work is unpaid labor for the benefit of families and communities, sometimes referred to as household production, which is devalued under capitalist industrialization. Unpaid women's work includes child care, food growing and production, fetching of water and firewood, production of clothing for their families, and nurturing of family members. Bennholdt-Thomsen (1988) argued that as capitalism advances, women are included as unpaid laborers by the process of "housewifization." In addition to activities that nourish and benefit children and other family members, there might be gender differences in participation in voluntary activities that benefit schools, churches, civic organizations, and the community (Briar-Lawson, Lawson, Hennon, & Jones, in press). These are services that help to maintain other people and enable them to participate in education and wage earning activities and are as important to social life as any other type of labor. But in the face of the social importance of this labor, labor for pay is often considered as the only "real" work. This is the work that is counted and statistically analyzed when the economy of a country is being considered.

Scholars have related the economic position of women to the worldwide structure of unequal labor markets. This scholarship also brings understanding of how labor, including home-based employment, can be both cause and consequence of conceptions of gender. Scholars have developed models of a household division of labor and an international division of labor with a reorganization of production that uses subcontracting to save costs and raise profits for organizations (Boris, 1996; Chafetz, 1991; Entwisle et al., 1995; Espinal & Grasmuck, 1997; Ferree, 1990; Hsiung, 1996; Osmond & Thorne, 1993; Prügl & Boris, 1996; van der Plas & Fonte, 1994; Wallerstein & Smith, 1991; Whatmore, 1991). Some have argued that transnational organizations, in particular, have exploited home-workers (Boris & Prügl, 1996; Briar-Lawson et al., in press; Wallerstein & Smith, 1991). When profits fall and cheaper labor can be found elsewhere, these corporations move on, leaving disorganization and economic destruction in their wake. Studies have shown the connections among subcontracting chains, home-based employment, export increase, and rising profits for corporations (Prügl & Boris, 1996). Home-workers worldwide and Third World women in particular have been called upon because of their cheap labor. To the extent that homes in any country can and "should" be used for employment sites, and that women can and "should" contribute to community and state economic development via home-based employment, this leads to the en-gendering of specific activities at the same time that it legitimizes specific forms of surplus value and capital accumulation. This surplus and accumulation can be obtained at the expense of the more fundamental interests of women.

Gender can be a factor in the choice of home-based employment. Subcultural norms, gender conceptions within a particular cultural group, other opportunities for employment, and idiosyncratic or more general values and goals all seem to play a part. More careful analysis of how gender is connected to and constructed through home-based employment in specific occupation types and cultures is required. Some home-based occupations are considered more appropriate for men, some more appropriate for women (Rowe et al., 2000). In the United States, for example, some home-based business occupations appear to be dominated by men (with 50% or more owned by men—i.e., contractors, mechanics, professional/managerial, shopkeepers, sales representatives, truck drivers) and others are occupations dominated by women (i.e., agricultural sales, beautician, clerical, crafts, food services, human services, income managers, sales agents, service managers, teachers) (Rowe et al., 2000). People who cross these gender conceptions can be perceived as odd by others and be affected by the residuals of this reverse stereotype. For example, a man engaged in home-based knitting as an occupation might be considered out of place by others (Loker, 2000) but a business partner by his wife. A woman running a construction business from her home might be admired or considered unusual.

Overall, although it appears there are some gender-related factors in who participates in home-based employment, why, and for what rewards and at what costs, it does not appear that there is one universal, global relationship. Universal statements of explanation for the relationships between gender and home-based employment might be misleading. More microlevel studies can possibly help in illuminating specific instances of how home-based employment is "gendered" in terms of its causes and its consequences.[5] Such studies, as they are cumulated and integrated, can help in building a more global and less culturally bound theory of gender and home-based employment. Quality studies also can help in understanding the processes involved in how home-based employment in particular cases is related to localized or familial conceptions of gender, that is, how home-based employment by either men or women is an instance of "doing gender" (Osmond & Thorne, 1993). Perhaps men performing some home-based for pay activities and women performing others will help to reinforce, or change, gender conceptions and how gender is constructed. Time will tell.

GENDER, HOUSEHOLD PRODUCTION, AND HOME-BASED EMPLOYMENT

Many scholars (e.g., Briar-Lawson et al., in press; Christensen, 1988b; Heck et al., 1995; Hunts, Danes, Haynes, & Heck, 2000; Mills, Duncan, & Amyot, 2000; Rowe et al., 2000) have suggested or studied the idea that home-based employment is an opportune way of combining activities for pay or profit with family and household production activities, including activities such as nurturing of spouse or child, child or other dependent care, cooking, and household management. It also includes propinquous production activities with outcomes that are important for the development of family members and/or for the social and spiritual vitality of families and communities.

Various authors in the book by Boris and Prügl (1996) demonstrated how women often ran businesses from their homes in order also to manage their households. Physical space was reorganized in some homes so women could keep watch over their children while managing their businesses, often with several employees. Loker (2000), Beach (1988, 1989), and the research presented in Winter (1992), Heck (1992), and Heck, Owen, and Rowe (1995) showed how home-based employment for profit or wages was bonded with family and household production activities. In many cases, accommodations had to be made either to family and household activities or to employment activities as a result of interruptions caused by activities in the other sphere. Other data showed that more women than men reported that running a home-based business included interruptions to their families, such as phone calls or clients stopping by the house (Trent, 2000). It is unclear whether this pattern of interruptions was due to the nature of the businesses run by women or to gender related factors. Loker (2000) also observed a pattern in which women home-based knitters were interrupted by family members and neighbors while attempting to knit.

Although some research indicates that, at least in the United States, home-based employment does not eliminate the necessity of hired child care (Ahrentzen, 1990; Heck, Saltford, Rowe, & Owen, 1992; Pratt, 1993), child care, food production, and household chores (i.e., household production and propinquous production activities) can be combined with employment activities so that more total work can be accomplished. In addition, workers might find new creative talents, gain self-confidence, earn income that is in many cases quite important for their families, increase their social class and quality of life, and embark on entrepreneurial activities that allow them to restructure their lives (Boris & Prügl, 1996; Hennon et al., 1998). It has also been argued that the lack of commuting time can either make people more productive or allow them more leisure or family time (Loker, 2000). In contrast, some scholars have suggested that such combinations of household production and work for pay have actually led to the stretching of the working day with the result that workers, especially women, are suffering exploitation by employers, family members, and even themselves (Prügl & Boris, 1996).

Time can be more easily allocated to a wider range of activities simultaneously or sequentially when home-based employment is the paid-work option. Time can also be perceived as more flexible and less structuring of one's activities (Beach, 1988; Loker, 2000). Beach (1988) concluded that for her sample of rural families running microbusinesses, it was the flexible use of time, rather than just its allocation, which was important for home-workers. Rather than thinking of time as a finite resource to be allocated among competing demands,

time for work-at-home families was not uniform but flexible and integrated with daily functions. Participants reported variable work days of nonuniform hours, punctuated by breaks for specific needs—a child's violin lesson, decorating a birthday cake, doing laundry, or reading to a child. In their nonroutinized work days and schedules, these families display a distinctive concept of "work time." As such, it may more closely approximate the older premodern rhythm . . . than the time discipline imposed by the industrial structure. (p. 139)

Women often report that home-based employment reduces employment-family stress (Mills et al., 2000). But men also indicate this. And some men also report that home-based employment helps them fulfill child care or other household duties or goals. Some women see their home-based employment income as secondary family income whereas men often see their home-based employment income as the primary family income (Gringeri, 1996), but not universally. For some households the income from women's home-based employment is the primary income. For some men as well as for some women, home-based employment is a second job, or "moonlighting" (Olson, Fox, & Stafford, 1995).

Gender determinations on how families intertwine enterprise and family should be assessed. Different life-style strategies—sharing, complementary, and segregated—are possible (Wheelock, 1994). Value shifts are often necessary to adapt to a more family-oriented life-style, which requires establishing family and home-centered activities as the focus of one's life, with concerns and ideas about income generation considered from this perspective. Sharing a set of goals that are regarded as worth pursuing is likely important for the home-based family business, the family, and each individual, to prosper and succeed.

Family dynamics are important determinants of success for home-based family businesses. Entrepreneurial families foster, enable, and enhance the efforts of their members (IFBPA, 1995). As Wheelock (1994, p. 33) wrote, "Families often need to adapt to a new way of life when they set up in business, and for some this . . . [is] much easier than for others." Weigel and Ballard-

Reisch (1996) and Hennon and colleagues (1998) also indicated the difficulties of integrating household and employment aspects in a family enterprise. Gender expectations and power relations might facilitate smooth business functioning, or get in its way. As home-based family businesses are promoted for social development agendas, the roles that gender plays in their formation, management, and success, as well as the business's impact on family dynamics, should be more carefully documented.

Throughout the world, parents can have their children with them while preparing products for sale, such as foodstuffs or crafts, and also have their children under watch while the products are being distributed. Or a parent can take the children along while calling on customers. Children can be studying for school while their parent who is a real estate agent is searching a computer data base for homes for sale and talking to a buyer on the phone. Parents can telecommunicate/telecommute, service equipment or animals, create products, or provide information services, while keeping a watchful eye on children and cooking supper. Although men and women are able to combine parenting, household, and employment activities, it often appears it is women who are left to do so (Baxter, 1997; Beach, 1988; Bruce, Lloyd, & Leonard, 1995; Boyden, 1993; Bryant & Zick, 1994; Demo & Acock, 1993; Godwin, 1991; Hennon & Brubaker, in press; Lewis & Cooper, 1995; Lobodzinska, 1996b). The social construction of gender in many cultures has attached these duties to women.

Some authors' conclusions support the contention that home-based employment can be a panacea for juggling the competing requirements of earning a living, managing a household, participating with family, and engaging in leisure. An alternative view would argue that when combining family and livelihood, the amount of interruption to livelihood activities could be stressful, detrimental to business, and perhaps not safe for children. Additionally, as it is women who conduct most of the child care and household production tasks, this scheme for linking nurturing activities with those for pay or profit serves to engender these arrangements as "women's" and serves to keep women marginalized in status and resources (e.g., Boris, 1994, 1996; Gringeri, 1995). The argument is that people with more human or social-cultural capital are likely to be less marginalized, be employed in the formal economic sector, and realize higher relative incomes. On the other hand, some studies (e.g., Beach, 1988; Loker, 2000) found women expressing satisfaction with the ability to accommodate both paid-work and family responsibilities through home-based employment. More theoretically motivated studies are necessary to ascertain the family and employment dynamics, how this is related to gender among families with members engaged in home-based employment, and whether the arrangement is satisfactory for women and men.

THE GLOBAL CONTEXT OF GENDER
AND HOME-BASED EMPLOYMENT

Global Economies

One way to think about the place of home-based employment in the world economy is to consider how such work can be en-gendered and shaped by the globalization of economies. Prügl and Boris (1996) noted that the recent interest in home-based employment has been partly due to the structural changes in the organization of international capitalism that have been detrimentally affecting the economic position of women. Such structural change has included a decentralization of production processes; this pattern has been labeled as the "global assembly line" within "the global factory" (Prügl & Boris, 1996; Rothstein & Blim, 1992). Companies can choose the most profitable production arrangements from geographically disparate areas. However, the control of these processes is centralized in what have been termed "global cities" such as Tokyo or New York. Prügl and Boris (1996) argued that this international restructuring is leading to changes in social class. By using flexible subcontracting arrangements, a middle class of largely male production workers is being eliminated. In the post World War II period, this middle class had achieved wages that were supportive of a family, job guarantees, and a variety of benefits that enhanced their social security. In this way, the structural changes of international capitalism are detrimentally affecting the economic position of many men.

Some now see that in place of this middle class, a disproportionately female (and immigrant) work force involved in export-processing industries is being created (Hsiung, 1996; Prügl & Boris, 1996). In what have been referred to as "subcontracting chains" within the global factory, both home-workers and others in economically advanced as well as newly industrializing and poor nations are being drawn into international production (Hsiung, 1996; Prügl & Boris, 1996; Rothstein & Blim, 1992). For example, a woman stitching shoe tops at her home in Italy can be contracting with a person who sells to a wholesaler who provides finished shoes to a large chain of department stores in Canada and the United States. In their homes, women in Taiwan can produce toys for American markets. Men and women in the United States can be self-employed and work at home as retailers of items that are partially fashioned by men and women working in their homes in several different countries.

It can be argued that the labor force is polarized and those who have flexible work arrangements appear to be benefiting less from the economic restructuring in that they are paid low wages, receive few if any employment benefits such as health insurance or vacations, and are without social security benefits, the protection of labor standards, or other government guarantees. So, although these people have employment, they might otherwise not have, it can be argued that they are being exploited for the benefit of others, both capitalists and consumers of sometimes lower priced goods (Briar-Lawson et al., in press). In Asia and Latin America some governments have created policies to establish and maintain these types of employment practices. Labor markets have been deregulated in order to help repay foreign debts and to respond to economic crises. Corporations in such countries have turned increasingly to subcontracting. These companies rely on the cheap labor of women, often working in the home (Hsiung, 1996; Prügl & Boris, 1996). This pattern of using cheap labor of women can also be found in various forms in North America (Fernandez-Kelly & Garcia, 1988; Gringeri, 1995, 1996; Stepick, 1989).

In summation, it can be argued that home-based employment as part of a larger scheme of global capitalism, production, and trade is having negative consequences for some people. The consequences are not only economic, but also extend to all that is associated with income—such as health, life opportunities, education, domestic relations, power, and control. To the extent that home-based employment is en-gendered and en-gendering, it would appear that such work would have differential costs and benefits for women and men. If home-based employment is considered an option mainly for women in some particular sociocultural contexts, these women can benefit in some ways and can be disadvantaged in other ways. More generally, women can be advantaged by the global spread of home-based employment such as through consumption of lower priced goods or employment in management level positions in transnational corporations. Women might also be disadvantaged by the lack of any meaningful employment possibilities. Some men lose their jobs to cheaper labor in other countries and are unemployed or underemployed. Other men can have better paying jobs. Continuing research into home-based employment and its connection to gender in the context of different regions and levels of society can help bring new insights into gender construction as well as who is advantaged or disadvantaged, and why.

Gender and Capitalist Structure of Labor

There is concern among some authors (Acevedo, 1990; Christensen, 1988a; Hennon et al., 1998; Hsiung, 1996; Prügl & Boris, 1996; Wieling et al., 1997) that home-based employment can be marginalizing to those who are so engaged. People engaged in such employment activities are often paid less, have few if any fringe benefits, do not benefit from collective labor politics such as that of unions, are sometimes at the mercy of agents or brokers, can suffer in terms of career advancement, might experience isolation, and often are women. Another concern is that industrialization as a process is detrimental to women.

Some writers (see for example Stølen & Vaa, 1991) argue that capitalist driven industrialization leads to barriers that constrain women's participation in formal sector economic activities. For example, Spencer-Walters (in press) pointed out that in Sierra Leone, the participation of women in the informal sector of the employment market is important and ongoing. However, when the government has intervened in the informal economic sector, it has given assistance mainly to those activities that are dominated by men, such as tailoring, metal work, or woodwork. Such assistance has not been extended to women petty traders, restaurateurs, or food sellers. Even so, the services of women petty traders are important not only as a source of income for them and their families, but also as a provider of affordable products in a country which experiences erratic economic conditions. Authors generally conclude that cross-culturally women are considered as making up a pool of cheap laborers (Grown & Sebstad, 1989) or secondary earners relegated to the informal economy. Men are considered to be more appropriately engaged as industrial or formal sector employees (Lobodzinska, 1996a, 1996b; Prügl & Boris, 1996).

Worldwide, observations can be made of how home-based employment, especially of a "blue" or "pink" collar variety, is a facet of the marginalization of laborers. Lack of other meaningful employment combined with home-based employment "opportunities" can keep wages low and laborers unorganized, readily disposed of, and on the fringes of the economic system. Although home-based employment can create opportunities for advancement in careers, class, and quality and standard of living, it can also create marginalization. Especially when societies are structured such that women are regarded as worthy of low pay, discriminated against in employment and career advancement, suffering from a lack of formal education, and considered as belonging in the family and household spheres, it is highly likely that it will be women who are the home-workers. Such social and cultural practices serve to perpetuate the marginalization of women with home-based employment.

Income earning at home has been subject to a variety of different social policies and laws (Boris, 1994; Boris & Prügl, 1996; Bryant, 1989; Christensen, 1988b; Entwisle et al., 1995; Hsiung, 1996; Loker, 2000; Loker, Owen, & Stafford, 1995; Owen, Rowe, & Saltford, 1995). It has also entered the arena of international politics (Prügl & Boris, 1996). Such groups as the European Union and the International Labour Organisation have produced documents and raised concerns about home-based employment.[6] In response to marginalization and exploitation several advocacy groups have organized an umbrella organization, Homenet International. An objective of this organization is "to coordinate an international campaign for the improvement of home-based workers' conditions of work at national, regional, and international levels" (Prügl & Boris, 1996, p. 4). More research is required for deeper understanding of how the marginalization-integration continuum is related to gender globally. Although home-based employment might be detrimental for some women, or some men, it might also be a viable employment choice that empowers individuals while contributing to the development of their families and communities.

Home-based employment can be viewed as a positive paid-work opportunity that can be especially useful to those living in areas with restrictive employment opportunities, to people with child care or other responsibilities, to families wishing to increase household income, or to those in industries that are particularly conducive to telecommuting (Beach, 1988, 1989; Christensen, 1988b; Heck, 1992; Heck et al., 1995; Hennon et al., 1998; Wheelock, 1994; Winter, 1992). Home-based employment, along with self-employment and the creation of family businesses including those of a microenterprise nature, have been suggested to be aspects of economic development strategies, alternatives to poverty, and pathways from welfare dependency (Balkin, 1989; Barrantes, 1997; Briar-Lawson et al., in press; Bryant, 1989; Espinal & Grasmuck, 1997; Garnier & Majeres, 1992; Hennon et al., 1998; Midgley & Livermore, 1997; Mingione, 1994, Raheim, 1997). When there are few other choices for gaining a livelihood, home-based employment might prove to be a viable alternative. This can be especially so in economies in transition and in rural areas.

Gender and Home-Based Employment in Transitional and Rural Economies

Families are increasingly being regarded as both the agents and beneficiaries of socioeconomic development (Aronson, 1991; Briar-Lawson et al., in press; Hennon, Jones, Hooper-Briar, & Kopcanová, 1996; Hennon et al., 1998; Livermore, 1996; Midgley & Livermore, 1997). Likewise, it is recognized that family businesses, including those that are home-based, are critical in developing and immature market economies (Briar-Lawson et al., in press; International Family Business Program Association [IFBPA], Kolb, 1993; Livermore, 1996; 1995; Midgley, 1995). For instance, in Eastern and Central Europe, families are interested in becoming better income generating units (Centre for Social Development and Humanitarian Affairs, 1991; Popescu & Roth, in press; Raabe, 1998), being entrepreneurial (Hennon et al., 1998; Lobodzinska, 1996a; *Report*, 1993; United Nations Industrial Development Organization, 1994), and being innovative in weaving together different pay or profit activities (Hennon et al., 1998).

As an illustration, microenterprises represented 94% of the total number of small and middle-sized enterprises in Romania in 1996. Many were home-based and the majority of these had fewer than five employees, often family members (Popescu & Roth, in press). Almost 47% of people in the private sector were self-employed. Of these, 26% were unpaid family members (National Commission for Statistics, 1996). These figures indicate that the private sector labor force in Romania is largely family based. Many of the businesses are located at, or the activities are conducted from, the home. Sensitive policies and practice (Hennon et al., 1998) can enhance and promote such income generating activities.

Rosenfeld (1981), Galeski and Wilkening (1987), Singh (1988), Price and Wilhelm (1988), Hennon and Brubaker (1988), Bryant (1989), UNIFEM (1990), Lowe and Murdoch (1993), Gasson and Errington (1993), Lustiger-Thaler and Salée (1994), Gringeri (1996), Wheelock and Baines (1998), and Briar-Lawson et al. (in press), among others, have also detailed the characteristics of the economies faced by rural families in various regions of the world, and the limiting economic opportunities often available. Home-based employment, often of a microenterprise nature and often in the informal economic sector, is an opportunity that some rural families choose as they weave together a pattern of lives and livelihoods. Teal (1981) presented the following description:

The economies of many rural areas are still made up of thousands of micro-businesses: cottage industries; one- or two-person shops; labor intensive manufac-turing operations out of kitchens, barns and sheds; small specialized mail-order outfits; artisans and crafters; and small-scale agriculture. (p. 28).

People who are made redundant and/or cannot obtain jobs as a result of economic downturns often choose other employment alternatives. Likewise, as a family/household strategy, additional members can be added to the work force. Globally, it appears that increasing household income through the efforts of multiple workers is a common strategy to deal with poor economic conditions. It also appears that women are increasingly involved in pay or profit activities because of family income requirements (Boyden, 1993; Bruce et al., 1995; Wieling et al., 1997). Home-based employment, sometimes with multiple fam-ily-member involvement, is being used worldwide to adjust to changing econ-omy and family life situations in which more than the male head of household must produce income to meet family needs. This is particularly true in rural and transitional economies. As the prevalence of home-based work activities for pay or profit increases, the study of their impact on individuals, families, and com-munities becomes more important.

Families can be seen as the engines of socioeconomic development, espe-cially as they create employment through their own, often home-based, entrepre-neurial activities. Policy in support of such activities is being promoted glob-ally especially in rural and transitional economies. However, it might be wise to know more about both the advantages and disadvantages to individuals, fami-lies, communities, and nations, and how rewards and costs of such activities can be differentially experienced by men and women, before these types of schemes are blindly promoted. In this way, policies and practices that are more capable of sustainable and equable development can be designed, implemented, and evalu-ated (Briar-Lawson et al., in press; Hennon et al., 1998).

CONCLUSIONS

The relation of gender to home-based employment in a global context is discussed in this chapter. Gender is considered a socially constructed variable, dependent upon both the women and men involved and societal expectations. The global context of home-based employment is significant both for its cultur-ally dependent social construction of gender and for the changing capitalist structures of labor that are influencing home-based employment. Home-based employment and its gendered nature continue to evolve and provide fertile grounds for study.

Significant relationships between gender and both home-based employment and the interaction between home-based employment and household production activities are described in the literature. Differential opportunities in home-based employment are afforded women and men, by both individual gender construction and the stereotypes of society. The ways women and men construct their home-based paid and unpaid work establish power relationships in the home and elsewhere and are a consequence of the power relationships expected and experienced by individuals within societal contexts. The division of labor in the home workplace and in family household activities is a result of how the women and men involved define themselves and the labor as well as societal expectations of the relationship between gender and the labor. Choosing to labor for love, for one's own money, or for money to maintain one's family can also be considered within the social construction of gender. An adequate categorization of the differences between the choices of women and those of men is still to be discovered.

The gendered nature of the interaction between home-based employment and household production is clear. The role of women in both realms is traditional. But how women and men are constructing these relationships is often dependent upon the individual, the particular family, and the context in which they find themselves. More research is needed to establish patterns within types of individuals, families, and cultural contexts.

Depending on the context—country, rural/urban, economic orientation—gender and home-based employment have developed unique relationships. Research considering home-based employment within specific socio-cultural contexts can illuminate these unique relationships. Such research can lead to the development of better categorizing schema as well as to the application of various context specific gender and home-based employment relationships in forming a broader, more inclusive cross-cultural theory.

NOTES

1. Several different terms are used to describe this phenomenon of working at or from one's home (that is, having no other office or regular place of employment even though the task might be performed elsewhere, such as in plumbing or construction work) for pay (i.e., wage labor, piecework or payment depending upon work completed, salary, or a commission) or profit (i.e., from a family-owned business or self-employment). Among the terms used are *homework, home-worker, homeworking, home-based worker, putting out work, being home-based, working at home, work-at-home families,* and *home-based worker.* The occupations of home-workers include both professionals and "blue" or "pink" collar jobs, and the jobs may be in the formal or informal economies. In this book, we have used the term *home-based employment* to describe work that is being conducted at home for pay or profit. In this chapter, *home-workers* is used extensively to describe the people who do this work, as this term is commonly used globally, though not as much in the United States.

2. The *construction of gender* (or gender construction) means that gender, as opposed to biological sex, is not "natural" or "a given." Rather, what it means to be a

man or a woman and the phenomena trussed with masculinity or femininity are arti-facts created through social interaction within a specific sociohistorical period and culture. Each cultural group holds values concerning what it means to be a man or a woman and through a variety of social control mechanisms shapes the attitudes and behavior of its members. Actual behavior thus comes to reflect, more or less, the gender ideology within a specific group. Differences between men and women are exaggerated and reinforced through a variety of socialization experiences, activities ("doing gender"), rewards, and sanctions. Members of a particular culture typically see gender and the role expectations that go along with it as normal and often do not question them. Certain activities, emotions, gestures, items, and so on, are taken to be normal for one gender and not for the other. However, gender role expectations are open to challenge, are negotiated and contested, at the same time that they are rela-tively enduring and "taken for granted" by members of any particular cultural group (Osmond & Thorne, 1993; Stølen, 1991; West & Zimmerman, 1991; Whatmore, 1991).

3. As Whatmore (1991) points out, although biological explanations of a gen-der division of labor have been discredited, some other accounts of the division of labor rely on the more innocent concept of family life cycle and associated gender roles. Such accounts, that might be used for example to explain the division of household and child-care responsibilities in households with home-workers, are inadequate in that they also do not account for diversity and variation found in gen-der divisions of labor in different times and places. These conceptualizations also do not address the issue of why it is women rather than men who undertake subsistence and reproductive labor. Explaining that women often do home-based employment so they can also do household management and child care might be an example of us-ing family life cycle or gender roles by taking such activities as given and then of= fering them as an explanation for the different patterns of involvement in paid and unpaid work between women and men. Such accounts are tautologous, not to men-tion sexist. These types of accounts tell little about the social relations and proc-esses through which labor is expropriated and resources distributed within a house-hold. These accounts also do not adequately explain the practices and ideologies by which women's and men's gender identity and labor activities are constructed.

4. *En-gendering* refers to the process of categorizing certain behavior (as well as attitudes, objects, places, emotions, etc.) as separate and unique for women, and other behavior as separate and unique for men. By this process of en-gendering, working at home for pay may be considered as acceptable for one gender, but not another. Or, a certain home-based employment occupation (for example, being a seamstress) might be considered acceptable for women, but not men. The illusion of a gender dichot-omy in the face of between sex similarity and within sex differences is thus perpetu-ated through en-gendering (Ferree, 1990).

5. *Gendered* refers to the fact that certain expectations about which gender is to be involved are associated with specific behavior. Thus home-based employment can be gendered to the extent that there are widely agreed upon social expectations about who, women or men, are to be involved. These expectations lead to decisions about who will participate in home-based employment, and participating in home-based employment perpetuates the expectation and reality for which gender this is an ac-ceptable activity. Gender is thus a "cause" as well as a "consequence" of home-based employment.

6. See Lotherington and Flemmen (1991) for a discussion of the International Labour Organisation and the negotiation of gender.

REFERENCES

Acevedo, L. A. (1990). Industrialization and employment: Changes in the pattern of women's work in Puerto Rico. *World Development, 18,* 231–255.

Aghajanian, A. (in press). Family and family change in Iran. In C. B. Hennon & T. H. Brubaker (Eds.), *Diversity in families: A global perspective.* Belmont, CA: Wadsworth.

Ahrentzen, S. B. (1990). Managing conflict by managing boundaries: How professional homeworkers cope with multiple roles at home. *Environment and Behavior, 22,* 723–752.

Aronson, R. (1991). *Self-employment.* Ithaca, NY: ILR Press.

Balkin, S. (1989). *Self-employment for low income people.* New York: Praeger.

Barrantes, C. (1997). *Política social, género y microempresas populares en Venezuela* [Popular microenterprises, gender, and social policy in Venezuela]. Universidad Central de Venezuela, Facultad de Ciencias Económicas y Sociales.

Baxter, J. (1997). Gender equality and participation in housework: A cross-national perspective. *Journal of Comparative Family Studies, 28,* 220–247.

Beach, B. (1988). Time use in rural home-working families. In R. Marotz-Baden, C. B. Hennon, & T. H. Brubaker (Eds.), *Families in rural America: Stress, adaptation and revitalization* (pp. 134–141). St. Paul, MN: National Council on Family Relations.

Beach, B. (1989). *Integrating work and family life: The home working family.* New York: SUNY.

Bennholdt-Thomsen, V. (1988). Why do housewives continue to be created in the Third World too? In M. Mies, V. Bennholdt-Thomsen, & C. von Werlhof (Eds.), *Women: The last colony* (pp. 159–167). London: Zed.

Bergmann, B. R. (1980). Occupational segregation, wages and profits when employers discriminate by race or sex. In A. H. Amsden (Ed.), *The economics of women and work* (pp. 271–282). New York: St. Martin's.

Boris, E. (1994). *Home to work: Motherhood and the politics of industrial homework in the United States.* Cambridge, England: Cambridge University Press.

Boris, E. (1996). Sexual divisions, gender constructions: The historical meaning of homework in Western Europe and the United States. In E. Boris & E. Prügl (Eds.), *Homeworkers in global perspective: Invisible no more* (pp. 19–37). New York: Routledge.

Boris, E., & Prügl, E. (Eds.). (1996). *Homeworkers in global perspective: Invisible no more.* New York: Routledge.

Boyden, J. (1993). *Families: Celebration and hope in a world of change.* London: Gaia Book, UNESCO.

Briar-Lawson, K., Lawson, H., Hennon, C. B., & Jones, A. (in press). *Family supportive policies and practices: International implications.* New York: Columbia University Press.

Bruce, I., Lloyd, C. B., & Leonard, A. (1995). *Families in focus: New perspectives on mothers, fathers, and children.* New York: Population Council.

Bryant, C. R. (1989). Entrepreneurs in the rural environment. *Journal of Rural Studies, 5,* 337–348.

Bryant, W. K., & Zick, C. D. (1994). Economics of housespousery: An essay on household work. *Journal of Family and Economic Issues, 15,* 137–168.

Centre for Social Development and Humanitarian Affairs. (1991). *1994 International Year of the Family: Building the smallest democracy at the heart of society.* Vienna: United Nations Office at Vienna, Author.

Chafetz, J. S. (1991). The gendered division of labor and the reproduction of female disadvantage: Toward an integrated theory. In R. L. Blumberg (Ed.), *Gender, family, and economy: The triple overlap* (pp. 74–94). Newbury Park, CA: Sage.

Christensen, K. E. (1988a). *Women and home-based work: The unspoken contract.* New York: Henry Holt.

Christensen, K. E. (Ed.). (1988b). *The new era of home-based work.* Boulder, CO: Westview.

Cindoglu, D. (in press). Turkish families: A story of modernization. In C. B. Hennon & T. H. Brubaker (Eds.), *Diversity in families: A global perspective.* Belmont, CA: Wadsworth.

Clark, T. A., & James, F. J. (1992). Women-owned businesses: Dimensions and policy issues. *Economic Development Quarterly, 6,* 25–40.

Clay, D. C., & Schwarzweller, H. K. (Eds.). (1991). *Household strategies. Research in Rural Sociology and Development, 5.*

Cockburn, C. (1986). The relations of technology: What implications for theories of sex and class? In R. Crompton & M. Mann (Eds.), *Gender and stratification* (pp. 74–85). Cambridge: Polity.

Deming, W. G. (1994, February). Work at home: Data from the CPS. *Monthly Labor Review, 117*(2), 14–20.

Demo, D. H., & Acock, A. C. (1993). Family diversity and the division of domestic labor: How much have things really changed? *Family Relations, 42,* 323–331.

de Vaus, D. (in press). Australian families: Social and demographic patterns. In C. B. Hennon & T. H. Brubaker (Eds.), *Diversity in families: A global perspective.* Belmont, CA: Wadsworth.

Edwards, L. N., & Field-Hendrey, E. (1996, November). Home workers: Data from the 1990 census of population. *Monthly Labor Review, 119,* 26–34.

Entwisle, B., Henderson, G. E., Short, S. E., Bouma, J., & Fengying, Z. (1995). Gender and family businesses in rural China. *American Sociological Review, 60,* 36–57.

Espinal, R., & Grasmuck, S. (1997). Gender, households and informal entrepreneurship in the Dominican Republic. *Journal of Comparative Family Studies, 28,* 103–125.

Fernandez-Kelly, M. P., & Garcia, A. M. (1988). Informalization at the core: Hispanic women, homework, and the advanced capitalist state. In A. Portes, M. Castells, & L. A. Benton (Eds.), *The informal economy: Studies in advanced and less developed countries* (pp. 247–264). Baltimore: Johns Hopkins University Press.

Ferree, M. M. (1990). Beyond separate spheres: Feminism and family research. *Journal of Marriage and the Family, 52,* 866–884.

Foglino, A. (1998, November). Women who do everything. *Redbook,* pp. 160–162, 174.

Galeski, B., & Wilkening, E. (1987). *Family farming in Europe and America.* Boulder, CO: Westview.

Garnier, P., & Majeres, J. (1992). Fighting poverty by promoting employment and socio-economic rights at the grassroots level. *International Labour Review, 131,* 63–75.

Gasson, R., & Errington, A. (1993). *The farm family business.* Wallingford, England: CAB International.

Godwin, D. D. (1991). Spouses' time allocation to household work: A review and critique. *Lifestyles: Family and Economic Issues, 12,* 253–294.

Greenstein, T. H. (1995). Gender ideology, marital disruption, and the employment of married women. *Journal of Marriage and the Family, 57,* 31–42.

Gringeri, C. E. (1995). Inscribing gender in rural development: Industrial homework in two midwestern communities. *Rural Sociology, 58,* 30–52.

Gringeri, C. E. (1996). Making Cadillacs and Buicks for General Motors: Homeworking as rural development in the Midwestern United States. In E. Boris & E. Prügl (Eds.), *Homeworkers in global perspective: Invisible no more* (pp. 179–201). New York: Routledge.

Grown, C., & Sebstad, J. (1989). Introduction: Toward a wider perspective on women's employment. *World Development, 17,* 937–952.

Heck, R. K. Z. (Ed.). (1992). Thematic issue: At-home income generation (Part Two) [Special issue]. *Journal of Family and Economic Issues, 13* (3).

Heck, R. K. Z., Owen, A. J., & Rowe, B. R. (Eds.). (1995). *Home-based employment and family life.* Westport, CT: Auburn House.

Heck, R. K. Z., Saltford, N. C., Rowe, B., & Owen, A. J. (1992). The utilization of child care by households engaged in home-based employment. *Journal of Family and Economic Issues, 13,* 213–237.

Hennon, C. B., & Brubaker, T. H. (Eds.). (in press). *Diversity in families: A global perspective.* Belmont, CA: Wadsworth.

Hennon, C. B., & Brubaker, T. H. (1988). Rural families: Characteristics and conceptualization. In R. Marotz-Baden, C. B. Hennon, & T. H. Brubaker (Eds.), *Families in rural America: Stress, adaptation and revitalization* (pp. 1–9). St. Paul, MN: National Council on Family Relations.

Hennon, C. B., Jones, A., Hooper-Briar, K., & Kopcanová, D. (1996). A snapshot in time: Family policy and the United Nations International Year of the Family. *Journal of Family and Economic Issues, 17,* 9–46.

Hennon, C. B., Jones, A., Roth, M., & Popescu, L. (1998). Family-enterprise initiatives as a response to socioeconomic and political change in Eastern and Central Europe. *Journal of Family and Economic Issues, 19,* 235–253.

Hildenbrand, B. (in press). Diversity in families: Germany. In C. B. Hennon & T. H. Brubaker (Eds.), *Diversity in families: A global perspective.* Belmont, CA: Wadsworth.

Hsiung, P-C. (1996). *Living rooms as factories: Class, gender, and the satellite factory system in Taiwan.* Philadelphia: Temple University Press.

Hunts, H., Danes, S. M., Haynes, D. C, & Heck, R. K. Z. (2000). Home-based employment: Relating gender and household structure to management and child care. In C. B. Hennon, S. Loker, & R. Walker (Eds.), *Gender and home-based employment* (pp. 79–117). Westport, CT: Auburn House.

International Family Business Program Association, Task Force. (1995). Family business as a field of study. *Family Business Annual, 1* (Section II), 1–8.

Kolb, B. (1993, October). *Capital funding for small business in Eastern Europe: A proposal for local development banks.* Paper presented at the international conference Privatization and Socioeconomic Policy in Central and Eastern Europe, Krakow, Poland.

Lewis, S., & Cooper, C. L. (1995). Balancing the work/home interface: A European perspective. *Human Resource Management Review, 5,* 289–305.

Lisk, F., & Stevens, Y. (1987). Government policy and rural women's work in Sierra Leone. In C. Oppong (Ed.), *Sex roles, population and development in West Africa* (pp. 183–202). Portsmouth, NH: Heinemann.

Livermore, M. (1996). Social work, social development and microenterprises: Techniques and issues for implementation. *Journal of Applied Social Services, 21,* 37–44.

Lobodzinska, B. (1996a). Women's employment or return to "family values" in Central-Eastern Europe. *Journal of Comparative Family Studies, 27,* 519–544.

Lobodzinska, B. (Ed.). (1996b). *Family, women, and employment in Central Eastern Europe.* Westport, CT: Greenwood.

Loker, S. (2000). Interweaving home and work spheres: A case study of Vermont knitters. In C. B. Hennon, S. Loker, & R. Walker (Eds.), *Gender and home-based employment* (pp. 189–212). Westport, CT: Auburn House

Loker, S., Owen, A. J., & Stafford, K. (1995). The community connection. In R. K. Z. Heck, A. J. Owen, & B. R. Rowe (Eds.), *Home-based employment and family life* (pp. 135–165). Westport, CT: Auburn House.

Loscocco, K. A., & Leicht, K. T. (1993). Gender, work-family linkages, and economic success among small business owners. *Journal of Marriage and the Family, 55,* 875-887.

Lotherington, T., & Flemmen, A. B. (1991). Negotiating gender: the case of the International Labour Organization, ILO. In K. A. Stølen & M. Vaa (Eds.), *Gender and change in developing countries* (pp. 273–307). London: Norwegian University Press/Oxford University Press.

Lowe, P., & Murdoch, J. (1993). *Rural sustainable development.* London: Rural Development Commission.

Lustiger-Thaler, H., & Salée, D. (Eds.). (1994). *Artful practices: The political economy of everyday life.* Montreal: Black Rose.

McLennan, W. (1996). *Persons employed at home, Australia, September, 1995* (Catalogue no. 6275.0). Belconnen, ACT: Australian Bureau of Statistics.

Michael, B. (1997). Female heads of patriarchal households: The Baggara. *Journal of Comparative Family Studies, 28* (2), 170–182.

Midgley, J. (1995). *Social development: The developmental perspective in social welfare.* Thousand Oaks, CA: Sage.

Midgley, J., & Livermore, M. (1997). The developmental perspective in social work: Educational implications for a new century. *Journal of Social Work Education, 33,* 573–585.

Mies, M. (1988). Capitalist development and subsistence production: Rural women in India. In M. Mies, V. Bennholdt-Thomsen, & C. von Werlhof (Eds.), *Women: The last colony* (pp. 27–45). London: Zed.

Mills, R. S. L., Duncan, K. A., & Amyot, D. J. (2000). Home-based employment and work-family conflict: A Canadian study. In C. B. Hennon, S. Loker, & R. Walker (Eds.). *Gender and home-based employment* (pp. 137–165). Westport, CT: Auburn House.

Mingione, E. (1994). Family strategies and social development in Northern and Southern Italy. In H. Lustiger-Thaler & D. Salée (Eds.), *Artful practices: The political economy of everyday life* (pp. 41–60). Montreal: Black Rose.

National Commission for Statistics. (1996). *Starea sociala si economica a Romaniei in anul 1995* [The social and economic situation of Romania in 1995]. Bucharest: Author.

Olson, P. D., Fox, J. J., & Stafford, K. (1995). Are women installing their own glass ceilings? *Family Economics and Resource Management Biennial, 1,* 163–170.

Osmond, M. W., & Thorne, B. (1993). Feminist theories: The social construction of gender in families and society. In P. G. Boss, W. J. Doherty, R. LaRossa, W. R. Schumm, & S. K. Steinmetz (Eds.), *Sourcebook of family theories and methods: A contextual approach* (pp. 591–623). New York: Plenum.

Owen, A. J., Carsky, M. L., & Dolan, E. M. (1992). Home-based employment: Historical and current considerations. *Journal of Family and Economic Issues, 13,* 121–138.

Owen, A. J., Rowe, B. R., & Saltford, N. C. (1995) The changing environment of work. In R. K. Z. Heck, A. J. Owen, & B. R. Rowe (Eds.), *Home-based employment and family life* (pp. 15–40). Westport, CT: Auburn House.

Popescu, L., & Roth, M. (in press). Stress and coping among Romanian families in the post-communist period. In C. B. Hennon & T. H. Brubaker (Eds.), *Diversity in families: A global perspective.* Belmont, CA: Wadsworth.

Potuchek, J. L. (1992). Employed wives' orientations to breadwinning: A gender theory analysis. *Journal of Marriage and the Family, 54,* 548–558.

Pratt, J. H. (1993). *Myths and realities of working at home: Characteristics of home-based business owners and telecommuters* (U.S. Small Business Administration, Office of Advocacy Contract SBA-647-OA-91). Washington, DC: U.S. Government Printing Office.

Price, D. Z., & Wilhelm, M. (Eds.). (1988). Socioeconomic stress in rural families [Special issue]. *Lifestyles: Family and Economic Issues, 9* (2).

Prügl, E., & Boris, E. (1996). Introduction. In E. Boris & E. Prügl (Eds.), *Homeworkers in global perspective: Invisible no more* (pp. 3–17). New York: Routledge.

Raabe, P. H. (1998). Women, work, and family in the Czech Republic—and comparisons with the West. *Community, Work, and Family, 1,* 51–63.

Raheim, S. (1997). Problems and prospects of self-employment as an economic independence option for welfare recipients. *Social Work, 42,* 44–53.

Report. (1993). United Nations Europe and North America Preparatory Meeting for the International Year of the Family, Valletta, Malta, April, 1993 (Document IYF/PM.2/9, May 1993). Vienna: United Nations, Secretariat for the International Year of the Family.

Rosenfeld, S. (Ed.). (1981). *Brakeshoes, backhoes and balance sheets: The changing vocational education of rural women.* Washington, DC: Rural American Women, Inc.

Rothstein, F. A., & Blim, M. L. (Eds.). (1992). *Anthropology and the global factory: Studies of the new industrialization in the late twentieth century.* Westport, CT: Bergin & Garvey.

Rowe, B. R., & Bentley, M. T. (1992). The impact of the family on home-based work. *Journal of Family and Economic Issues, 13,* 279–297.

Rowe, B. R., Stafford, K., Walker, R., Haynes, G. W., & Arbuthnot, J. (2000). Unexpected outcomes: The economics of genderized home-based business. In C. B. Hennon, S. Loker, & R. Walker (Eds.). *Gender and home-based employment* (pp. 45–77). Westport, CT: Auburn House.

Singh, R. (1988). *Economics of the family and farming systems in Sub-Saharan Africa.* Boulder, CO: Westview.

Spencer-Walters, T. (in press). Family patterns in Sierra Leone. In C. B. Hennon & T. H. Brubaker (Eds.), *Diversity in families: A global perspective.* Belmont, CA: Wadsworth.

Sprey, J. (1995). Explanatory practice in family studies. *Journal of Marriage and the Family, 57,* 867–878.

Stepick, A. (1989). Miami's two informal sectors. In A. Portes, M. Castells, & L. A. Benton (Eds.), *The informal economy: Studies in advanced and less developed countries* (pp. 111–134). Baltimore: Johns Hopkins University Press.

Stølen, K. A. (1991). Introduction: Women, gender and social change. In K. A. Stølen & M. Vaa (Eds.). (1991). *Gender and change in developing countries* (pp. 1–10). Oxford: Norwegian University Press.

Stølen, K. A., & Vaa, M. (Eds.). (1991). *Gender and change in developing countries.* Oxford: Norwegian University Press.

Teal, P. (1981). Women in the rural economy: Employment and self-employment. In S. Rosenfeld (Ed.), *Brakeshoes, backhoes and balance sheets: The changing vocational education of rural women* (pp. 27–65). Washington, DC: Rural American Women, Inc.

Trent, E. S. (2000). Industry and self-employment analysis by gender. In C. B. Hennon, S. Loker, & R. Walker (Eds.). *Gender and home-based employment* (pp. 167–187). Westport, CT: Auburn House.

UNIFEM (Producer), Montoro, T. S., Woortman, E. B., & Gramkow, M. M. (Consultants). (1990). *Women of the sand* (video). Brasilia: University of Brasilia.

United Nations Industrial Development Organization. (1994). *Practice guidelines for business incubators in Central and Eastern Europe.* Vienna: Author.

U.S. Bureau of Labor Statistics. (1998). *Work at home in 1997.* Available at *http://stats.bls.gov/newsrels.htm.*

van der Plas, L., & Fonte, M. (Eds.). (1994). *Rural gender studies in Europe.* Assen, The Netherlands: Van Gorcum.

Wallerstein, I., & Smith, J. (1991). Households as an institution of the world-economy. In R. L. Blumberg (Ed.), *Gender, family, and economy: The triple overlap* (pp. 225–242). Newbury Park, CA: Sage.

Weigel, D. J., & Ballard-Reisch, D. S. (1996). Merging family and firm: An integrated systems approach to process and change. *Journal of Family and Economic Issues, 18,* 7–31.

West, C., & Zimmerman, D. H. (1991). Doing gender. In J. Lorber & S. A. Farrell (Eds.), *The social construction of gender* (pp. 13–37). Newbury Park, CA: Sage.

Whatmore, S. (1991). Life cycle or patriarchy? Gender divisions in family farming. *Journal of Rural Studies, 7,* 71–76.

Wheelock, J. (1994). Survival strategies for small business families in a peripheral local economy: A contribution to institutional value theory. In H. Lustiger-Thaler & D. Salée (Eds.), *Artful practices: The political economy of everyday life* (pp. 21–40). Montreal: Black Rose.

Wheelock, J., & Baines, S. (1998). Dependency or self-reliance? The contradictory case of work in UK small business families. *Journal of Family and Economic Issues, 19*, 53–73.

Wieling, E. A., Winter, M., Morris, E. W., & Murphy, A. D. (1997). *Working for pay or profit by women in Oaxaca de Jurez, Mexico, 1987–1992: Integration or marginalization?* Unpublished manuscript, Texas Tech University, Lubbock, TX.

Winter, M. (Ed.). (1992). Thematic issue: At-home income generation (Part One) [Special issue]. *Journal of Family and Economic Issues, 13* (2).

Wood, J. T. (1999). *Communication, gender, and culture* (3rd ed). Belmont, CA: Wadsworth.

Chapter 3

Unexpected Outcomes: The Economics of Genderized Home-Based Businesses

Barbara R. Rowe, Kathryn Stafford, Rosemary Walker, George W. Haynes, and Jeanette Arbuthnot

INTRODUCTION

The majority of jobs in the United States are full time, Monday through Friday, performed eight to five at a centralized work site (Robinson & Bostrom, 1994). However, the proliferation of relatively inexpensive personal computers, fax machines, electronic mail, and advanced telephone systems, in combination with a growing number of "information workers," has made it possible to move paid-work to a number of locations, including the home (Christensen, 1987; Kraut, 1989).

Depending upon the definition used, 8% to 31% of the U.S. population are either full- or part-time home-workers (Heck, Owen, & Rowe, 1995; Sloane, 1993).[1] Most home-workers are self-employed, responsible for all of the activities of their business and selling their products or services in the marketplace. Other home-workers function as employees, working at or out of their home for wages and commissions from a single employer.

The work-at-home movement is seen as particularly beneficial for women, who are in the paid labor force in record numbers, as a means of easing some of the tensions between the employment roles and family roles they typically fulfill. It also provides an alternative for women who have bumped their heads against the "glass ceiling" or been laid off as a part of industrial restructuring. For employers, the transfer of jobs from the central workplace to homes leads to a reduction in office space with its attendant costs, allows for recruiting the services of people who might not otherwise be employable (e.g., as a result of social or physical handicaps), and keeps the demand for labor flexible (Kraut & Grambsch, 1987; Lozano, 1989).

Home-based employment might present women with fewer barriers to success than the traditional labor market. Historical accounts (discussed later in this chapter) of home-based employment in the United States focused on women doing piecework for low wages in miserable working conditions (Boris, 1985; Dangler, 1986). Today's news stories about work at home highlight home-based self-employment as a means of balancing employment and family, controlling one's own work environment and pace, and gaining flexibility. In 1991, the Bureau of the Census reported that 15.4% of women 16 years and older were both self-employed and working at home at least 8 hours a week (Deming, 1994).

Research on gender in the traditional labor market has documented differences in compensation received by men and women (England, Herbert, Kilbourne, Reid, & Megdal, 1994; Groshen, 1991; Kilbourne, England, & Beron, 1994; Marini, 1989; O'Neill & Polachek, 1993; Sorensen, 1989; Witkowski & Leicht, 1995). The persistence of occupational segregation and perceptions of a glass ceiling—the level beyond which promotions are no longer expected—are considered by many women as immovable barriers of the traditional labor market. One response could be self-employment. Over the past two decades the self-employment rate among women has rapidly increased. In 1990, 1 of 15 employed women was self-employed in her main job, and women represented one-third of all self-employed workers, a 63% increase (Devine, 1994).

However, do self-employed women improve their earnings differential compared to self-employed men? More particularly, is there an earnings gap when work is conducted within the domain of the home? Do women with home-based businesses self-segregate into traditionally female-dominated occupations? Are they willing to trade flexibility in the hours and days they work for lower earnings? Because the business owner is his or her own employer, selects his or her own occupation, and determines the asking price for the product or service provided, it is presumed that there are no labor market factors which would impose an earnings gap between self-employed men and women or between self-employed women and their wage-and-salary counterparts. But there is little empirical evidence to support this assumption.

In this chapter, the aim is to collect and summarize the existing research in an attempt to answer these questions. First, a summary of current theories on the reasons for earnings differentials between female and male workers is presented. This is followed by a description of factors affecting the growth of home-based employment—what is known from the research to date. The final section is a discussion of prospects for the future and the implications of the research for home-workers and their families.

REVIEW OF LITERATURE

Gender Differences in Earnings

On average, women earn less than two-thirds the earnings of men. Depending upon which median earnings data set is used, estimates range from 40% to

42% less, a differential that has persisted at approximately the same level for several decades. The gender difference in wages tends to be lowest for the young, rising with age. Gender difference is larger in male-dominated occupations and varies with racial and ethnic categories (Greenberger & Steinberg, 1983). What accounts for this earnings gap? Four explanations have been proposed: (a) differences in the individual or labor market characteristics of women and men (human capital theory), (b) differences in the distribution of women and men among different occupations (occupational segregation), (c) discrimination in the labor market, and (d) unequal sharing of domestic responsibilities.

Human Capital Theory

The human capital approach implies that wage differences among workers are primarily a result of differences in their productivity. Therefore, women perhaps earn less than men do because they bring to the labor market different productive capacities. For example, women might not have invested as heavily in education and training to develop labor market skills (Smith & Ward, 1989). Second, women might interrupt their market work to bear and rear children, therefore spending less time in the labor force than men might. While they are out of the labor force, workers' existing stock of human capital possibly deteriorates rather than appreciates as it would if they were in a paid job (Jacobsen & Levin, 1995; Mincer & Ofek, 1982). When women are employed, their jobs provide fewer opportunities for skill enhancement. Thus, women acquire less experience and on-the job training than do men. Men are assumed to be relatively continuous labor force participants, enhancing their productivity through additional experience and seniority. Women's shorter and more intermittent labor force experience results in lower productivity, which in turn accounts for their lower wages (Stevenson, 1988). This pattern of labor force participation also reduces wages indirectly because women choose to invest less in their own human capital, reasoning that because they will reap fewer rewards, the negative cost of investing in human capital is too large. Therefore, women perhaps choose jobs with low penalties for intermittent employment (England, 1982; Marini, 1989).

There is some validity to the belief that family responsibilities affect women's earnings. Coverman (1983) showed that time spent in housework affects the earnings of *both* men and women, although few men do enough housework to make much of a dent in their earnings (Berk, 1984; Hochschild, 1989). However, even single women, who would be expected to have the same employment characteristics as men, earn substantially less than men and have the same flat age-earning profile as married women (Barrett, 1979).

Mincer and Ofek (1982), while exploring the depreciation effect, also found a rapid growth in wages after a return to work that followed a period out of the labor force. They believed that it is quicker to restore human capital than to build it anew. The consequent rebound effect on wages implies that skill depreciation during step-outs, although of great importance in explaining the wage rates of recent re-entrants, diminishes in the long run as earnings continue to rise. However, Jacobsen and Levin (1995) noted that the wages of women who take a leave from the labor market do not completely catch up to the wages of women who never left, even after 20 years.

Empirical studies exploring the characteristics of women in the labor market generally explain only about one-third of the wage differential between women and men by controlling for a variety of individual productive (e.g., education and age) and personal (e.g., marital status and race) characteristics (Corcoran & Duncan, 1984). Thus a substantial proportion of the earnings gap between women and men remains unexplained. One unresolved issue in the human capital argument is the extent to which low levels of human capital are the cause or the effect of labor force instability (Sandell & Shapiro, 1978). Low wages might discourage women from investing in human capital, and limited investments in human capital perpetuate women's lower earnings.

Evidence using data from the Current Population Survey (CPS), the Panel Study of Income Dynamics (PSID), and the National Longitudinal Survey (NLS) showed that the gender gap in wages declined at about 1% a year between 1976 and 1989. Giving credence to the human capital argument, it appears that between one-third and one-half of this decline is due to increases in women's work experience, schooling, and other skill training (O'Neill & Polacheck, 1993). Nevertheless, the most ambitious studies using individual characteristics still leave a substantial earnings gap unexplained, indicating that there must be other factors involved. Some of that earnings gap might arise from the types of jobs women and men hold.

Occupational Segregation

Economists and sociologists have argued that labor markets are segregated by occupation and job title. Discriminatory hiring practices crowd women into gender-typed jobs. The clustering of a large number of women into a limited number of occupations exerts a downward pressure on their pay. A number of studies on wage differentials have supplemented information on productivity-related individual characteristics with data on occupation, industry, unionization status, and type of employer (for example, government versus private, or large versus small firms). These studies have been able to explain a substantially larger portion of the earnings gap than human capital theory alone (Bergmann, 1980; England et al., 1994; Jacobsen, 1994; Kodras & Padavic, 1993; Parcel & Mueller, 1989; Treiman & Hartmann, 1981). Groshen (1991) found that the largest source of the gender wage gap is the association between salaries and the proportion of women in occupations, which accounts for a wage difference of 11% in manufacturing and 26% in services. Treiman and Hartmann (1981) estimated that occupational differences accounted for between 35% and 40% of the wage gap between men and women.

Despite marked increased progress in women's educational attainment and large increases in their labor force participation, occupational sex segregation has declined slowly (Jacobsen, 1994). Researchers who study occupational segregation rely on a dissimilarity index developed by Duncan and Duncan (1955). Using the Duncan Index, Cotter, DeFiore, Hermsen, Kowalewski, and Vanneman (1995) reported a drop of only 11% in occupational gender segregation between 1980 and 1990 among full-time, year-round workers. More women shifted into predominantly male occupations than men moved into predominantly female occupations. The higher the percentage of women workers in an occupation, the lower the average income is in that occupation. A small shift in occupational sex segregation experienced in the previous decade (i.e., between 1960 and 1970) was due more to the entry of men into a few female occupations—elementary school teaching, librarianship, nursing, and social work—than vice versa (Blau & Hendricks, 1979). Reskin and Roos (1990) concluded that growth in the number of women in the labor force is accompanied by increased segregation *within* occupations and by job deskilling, as well as declines in wages. There is some evidence that changes in occupational desegregation could be part of a "job tipping" process—the eventual abandonment by men of occupations as they are entered by a critical mass of women (for example, typists and bank tellers)—resulting in wage stagnation.

No single explanation exists for the high degree of gender segregation in the labor force. The influence of protective labor legislation (e.g., legally limiting the number of hours women could work and the amount of weight they could lift), in effect until the early 1970s, is still felt in some areas (Fox & Hesse-Biber, 1984). Occupational distributions are also the result of a number of individual decisions by employers and workers. Anticipation of leaving the labor force can lead to lower earnings over a woman's work life if she forgoes training that would prepare her for many male-dominated professions (Jacobsen & Levin, 1995). When women choose to qualify and apply for "men's" jobs, other forces such as employer discrimination in hiring or harassment by other workers might come into play (O'Farrell & Harlan, 1982; Spitze, 1988). Moreover, access to the training necessary for some occupations is often controlled by employers, unions, and/or educational institutions and is not entirely at the discretion of the individual worker (Bergmann, 1984).

Reskin and Roos (1990) examined various institutional barriers that hinder movement into nontraditional employment for women. They described how such restrictions operate in private apprenticeship and federal job training programs. Factors such as job access and assignment, employer and/or co-worker preference, entrance requirements such as preferred status for veterans, occupational mobility, and job retention programs, including provision or nonprovision of family support plans such as pregnancy leave, flextime, and child care, limit women's access into certain occupations.

One popular explanation for occupational sex segregation is that women choose traditionally female jobs because such jobs are geographically dispersed and can be re-entered easily after a period out of the labor force. This makes it easier for a woman to find work after staying home with children for a few years. England (1982) showed that women-typed occupations penalize worker earnings for intermittent employment to the same degree that men-typed occupations do, and Ferber (1982) reported that women-typed jobs are no more geographically dispersed than are men-typed ones. Women's home responsibilities can affect their occupational choices as well because some traditional occupations for women can be part-time or have hours and seasonal schedules that are compatible with caring for preschool or school-age children (Hayghe & Bianchi, 1994).

Discrimination by Employers

Most of the studies on pay disparity between women and men have been motivated by a desire to quantify the effects of discrimination in the labor market on women's earnings. These studies have measured what women would earn, on average, if they had the same education, training, and other productive characteristics as men given the skill requirements and working conditions (riskiness, dirtiness, unpleasantness, and so forth) of an occupation. The earnings gap remaining (that is, the differential that is left unexplained) has often been interpreted as a measure of discrimination.

Discrimination can take many forms; the two most often discussed are wage discrimination—paying different wages to equally qualified individuals performing equal or similar work—and job discrimination. The first is the sort of discrimination at issue in comparable worth legislation, that is, women's doing work that requires as much or more education, skill, or training as masculine-type jobs but pays less because the work is done by women. Job discrimination also takes the form of denying access to well-paid jobs with advancement opportunities to a particular group of qualified individuals (women, minorities). Gender discrimination in the labor market has been an overtly acknowledged factor in job segregation by sex and is the basis for affirmative action laws (England & McCreary, 1987).

Two-sector models of labor market discrimination propose that the work force is divided into distinct segments that compete differently in the labor market. In contrast to a single pool of workers that enters the labor market with everyone having equal chances to compete for jobs in terms of education and skill requirements, the work force is split along class, race, and gender lines so that different groups are sorted into separate areas of the occupational structure. Secondary sector employment is characterized by low wages and no fringe benefits, little or no job security or advancement opportunities, and unsafe working conditions. This sector is composed of a variety of jobs that include unskilled work in nonunionized factories; clerical, retail, and wholesale trade; service industries in general; and migrant agricultural work. In general, women, racial minorities, and immigrants are concentrated in secondary sector employment. In contrast, primary sector jobs are characterized by relatively stable employment, good working conditions, high wages, and built-in advancement and promotion opportunities (Dangler, 1994; Marini, 1989). Empirical investigations of dual labor market theories tend to find that these structural variables are as important as or more important than individual variables in accounting for wage differences among workers (Coverman, 1988; Figart, 1997).

Several studies have found that women are more likely than men to be employed in the secondary sector with its attendant low wages (Taylor, Gwartney-Gibbs, & Farley, 1986; Ward & Mueller, 1985). However, Reskin and Roos (1990) argued that the concentration of women in a small number of female-dominated industries has been more detrimental to earnings than has being employed in the secondary sector. Some evidence exists that even when women are employed in primary sector jobs, they receive lower economic payoffs for their qualifications (such as education and work experience) than men do *within* the same sector (Chauvin & Ash, 1994).

Economists have been slow to accept that discrimination accounts for part of the wage gap, believing that it disappears in competitive labor markets. For example, in this model employers with a preference for majority workers (white men) would hire them rather than minorities (women, men of color) who are equally productive, even if they had to pay the majority workers a higher rate. Majority workers gain from employer discrimination; they still compete with each other for jobs, but they are protected from competition with minority workers. However, employers who exercise their preference to discriminate would incur higher costs and reap lower profits, eventually being forced out of business by nondiscriminating competitors (Hersch, 1991).

One view of the labor market assumes that workers are allocated and wages determined through the competitive forces of supply and demand. However, internal labor market theory states that administrative decisions insulate many jobs from direct supply and demand market forces (Coverman, 1988). It is often suggested that women's earnings are lower than men's because more women work part-time and because women are not steadily employed over their lifetime. Differences in employment patterns by gender do exist, although earnings differentials remain even when those patterns are controlled (Chauvin & Ash, 1994; Hersch, 1991). However, if employers assume that women workers are less likely to stay on the job or will be absent more often than men, these attitudes will negatively affect their willingness to hire women for jobs with opportunities for advancement and training, or they will pay women somewhat less (Goldin, 1989; Heilman, 1995; Olson, 1990).

Women are more likely to have part-time or part-year employment than men. Part-time employment yields lower wages to both women and men, but most men in such work tend to be just entering the labor force or semi-retired (Fullerton, 1991). Women also work slightly fewer hours than men on average even when they are employed full-time, perhaps because home responsibilities do not allow them to take overtime work or because women-typed jobs are less likely to be structured for overtime. Some part-time employment might occur because people are unable to find jobs with more hours or because child care or transportation is costly or unavailable. Employers perhaps also structure jobs as part-time because such work does not have to offer the same fringe benefits as does full-time employment, thus cutting labor costs (Spitze, 1988).

Women are not absent from their jobs more often than men, as is often assumed. When women's absenteeism rates are compared to those of men in the same job category, they are found to be related to the job's status, and not to gender (Stroh, Brett, & Reilly, 1996). The same is true of turnover rates; women are no more likely to quit a job than are men in the same category. Rather, people in general are more likely to be absent or leave a job if there are few incentives to stay, such as prospects for advancement or pay increases (Martins-Crane, Beyerlein, & Johnson, 1995).

Gender and Housework

The final explanation for the sex differences in earnings to be reviewed is that competing demands on women's time place them at a disadvantage in comparison to men. Gender specialization still exists in most families; men are primarily responsible for earning income and women are primarily responsible for homemaking (Bryant & Zick, 1994; Thompson & Walker, 1989). All studies agree that husbands do much less housework and child care than wives, even when the wives are employed full-time. Whereas women's housework hours drop dramatically when they are employed 35 hours or more a week, men's housework time increases only slightly when their wives are employed full-time (Berk, 1984; Gershuny & Robinson, 1988; Hochschild, 1989; Sanik & Mauldin, 1986). Even under the most optimistic projections (Pleck, 1985), men have proved extremely resistant to assuming more family responsibilities. As Bernard (1981, p. 36) explained, "The old fear that women would de-sex themselves if they entered the labor force has been overcome; but the fear that men will become de-sexed if they share child care and household responsibilities remains."

Clearly, the time spent in domestic labor has implications for women's lives outside the household. There are only so many hours in a day and the time spent on one type of activity will reduce the time (and energy) expended on another. Coverman (1983) and Shelton and Firestone (1989) found that time spent on housework decreases the earnings of both women and men; Shelton and Firestone (1989) have estimated that about 8% of the earnings gap by sex is due directly to the greater amount of time women spend in household work. They suggested that the total effect might be larger than this because women's primary responsibility for domestic work can lead to fewer hours in paid employment, fewer years of work experience, and discriminatory hiring and promotion practices, all of which contribute to the earnings gap (see previous discussion).

Kanter (1977), Lambert (1990), and others argued that there are dual linkages between the occupational and family systems. Family responsibilities have also constrained men's careers. For example, early studies showed that married men were less geographically mobile than were unmarried men (see reviews in Markham, 1987) and men in dual-career families had less professional success than men with wives who were not employed (Ferber & Huber, 1979). But more recent research has indicated that family constraints are more relevant to women's occupational achievement. Marini (1989) showed that early marriage inhibits women's educational attainment but has no effect on men's schooling after marriage. Women with family responsibilities are less likely than men to be in the labor force, especially when children are young (Hayghe & Bianchi, 1994). In addition, the rate of part-time employment varies by marital status and family responsibility.

There seems to be no one theory that accounts for the source of the wage gap between women and men. Any comprehensive explanation of wage inequality in the labor market must take into account the many individual and structural factors that economic and sociological research has shown to affect earnings (Kalleberg & Rosenfeld, 1990; Miller & Garrison, 1982). Individual characteristics, occupational sex segregation and other structural mechanisms, and women's greater involvement in housework and child care than men's are all related. Constraints in one area structure roles in the other, shaping women's opportunities in the U.S. national economy.

FACTORS AFFECTING THE GROWTH OF
HOME-BASED EMPLOYMENT

Working at home for pay is nothing new in U.S. society. Until the Industrial Revolution, agriculture and cottage industries dominated the economy. However, industrialization and urbanization have moved the production functions of the family to factories, and city life halted much of the domestic manufacture of food, clothing, and household goods that had previously occurred on farms. Men and single women began exchanging their labor for wages, and married women became responsible for managing the family's consumption (Mintz & Kellogg, 1988). The idea that employment and family occupy separate and relatively autonomous spheres grew out of this physical separation of the centralized workplace and home (Kanter, 1977).

Mechanization and centralization of production did not completely eliminate home-based manufacturing production; instead it was incorporated into the factory system. Manufacturers would subcontract unfinished work (i.e., homework) out to women (i.e., home-workers), often the wives or daughters of inside workers, who would be paid by the finished piece or unit. Any work that could be segmented into discrete units (e.g., hat-braiding, knitting, sewing and embroidery, button-making, cigar-rolling, stitching shoes) was done in the home (i.e., home-working) (Boris, 1985). Home-working reached its peak in the late 19th century with the garment or apparel industry employing the largest number of workers. Garment manufacturers would contract out stitching and finishing to women, who lived and worked in tenement housing. A continuous flow of

Eastern European and Italian immigrants provided cheap home-based labor, which employers used to keep factory wages low and to ward off unionization. During the 1930s, social reformers campaigned against home-work; the result was the passage of anti-sweatshop laws that prohibited the use of home-workers in seven apparel-related industries and set up mechanisms for the regulation of home-workers in the remaining industries where it was allowed. Yet home-work never completely disappeared, and, in the unstable economy of the 1970s and 1980s, reports began to surface of a resurgence of home-work in old industries, as well as in new ones unregulated by the act (Silver, 1989).

Home-working was given extensive media attention after a dispute between a home-knitter and a sporting goods manufacturer over wage and hour violations. The roots of the episode went back to the 1940s, when the Labor Department decided that the production of goods in the home for an employer threatened the maintenance of labor standards. In 1941–1943, the labor secretary banned the home manufacture of women's apparel, knitted outerwear, gloves and mittens, buttons and buckles, embroidery, jewelry, and handkerchiefs. These restrictions stayed on the books until 1979, when a home-knitter complained that she was not being paid the minimum wage by CB Sports, who, along with other Vermont-based companies, had for several years been employing home-knitters to manufacture apparel. The Department of Labor (DOL) filed suit against the apparel firms, generating a series of hearings. Despite union opposition, in 1986 the DOL lifted the home-work ban on knitted outerwear and five of the six other restricted industries, replacing it with a certification system. Under this system, an employer could employ home-workers after obtaining a certificate from the department which committed them to paying at least the minimum wage plus pay for overtime (Hukill, 1990).

The controversy over home-work in manufacturing industries occurred at the same time that the incidence of home-based employment among white-collar workers, which is not covered by DOL restrictions, increased. Recent technological advances in the development of inexpensive personal computers, associated software, and electronic communications systems have made it feasible to move office work to other locations, including homes and prisons (Berch, 1985). Home-based employment has also arisen in the insurance, banking, and telephone industries, leaders in the use of computer and telecommunication technologies.

The forces that can lead to or allow a growth in the number of people working at home for pay are not only technological. Persistently high levels of unemployment in large sections of the country and increasing difficulties in entering the regular labor market; the growing number of dual-earner families and the opportunity to link employment, family time, and leisure; disappointment with the corporate setting; the challenge and autonomy of being one's own boss; and the move toward flatter, more decentralized organizations can all be seen as potential nontechnological contributors to increased home-based employment (Shamir, 1992; Wolfgram, 1984).

It has been challenging, using available data sets, for researchers to count the number of people in the United States who work at home for pay, including those running their own businesses. Differing estimates depend upon definitions of home-based employment as well as the population surveyed. Kraut (1988) used the 1980 Census data to compute that 750,000 white-collar, non-farm home-workers work at home for pay. Christensen (1988) and Silver (1989), using Bureau of Labor statistics for 1985, estimated 1.9 million home-workers, of whom 953,000 were full-time. Horvath (1986), using U.S. Bureau of Census data, estimated that 8.4 million people worked at least 8 hours a week at home as their primary job. Of these, 1.9 million worked exclusively in their home. LINK Resources, after conducting a national survey, reported in February 1993 that 39 million, or 31.4% of adults in the United States, were employed either part- or full-time at home (Sloane, 1993). Using the 1991 Current Population Survey, Deming (1994) estimated that approximately 20 million non-farm employees were engaged in some at-home work as part of their primary job, accounting for 18.3% of those employed. However, only 8 million were being compensated for their work at home. Of those who were paid or were self-employed, only about 4 million worked at home for 8 hours or more per week.

The majority of people with home-based employment are self-employed. The Census Bureau reported that the number of home-based business owners had increased to 5.6 million in 1991, over 2 million of whom were women (Pratt, 1993). The term *self-employment* is usually synonymous with small business and can include organizing as a sole proprietorship, partnership, or corporation. According to the limited information available, in comparison with non-home-based businesses, home-based businesses: (a) are more often started as sole proprietorships, (b) are less able to obtain start-up capital from commercial lenders, (c) operate with fewer employees, (d) have lower costs of doing business, and (e) generate less business income. Some recent studies portrayed home-based businesses as "an informal shaping of hobbies and casual activities into business dress" and their owners as women with young children who select the home as the location for their business to spend more time with their families (Pratt, 1993, p. 7). Most of what is known about home-based businesses is derived from anecdotal reports in the popular press, but some exploratory research has been conducted on gender differences and wages for home-based employment. Selected findings from several studies are presented next.

FINDINGS FROM THE RESEARCH

A rich source of data about home-based employment is a nine-state regional research project which focused on households in which at least one individual generated income by working at or from the home. During the spring of 1989, a 30-minute telephone interview was conducted with the household's manager (defined as the person who took care of most of the meal preparation, laundry, cleaning, child care, and scheduling of family activities).[2] Home-based employment was defined as income-generating labor done at or from the home and for which the worker had no regular alternate work site. The home-worker must have engaged in this work at least 6 hours a week in the previous year or worked at least 312 hours (6 hours per week for 52 weeks) and must have been in business for at least the previous 12 months. Farmers were excluded except those involved in retail sales and/or selling of value-added farm products. The unit of analysis was the household and the data were weighted to be representative of the population of the nine states and the rural and urban areas in the states.[3] More information on sampling, methodology, and definitions is contained in Stafford, Winter, Duncan, and Genalo (1992).

Walker and Haynes (1995) looked at only the family-owned home-based businesses in the nine-state sample and the financial rewards that accrued to their owners.[4] Their study asked (a) whether the earnings of men and women home-based family business owners were similar, and (b) if not, what were the differential determinants of these dissimilar outcomes. Table 3.1 provides a list of variables used in the analyses.

Control variables included in the model were those characteristics of the home-based family business owner that have been shown to be related to earnings, income, or business success of individuals (Blau & Ferber, 1992; Heck, 1992; Rowe, Haynes, & Bentley, 1994). These variables were the owner's education, age, number of hours worked annually, years in this business; whether or not the business was seasonal; and whether or not the residential location was rural.[5] Other variables included in the model were the form of legal ownership (sole proprietor, partnership, or corporation), female-dominated occupations, children younger than 6 years, and whether or not the owner also had an outside job.

The variable "female-dominated occupation" was created from answers to the question "What does the (home-based) worker do?" These responses were coded into 20 occupational categories, displayed in the first column in Table 3.2. Shown at the end of each row in Table 3.2 is the total number of businesses in that occupation in the sample. The middle column shows the percentage of women-owned businesses in the study by occupation. An occupation was considered to be female-dominated if 75% or more of the owners were women. Using this criteria, the following businesses were considered female-dominated: food service, beautician, human services, other services, service managers, and crafts.

Examples of the jobs performed within the six most female-dominated occupations were caterer, beautician, child- or elder-care, housecleaning, janitorial service, sewing, and ceramics. Although there are exceptions, these are jobs generally associated with low pay. Some occupations were totally or predominantly male: sales representatives, mechanics, contractors, shopkeepers, professional/managerial, and truck-drivers. Some examples of the jobs within the male-dominated occupations were manufacturer's representative, electronic repair, auto mechanic, building contractor, electrician, grain elevator owner, architect, certified public accountant, and backhoe operator. Although not all of these jobs are associated with high pay, men in sales and the professions were among the highest paid in the nine-state sample.

Table 3.1
Definition of Variables

Variable	Definition
Main effects	
Sole owners	equals 1 if business was solely owned; equals 0 if partnership or corporation
Female-dominated occupation	equals 1 if workers in the occupation consisted of at least 75% women; equals 0 otherwise
Children < 6	equals 1 if one or more child's age was less than 6 years; equals 0 otherwise
Outside Job	equals 1 if home-based business owner is employed outside the home; equals 0 otherwise
Control variables	
Education	years of education of home-based business owner
Age	years of age of home-based business owner in three brackets, < 35, 35–54, and > 54
Hours worked	total number of annual hours of paid-work by one or more workers in household and whose employment was covered by the survey interview
Experience	number of years worker has been doing the employment covered by the survey interview
Seasonal business	equals 1 if home-based employment was seasonal in nature, such as retail farm sales or landscaping services; equals 0 otherwise
Rural location	equals 1 if community lived in was town < 2,500, rural area, or farm; equals 0 otherwise
Dependent variables	
Annual earnings	total net 1988 annual income earned from the home-based business
Hourly earnings	annual income divided by hours worked

Note: From "Economic Outcomes: The Gender Factor" by R. Walker and G. Haynes, 1995, *Proceedings of the International Family Business Programs Association Annual Conference* (pp. 94–101), Nashville, TN.

Profiles of the business owners showed that both men and women had slightly more than a high school degree and were predominantly in the 35–54 age range. Women had owned their businesses, on average, about 2 years less than men had, 8.4 years compared to 10.5. Less than 20% of the businesses owned by either gender were operated seasonally. The sample was about evenly split by rural and urban location. Regardless of gender, more than 80% of the owners had organized their businesses as a sole proprietorship. Almost 60% of the women were in female-dominated occupations compared to 4% of the men. Thirty-one percent of the women lived in a household with a child younger than 6 years of age. A smaller percentage of women than men had outside jobs, that is, paid-work other than their home-based business.

Table 3.2
Occupation by Percentage of Home-Based Businesses Owned by Women ($n = 620$)

Occupation	Home-Based Businesses Owned by Women %	Total Businesses in Sample n
Female-dominated occupations		
Food service	100.0	1
Beautician	100.0	22
Human services	100.0	65
Other services	100.0	5
Service managers	83.0	12
Crafts	80.5	65
Mixed-gender occupations		
Agricultural sales	63.7	16
Sales agents	61.6	28
Teachers	60.4	16
Clerical	59.7	22
Livestock sales	55.2	4
Manager of income	53.8	9
Other sales	36.7	47
Creators	34.2	27
Male-dominated occupations		
Truck drivers	18.1	35
Professionals/managerial	15.4	51
Shopkeepers	14.4	8
Contractors	6.8	118
Mechanics	0.0	64
Sales representatives	0.0	5

Note: From "Economic Outcomes: The Gender Factor" by R. Walker and G. Haynes, 1995, *Proceedings of the International Family Business Programs Association Annual Conference* (pp. 94–101), Nashville, TN.

On average, men worked more hours a year than women did, 2,023 versus 1,547 hours. Table 3.3 shows the effects of the variables included in the model on hourly and annual earnings for women and men based on results of multivariate regression analysis.[6] The overall F statistic was significant for each of the four linear regressions, indicating the model was useful in explaining the variation in women's and men's earnings. Results of Chow tests[7] corroborated that the models of hourly and annual earnings were different for women and men, indicating that at least some of the influences on the earnings of home-based family business owners do differ by gender.

Table 3.3
Direction of Significant Effects of Research Variables on Earnings by Gender[a,b]

Variables	Hourly Earnings		Annual Earnings	
	Women	Men	Women	Men
Main effects				
Sole owners	−	n.s	−	n.s.
Female-dominated				
occupation	−	n.s.	−	−
Children < 6	−	n.s.	−	+
Outside job	n.s.	n.s.	−	−
Control variables				
Education	+	+	+	+
Age	−	+	−	n.s.
Hours worked	c	c	+	+
Experience	−	n.s.	n.s.	n.s.
Seasonal business	n.s.	n.s.	n.s.	n.s.
Rural location	n.s.	n.s.	n.s.	n.s.
F ratio	8.62*	3.89*	17.90*	9.09*
Adjusted R^2	24	09	42	21
Number of observations	262	358	262	358

Note: From "Economic Outcomes: The Gender Factor" by R. Walker and G. Haynes, 1995, *Proceedings of the International Family Business Programs Association Annual Conference* (pp. 94–101), Nashville, TN.
[a]Based on OLS regression.
[b]Weighted to represent the nine states' population.
[c]Hours worked was used to calculate hourly earnings and thus is not included as a variable.
n.s. indicates the effect is not significant.
*Significant at the $p < .1$ level.

Two control variables with significant influences on women's earnings were education and age. The interpretation was that, holding other influences constant, an additional year in school was associated with additional earnings; in contrast, being in the over-55 age group reduced earnings. The strongest influence on women's earnings was sole owner, and the effect was negative. Compared to organizing the business as a partnership or corporation, being a sole owner reduced annual earnings by more than $11,500. Being in a female-dominated occupation had a negative and significant effect on women's earnings. Compared to women in other occupations, doing "women's work" reduced annual earnings by more than $3,500. The presence of children under the age of 6 years reduced the annual earnings of women by more than $4,000, and working in an additional outside job had the expected negative effect on annual earnings from the business.

Two variables had similar effects on both measures of earnings regardless of gender: education and hours worked. Higher levels of education contributed to annual earnings, independent of other influences, for both men and women. Being in a seasonal business had no significant influence on earnings for either gender. Working more hours increased earnings from the business, regardless of gender, although the actual effect of an additional hour of work on annual earnings was quite different for women than for men. An additional hour of work added $1.89 to women's annual earnings, compared to $3.15 for men. Having children younger than 6 years of age increased men's annual earnings by more than $6,000.[8] Being a sole proprietor had no effect on men's earnings, in contrast to having a negative effect for women. Being in a female-dominated occupation reduced annual earnings of both women and men.

Walker and Haynes (1995) concluded that not only were the earnings of women who owned home-based businesses significantly lower than men's, the determinants of women's earnings were different from those of men. The strong negative effect of sole ownership for women is consistent with findings from Haber, Lamas, and Lichtenstein (1987), who found that women sole owners working full-time had average earnings 30% less than their men counterparts, and lower earnings than women owners who had incorporated. Additionally, they found that more women than men were engaged in casual and side businesses, and women were less likely to work full-time in their businesses.[9] The 37% of casual owners in their study who reported working full-time explained their low earnings by the fact that they were doing other things while working, such as watching children. Earning income was not their only motive. Walker and Haynes (1995) concluded that for some sole owners, the goal of running a profitable business was not the only concern.

The negative influence of being in a female-dominated occupation on women's earnings was not surprising. Women in these occupations were mainly involved in providing labor-intensive services or products with low capital requirements. The opposite effects by gender of the presence of children under 6 years of age are striking and support the generally held belief that female and male business owners behave quite differently (Korenman & Neumark, 1991). In families in which business work is synonymous with "men's work," the presence of young children might stimulate more intense work and a stronger profit motive. Because hours worked was held constant in the analysis, possible explanations could be that men who were business owners worked harder and more efficiently in the time they spent on their home-based business. In contrast, relative to other women who were home-based business owners, those with young children have lower earnings, independent of the number of hours worked, suggesting that these women perhaps dovetail paid-work with child-care responsibilities.

Using the same data set but a different statistical model and different criteria for inclusion, Olson, Fox, and Stafford (1995) selected a subsample containing only home-based business owners ($n = 679$) to determine whether factors associated with hourly gross business income differed by gender. Ordinary least squares (OLS) multiple regression analysis was used to determine which individual factors were significantly different between women and men home-based business owners. The dependent variable was the log of hourly gross business income. Explanatory variables included demographic characteristics, business characteristics, and occupations, as well as a dummy variable for gender. Explanatory variables were chosen to correspond with previously conducted research on wage rate determination (Blinder, 1973; Corcoran & Duncan, 1984; Oaxaca, 1973) and home-based business financial success.

About one-quarter of the home-based business owners had multiple workers involved in the business (27% of women-owned and 26% of men-owned), and men utilized a greater total number of workers. Male business owners averaged 0.61 employee who was a relative and 3.24 paid workers or independent contractors, compared to 0.27 worker who was a relative and 2.25 paid workers for female business owners. Men were also more likely to have another job in addition to their home-based business (32% versus 23% women) (Olson et al., 1995).

The researchers collapsed occupation titles into nine categories based on the *Standard Occupational Classification Manual* (1980) used by the U.S. Department of Commerce. Of the nine occupation codes in the prediction equation, some similarities and some glaring differences were found between women and men. Few women or men were in the agriculture and related products category (3% and 4%, respectively) or were managers (5% and 3%, respectively). The largest proportion of the women (35%) had a service-related business whereas only 1% of the men had a service business. A quarter (25%) of the women owners had businesses in the crafts/artisan category, whereas only 12% of the men were in this field. Fourteen percent of the women's businesses were in marketing/sales, about the same percentage as men's (13%). Eight percent of the women's businesses were professional/technical in nature, and 7% were clerical/administrative support (the proportion of businesses that were owned by men in those fields were 12% and 2%, respectively). Almost one-quarter (23%) of the male business owners were in mechanical/transportation trades, compared to 2% of the female business owners. The contractors group showed a similar discrepancy: 30% of the men but only 1% of the women had a contracting business (Olson et al., 1995).

Table 3.4 compares gross business income by gender and occupation. Both the selection of occupation and the differences in income between the genders in the same occupational category are worth noting. Gross business income was lower for women in all occupations except the contractor category, in which women made an average of over $115,000 annually and men made over

$104,000. However, only less than 1% of the women-owned businesses were in this category compared to 30% of the men's. Women in service businesses had the lowest gross incomes of workers in all occupational categories (Olson et al., 1995).

Table 3.4
Comparison of Gross Business Income by Gender and Occupation

Occupation	n	Women's Income in Dollars	n	Men's Income in Dollars
Professional/Technical	22	26,855.97 (44,486.55)	45	37,256.32 (33,557.82)
Marketing & Sales	39	50,452.07 (60,064.94)	51	96,168.95 (80,616.46)
Clerical & Adm. Support	20	26,921.04 (34,096.28)	8	59,221.01 (36,544.03)
Mechanical & Trans.	6	21,391.12 (16,606.22)	88	42,971.82 (45,756.11)
Crafts & Artisans	71	11,753.78 (20,813.86)	45	38,665.01 (43,069.51)
Managers	13	36,727.72 (57,938.69)	10	39,268.40 (32,105.08)
Services	101	11,178.38 (22,393.92)	3	24,666.67 (26,652.08)
Contractors	6	115,422.68 (191,112.10)	125	104,195.84 (120,892.33)
Ag. Products & Sales	10	30,695.88 (31,629.68)	16	58,140.27 (95,046.71)

Note: From "Are Women Installing Their Own Glass Ceilings?" by P. D. Olson, J. J. Fox, and K. Stafford, 1995, *Family Economics and Resource Management Biennial, 1.*
( ) = standard deviation.

A professional practices scale developed by Olson (1994) was used to provide information on how the business was managed. The score was the sum of responses to four of the variables in the data set which were thought to reflect the professionalism with which business was conducted: advertising in the Yellow Pages, incorporation of the business, use of a lawyer, and telephone answering protocol. Male home-based business owners used a higher number of professional practices than women (1.15 versus 0.71, respectively).

The results of their (Olson et al., 1995) OLS regression are reported in Table 3.5. The prediction equation performed better for female home-based business owners than it did for male home-based business owners (adjusted R^2 = 0.35 versus adjusted R^2 = 0.17). Twelve variables were significant in the women's equation, whereas only eight were significant predictors of the log of men's gross business earnings. Five variables were significant in both equations: the number of professional practices and the number of paid workers, which were positively related to gross business income for women and men; and the categories of professional/technical, mechanical/transportation, and crafts/artisans-related businesses, which were negatively related to gross business earnings for both men and women. Being married and having employment in addition to the business significantly lowered women's business income, whereas living in an urban county increased it. Earnings for women in all of the occupation categories were significantly lower than the earnings for men, except in marketing/sales (contracting being the omitted category). There were three additional variables significant for men's gross business earnings. Age of owner and number of years of education both had significant and positive effects, whereas having multiple workers in the household had a negative impact.[10]

All of the significant occupation variables, when interacted with gender, indicated higher earnings for men compared to women home-based business owners, except contracting, in which the few women in the sample earned more income than men. Other factors equal, male owners in clerical/administrative support businesses earned 117% more than women in the same occupation. Men with mechanical/transportation, crafts/artisans, managerial, service-related, and agricultural produce/sales businesses earned more than women in the same occupations (139%, 116%, 132%, 178%, and 153%, respectively).

Olson et al. (1995) also compared predicted earnings to actual earnings by gender (see Table 3.6). The actual hourly earnings, based on the sample means, showed a difference of over $28.00 an hour in gross hourly earnings between women and men who were business owners. By placing data containing the men's characteristics into a regression model created for men and the women's characteristics in a model for women, the men had a predicted gross hourly earning of $28.87 from the business. Women were predicted to earn $11.00 hourly in the women's equation. Yet when women's characteristics were substituted into the men's model, their earnings were predicted to be higher ($30.75) than the men's earnings in the same model ($28.87). In other words, if female home-based business owners kept their own characteristics (e.g., age, education, and marital status) but owned businesses in male-dominated occupations, their average wage would be greater than men's. Likewise, if men were in female-dominated occupations, their predicted hourly earnings would be less ($26.01) than their current earnings ($28.87).

In a third analysis of the nine-state data, Montalto, Olson, and Stafford (1995) focused on rural home-based business owners (rural counties were identified as those containing cities with populations of fewer than 25,000 residents) to determine whether the factors associated with gross income of the home-based business differed by gender. Ordinary least squares (OLS) multiple regression analysis was used in separate prediction models for women and men. The explanatory variables selected were categorized into four groups identified in the

Gender and Home-Based Employment

literature on small business success: community demographics, work commitment, worker characteristics, and business characteristics.

Table 3.5
Predictors of Log of Gross Business Income for Women and Men Who Are Owners of Home-Based Businesses

Variable	Women		Men	
	Coefficient	Standard Error	Coefficient	Standard Error
Intercept	3.191**	0.712	2.085**	0.486
Age of owner	0.008	0.007	0.011*	0.006
Marital status	-0.334*	0.184	-0.136	0.166
Dependents	0.053	0.052	0.001	0.057
Owner's education	-0.010	0.035	0.060**	0.030
Years in home-based business	-0.002	0.010	0.004	0.008
Urban	0.278**	0.139	0.128	0.114
Professional practices	0.395**	0.091	0.149**	0.062
Related employees	0.028	0.090	-0.060	0.047
Paid workers	0.021*	0.012	0.055**	0.013
Multiple workers in household	0.084	0.167	-0.324**	0.127
Additional employment	-0.283*	0.163	-0.165	0.124
Occ1 = Professional/Technical	-1.096**	0.531	-0.930**	0.221
Occ2 = Marketing/Sales	-0.456	0.497	-0.115	0.188
Occ3 = Clerical Admin. Sup.	-1.427**	0.530	-0.261	0.405
Occ4 = Mechanical/Trans.	-1.928**	0.649	-0.534**	0.154
Occ5 = Crafts/Artisans	-1.871**	0.484	-0.713**	0.198
Occ6 = Managers	-1.633**	0.558	-0.311	0.364
Occ7 = Services	-2.086**	0.472	-0.307	0.629
Occ9 = Ag Product/Sales	-2.003**	0.581	-0.470	0.293

Note: From "Are Women Installing Their Own Glass Ceilings?" by P. D. Olson, J. J. Fox, and K. Stafford, 1995, *Family Economics and Resource Management Biennial, 1.*
Women $n = 288$, $R^2 = 0.39$, Adjusted $R^2 = 0.35$; men $n = 391$, $R^2 = 0.21$, Adjusted $R^2 = 0.17$; omitted category = contractors.
*Significant $p = 0.10$.
**Significant $p = 0.05$.

There were no significant differences between the communities in which women and men's home-based businesses were located on the basis of analysis of data on community characteristics taken from the U. S. Bureau of the Census data on population and housing (1991). Counties in which home-based businesses were located were consistent with variables representative of rural counties nationally and also representative of the country as a whole, excluding minority comparisons.[11] The percentage of African Americans in counties where home-based businesses were located was significantly lower than the national rural average (6.1%) and the overall national average (12.0%), probably because the majority of the sample households were located in the Midwest region of the United States.

Table 3.6
Home-Based Business Owners: Men and Women's Predicted and Actual Earnings

	Mean	Standard Deviation
Actual hourly earnings based on sample means:		
Men's gross hourly earnings	45.49	(80.42)
Women's gross hourly earnings	17.26	(32.97)
Predicted hourly earnings rates based on regression equations:		
Men's predicted earnings with men's coefficients	28.87	(28.19)
Men's predicted earnings with women's coefficients	26.01	(30.75)
Women's predicted earnings with women's coefficients	11.19	(17.26)
Women's predicted earnings with men's coefficients	30.75	(123.26)

Note: From "Are Women Installing Their Own Glass Ceilings?" by P. D. Olson, J. J. Fox, and K. Stafford, 1995, *Family Economics and Resource Management Biennial, 1.*
Men $n = 391$; women $n = 288$.

Two variables chosen to represent worker commitment (i.e., years of experience in home-based business and annual hours the business owner worked) were significantly higher for men who were home-based business owners than for women who were home-based business owners. Male owners had worked approximately 11 years in their home-based business compared to 8 years for women (Montalto et al., 1995). Both tenures are about what would be predicted by survival rates for small businesses (Kalleberg & Leicht, 1991).

Business characteristics were grouped by occupation, utilization of employees, business management, and time management (Montalto et al., 1995). Although women and men were about equally represented in marketing and sales, the crafts/artisans occupation was composed predominately of women, and only 2% of the women were contractors (compared to 31% of the men). Women had fewer paid employees than men (1.4 and 2.7, respectively) and men were more likely to use household members and/or relatives not living in the household as employees.

Two scales provided information on how the business was managed. One was the professionalism scale (Olson, 1994) discussed previously; the second scale was a summation of responses to questions dealing with time use when work for the home-based business was especially hectic. Four time-use strategies were included: reduction of time spent with the family, reduction of sleeping time, hiring of help for the home-based business, and help from family or friends. Men used a higher number of professional practices (1.08 versus 0.51) and relatively more time-management strategies (2.25 versus 1.61) than did women who were home-based business owners. Further, men were more likely to use a delivery service (63% versus 56%) and a specially equipped vehicle (61% versus 16%) rather than the family vehicle.

The researchers then compared female and male rural home-based business owners in another regression model equation to predict gross business income using the same community characteristic, owner commitment, business characteristics, and responses to the time and professional management scales discussed. The prediction variables performed well for women, with an adjusted R^2 of 0.53, and for men, with an adjusted R^2 of 0.51, meaning that over 50% of the variance was explained for each model (Montalto et al., 1995). Twelve variables were significant predictors of men's gross business income; seven variables were significant predictors of women's gross business income. Some variables were significant for both: annual hours on the job, number of paid employees, use of a delivery service, use of a specially equipped vehicle, and the occupations of marketing/sales and contractors. A dual-use vehicle was related to decreased gross business income for women, but not for men. Community characteristics performed better in the men's equation than the women's. The professionalism scale, number of relatives employed, and the crafts/artisan occupation were also significant predictors for men, but not women.

Some variables had significantly greater effects for men who were home-based business owners. Each additional paid employee was associated with $2,713.25 more in gross business income annually for men than for women. Men owning crafts/artisan businesses earned $21,831 more each year than did women owning crafts/artisan businesses. Finally, each professional practice used increased men's gross business income $10,355 each year (Montalto et al., 1995).

SUMMARY

Perhaps the most important finding of these three studies is that traditional gender effects in the labor market carry over into home-based self-employment. Male home-based business owners are more likely to be in the highest-grossing occupations and earn more than female home-based business owners even when they are in the same occupations. King (1992) proposes that previous studies suggest that it is occupational choice, rather than education or experience, that drives gender differences in earnings, and the results of these studies are consistent with that premise. Education is not significantly correlated with earnings; nor is experience (years in business). Men in marketing/sales and crafts/artisans earn more than men earn in other occupations. Women who are contractors and in sales earn more than their female counterparts earn in other occupations. Considerable variation exists within occupations. For example, the crafts/artisans occupation contains women who crochet and sew for low pay and men who sculpt and work with wood for high pay.

Of course, occupational choice is not the whole story. There are significant gender differences in the effects of paid employees and professional practices on annual gross income from the home-based business even when controlling for occupation, experience, and hours worked. These variables have a larger effect on men's gross income than on women's gross income.

The questions posed by these results include, Do women underprice what they sell and if so, why? Does the anchor women use in setting prices differ from that of men? Will the market permit women to set prices equivalent to those set by men? Do women, as well as others, perceive their income to be supplemental (the "pin money" theory), and does this view affect their price setting? Why does the adoption of a few professional practices pay off so much more for men than for women? Why do women choose lower-paying occupations and work fewer hours in their home-based businesses? Also, why is it more profitable for men to hire employees than for women?

These findings show that home-based self-employment does not guarantee women an escape from the influence of gender in the workplace, particularly in realized income. Although home-based businesses permit greater flexibility and control of their work, flexibility and control do not necessarily translate into more money for female owners of home-based business.

WHAT DOES THIS MEAN FOR HOME-BASED BUSINESS OWNERS AND THEIR FAMILIES?

Discovering that women who own home-based businesses are earning so much less than their counterparts who are men is unexpected. Rational economic theory predicts that an independent business owner would set his or her hours of operation, choose his or her product or service, and set prices that would seek to maximize profits. But several factors can circumscribe the profitability of women-owned businesses. First, many women seek to own their own businesses in order to accommodate their family and child-care responsibilities in a way that other paid employment does not. "Care of family" and "flexibility to work in my own way at my own pace" figure prominently as the reasons women in the nine-state study chose home-based employment (compared to men, who say they "wanted to be their own boss") (Rowe & Bentley, 1992). Using home-based employment as a means to coordinate paid-work and family responsibilities better is also documented in studies by Allen (1983), Dangler (1994), and Beach (1993). There is a significant difference in the number of hours spent on home-based employment by gender in the nine-state study, with women spending approximately 1,350 hours compared to men's 1,750 hours per year. The number of hours spent in home-based employment is highly dependent upon the family situation of the business owner. Only women living alone match the number of hours spent on home-based employment by men (Rowe & Bentley, 1992). Ahrentzen (1990), Christensen (1987), and Pratt (1993), contrary to popular opinion, find that working at home for pay or profit does not necessarily eliminate the necessity of outside child care. Similarly, few women (or men) in the nine-state study cared for their children during the time they were engaged in home-based employment activities (Heck, Saltford, Rowe, & Owen, 1992).

Second, the size and type of many women's firms position them poorly in terms of financial rewards. Many of the women in the nine-state study own home-based businesses which are labor-intensive but are operating with only one or two employees. Men's home-based businesses are far more likely to have either paid employees or paid and unpaid family assistance (Heck & Walker, 1993). Owners who have to rely on only their own labor are at a disadvantage, and attaining higher incomes is extremely difficult (Aldrich & Weiss, 1981). Then, too, positioning one's business in the home can limit the preferred size of many businesses. The physical size of the building, the need for business deliveries, the disposal of waste products, and the number of employees who can be accommodated might possibly all be restricted by zoning laws or concern for the character of the owner's neighborhood, but the nine-state study contains no data which can illuminate these issues.

Third, many women opening home-based businesses have little capital or background in business. It appears that many men, but fewer than women, also start businesses with little capital or little experience. Men's enterprises are more likely than women's are to grow out of their technical training or management experience. Commercial lenders are reluctant to advance loans to business owners of either gender who do not have a track record and/or substantial assets for collateral. As a result, women's enterprises are frequently in sectors in which they can gain market share with a relatively small front-end investment (Brophy, 1989; Clark & James, 1992). In addition, 60% of all female business owners report little managerial training prior to owning their own business (Clark & James, 1992), or their administrative experience has been limited to middle-management positions (Hisrich, 1989). There is some evidence that women have more direct experience in the field in which they start their venture (Brophy, 1989) than do men, but not necessarily in a management position. In contrast, men's enterprises tend to grow out of their own technical education or specialization and previous work experience. A lack of experience can manifest itself in several ways. One can be price setting. There is anecdotal evidence that home-based business owners based their prices on what their neighbors or friends and family would pay for an item or service rather than what the market would bear, thereby limiting rather than maximizing the profitability of the business (Heck et al., 1995).

Businesses can be organized as sole proprietorships, partnerships, limited liability companies, or corporations. A sole proprietorship is owned by a single individual, a structure which limits the size of both human and financial capital available to the firm. While owners might incorporate for a variety of reasons (e.g., to reduce personal legal liability, to lower marginal tax rates, or to make themselves eligible for unemployment insurance), the act of incorporating suggests that the owner has a certain level of sophistication about the business environment and a seriousness about the profit motive that might not be characteristic of owners who do not incorporate. Also, small businesses begun as sole proprietorships are open to exploitation by larger firms and highly vulnerable to economic setbacks. In the nine-state study, having an incorporated business means having higher business income than either sole proprietorships or partnerships regardless of whether the owner is a woman or a man (Heck et al., 1995).

Finally, not only do women's home-based businesses in the nine-state study cluster into service-type occupations, there appears to be a second tier of gender segregation within occupational categories. For example, women in sales are more likely to be selling cosmetics or plastic refrigerator dishes than pharmaceutical products. Women are over-represented as beauticians and child-care providers and under-represented in the professions such as architects or attorneys. Why have women chosen to own businesses in such low-earning occupations? One explanation is that women tend to choose businesses in occupations in which they are familiar with the nature and function of the work. Until the 1970s, women were not presented with a wide variety of occupational choices—generally they could be secretaries, salesclerks, teachers, librarians, nurses, seamstresses, waitresses, or domestics. To some extent, past socialization and the widespread allocation of household responsibilities to women still slot them into traditional job categories. Female business owners, already lacking experience in business skills, might not look at businesses they perceive as being predominantly ones for men (just as most men do not look at operating a yarn shop or day care center). However, the rewards are there when they do—in the nine-state study, female contractors make more from their businesses than male contractors (Olson et al., 1995).

Women who are home-based business owners face many of the same challenges that non-home-based owners face. Their earnings from self-employment are negatively impacted by the limited number of hours they have available for paid-work; by the size, age, and legal structure of their businesses; by lack of business credentials; and by segmentation into traditional "women's" occupations. On the positive side, if women are choosing to base their businesses at home because they can make their paid-work fit around child and family responsibilities or to control growth, the experience of owning and managing a business can increase self-confidence and awareness of hidden talents and abilities translatable into other, more financially remunerative enterprises. A home-based business allows a woman an opportunity to obtain business expertise and to move her enterprise into a Main Street location when it is more compatible with her life-style. This points out the necessity to encourage women to think through a wide variety of business possibilities and not be circumscribed in generating ideas for their ventures.

NEEDS FOR ADDITIONAL RESEARCH

By most judgments, businesses that are owned by women and home-based businesses are the fastest growing in the country. However, more research is needed to flesh out the limited number of studies to date. Future research needs to focus on the longitudinal dimensions of home-based businesses and on the aspirations and ambitions of their owners. How much does profit and/or the employment picture in their home counties motivate the entry into and exit from home-based businesses? To what extent does generated income influence occupational choice? What are owners' strategies for growth and expansion of their businesses? How do these differ between home-based businesses owned by women versus men, or women who are non-home-based business owners? How many more home-based businesses would be created if tax, insurance, and zoning reforms were instituted? What is the survival rate of home-based businesses (e.g., how many exits are really quits once financial objectives are achieved)? How do home-based business owners coordinate their family responsibilities with business demands without sacrificing income? How do they meet and overcome obstacles to profitability as their businesses mature? What is the level of participation by minorities and by persons whose activities are physically limited, and are their financial pictures the same as or different from those of others? Are home-based businesses an avenue out of welfare dependency? If so, under what conditions? Last, there is an urgent need for well-designed qualitative studies so that researchers, practitioners, and policymakers can better understand the impact of home-based self-employment in this vitally important segment of the economy.

NOTES

This chapter reports results from the Cooperative Regional Research Project, NE-167, entitled *At-Home Income Generation: Impact on Management, Productivity and Stability in Rural and Urban Families*, supported by Cooperative States Research Service, U.S. Department of Agriculture, and the Experiment Stations at the University of Hawaii, Iowa State University, Lincoln University (Missouri), Michigan State University, Cornell University (New York), The Ohio State University, Pennsylvania State University, Utah State University, and University of Vermont.

1. In this chapter, the term *home-worker* is used to refer to someone who works at home for pay (i.e., home-working), either as an employee or in his or her own business.

2. Details of the study, *At-Home Income Generation: Impact on Management, Productivity and Stability in Rural and Urban Families*, can be found in Heck, Owen, and Rowe (1995).

3. Respondents were selected at random from a list of telephone numbers supplied by Survey Sampling of Fairfield, CT.

4. The total sample of home-workers was 899; those who were not business owners were employees working at home. Seventy-five percent ($n = 670$) of the total sample were home-based business owners. The subsample for the analyses in the

discussion that follows consisted of the 620 families who owned and operated a business at home: 262 owned by women and 358 owned by men. The family business designation rested upon respondents' answers to a screening question about family functioning. Because family membership was self-identified by the respondents, there were some informal families in the subsample (i.e., unrelated individuals who shared a household but who defined themselves as a family). Ninety percent of the businesses analyzed here were legally categorized as sole proprietorships; the remaining 10% were split between partnership and corporate legal structures.

5. Location was defined as rural if the home-worker lived in a town of fewer than 2,500 residents, a rural area, or a farm.

6. A major advantage of regression analysis is that it enables the researcher to isolate the effects of a particular variable of interest (such as children younger than 6 years of age) on earnings while holding constant the effects of the other variables.

7. A statistical test to determine whether two sets of observations belong to the same linear regression model (Chow, 1960).

8. Net income from home-based businesses varied significantly by gender. Male home-based business owners earned, on average, $21,298 in 1988 whereas female home-based business owners had net incomes of $7,691 annually. Net incomes from home-based businesses provided nearly 39.7% of the family's total income (Heck, Owen, & Rowe, 1995).

9. Defined in their study as one in which the owner expected annual gross receipts of less than $1,000.

10. Negative coefficients for the occupation variables are interpreted by comparing that occupation with the omitted occupation, which in this analysis was the contractor occupation, which had the highest income of all the occupation categories. For example, when the crafts/artisans occupation was a significant predictor of the log of women's hourly gross earnings, the coefficient was interpreted to mean that women in crafts/artisan businesses earned less than female contractors. Similarly, men's crafts/artisan businesses earned less than did those of men who were contractors.

11. The Federal Information Population Statistics (FIPS) codes enable researchers to link county location and county-level aggregate information from Census data to other data sets. Here, data from counties where each participant in the nine-state study resided were matched to the same variables in the U.S. population using FIPS. The context in which community variables were evaluated was clarified with this comparison technique, providing information that distinguishes the communities in which home-workers live from the general U.S. population.

REFERENCES

Ahrentzen, S. B. (1990). Managing conflict by managing boundaries: How professional homeworkers cope with multiple roles at home. *Environment and Behavior, 22*, 723–752.

Aldrich, H., & Weiss, J. (1981). Differentiation within the United States capitalist class: Workforce size and income differences. *American Sociological Review, 46*, 279–290.

Allen, S. (1983). Production and reproduction: The lives of women homeworkers. *Sociological Review, 31*, 649–665.

Barrett, N. S. (1979). Women in the job market: Occupations, earnings, and career opportunities. In R. E. Smith (Ed.), *The subtle revolution* (pp. 36–48). Washington, DC: Urban Institute.

Beach, B. (1993). Family support in home-based family businesses. *Family Business Review, 6,* 371–379.

Berch, B. (1985). The resurrection of out-work. *Monthly Review, 37,* 37–46.

Bergmann, B. R. (1980). Occupational segregation, wages and profits when employers discriminate by race or sex. In A. H. Amsden (Ed.), *The economics of women and work* (pp. 271–282). New York: St. Martin's.

Bergmann, B. R. (1984). Feminism and economics. *Challenge, 27,* 46–49.

Berk, S. (1984). *The gender factory: The apportionment of work of American households.* New York: Plenum.

Bernard, J. (1981). *Family life cycles and work: Myth and realities.* Washington, DC: American Association of University Women.

Blau, F. D., & Ferber, M. A. (1992). *The economics of women, men, and work.* Englewood Cliffs, NJ: Prentice-Hall.

Blau, F. D., & Hendricks, W. E. (1979). Occupational segregation by sex: Trends and prospects. *Journal of Human Resources, 14,* 197–210.

Blinder, A. (1973). Wage discrimination: Reduced form and structural variables. *Journal of Human Resources, 8,* 436–455.

Boris, E. (1985). Regulating industrial homework: The triumph of "sacred motherhood." *Journal of American History, 71,* 745–763.

Brophy, D. .J. (1989). Financing women-owned entrepreneurial firms. In O. Hagan, C. Rivchun, & D. Sexton (Eds.), *Women-owned businesses* (pp. 55–75). New York: Praeger.

Bryant, W. K., & Zick, C. D. (1994). The economics of housespousery: An essay on household work. *Journal of Family and Economic Issues, 15,* 137–168.

Chauvin, K. W., & Ash, R. A. (1994). Gender earnings differentials in total pay, base pay, and contingent pay. *Industrial and Labor Relations Review, 47,* 634–649.

Chow, G. C. (1960). Tests of equality between sets of coefficients in two linear regressions. *Econometrics, 28,* 591–605.

Christensen, K. E. (1987). Women, families, and home-based employment. In N. Gerstel & H. E. Gross (Eds.), *Families and work* (pp. 478–490). Philadelphia: Temple University Press.

Christensen, K. E. (1988). Independent contracting. In K. E. Christensen (Ed.), *The new era of home-based work: Directions and policies* (pp. 79–91). Boulder, CO: Westview.

Clark, T. A., & James, F. J. (1992). Women-owned businesses: Dimensions and policy issues. *Economic Development Quarterly, 6,* 25–40.

Corcoran, M., & Duncan, G. (1984). Do women "deserve" to earn less than men? In G. Duncan (Ed.), *Years of poverty, years of plenty* (pp. 153–172). Ann Arbor, MI: Institute for Social Research.

Cotter, D. A., DeFiore, J. M., Hermsen, J. M., Kowalewski, B. M., & Vanneman, R. (1995). Occupational gender desegregation in the 1980s. *Work and Occupations, 22,* 3–21.

Coverman, S. (1983). Gender, domestic labor time, and wage inequality. *American Sociological Review, 48,* 623–637.

Coverman, S. (1988). Sociological explanations of the male-female wage gap: Individualist and structuralist theories. In A. H. Stromberg & S. Harkess (Eds.), *Women working: Theories and facts in perspective* (2nd ed., pp. 101–115). Mountain View, CA: Mayfield.

Dangler, J. (1986). Industrial homework in the modern work-economy. *Contemporary Crises, 10,* 257–279.

Dangler, J. F. (1994). *Hidden in the home: The role of waged homework in the modern world-economy.* Albany: State University of New York Press.

Deming, W. G. (1994, February). Work at home: Data from the CPS. *Monthly Labor Review, 117*(2), 14–20.

Devine, T. J. (1994). Characteristics of self-employed women in the United States. *Monthly Labor Review, 117*(3), 20–34.

Duncan, O. D., & Duncan, B. (1955). A methodological analysis of segregation indexes. *American Sociological Review, 20,* 210–217.

England, P. (1982). The failure of human capital theory to explain occupational sex segregation. *Journal of Human Resources, 17,* 358–370.

England, P., Herbert, M. S., Kilbourne, B. S., Reid, L. L., & Megdal, L. M. (1994). The gendered valuation of occupations and skills: Earnings in 1980 census occupations. *Social Forces, 73,* 65–99.

England, P., & McCreary, L. (1987). Gender inequality in employment. In B. B. Hess & M. M. Ferree (Eds.), *Analyzing gender: A handbook of social science research* (pp. 286–320). Newbury Park, CA: Sage.

Ferber, M. A. (1982). *Women and work: Issues of the 1980s.* Palo Alto, CA: Mayfield.

Ferber, M., & Huber, J. (1979). Husbands, wives, and careers. *Journal of Marriage and the Family, 41,* 315–325.

Figart, D. M. (1997). Gender as more than a dummy variable: Feminist approaches to discrimination. *Review of Social Economy, 55,* 1–32.

Fox, M. F., & Hesse-Biber, S. (1984). *Women at work.* Palo Alto, CA: Mayfield.

Fullerton, H. N. (1991). Labor force projections: The baby boom moves on. *Monthly Labor Review, 114*(11), 31–44.

Gershuny, J., & Robinson, J. P. (1988). Historical changes in the household division of labor. *Demography, 25,* 537–552.

Goldin, C. (1989). Life-cycle labor-force participation of married women: Historical evidence and implications. *Journal of Labor Economics, 7,* 20–47.

Greenberger, E., & Steinberg, L. D. (1983). Sex differences in early labor force experience: Harbinger of things to come. *Social Forces, 62,* 467–486.

Groshen, E. L. (1991). The structure of the female/male wage differential: Is it who you are, what you do, or where you work? *Journal of Human Resources, 26,* 457–472.

Haber, S. E., Lamas, E. J., & Lichtenstein, J. H. (1987). On their own: The self-employed and others in private business. *Monthly Labor Review, 110*(5), 17–23.

Hayghe, H. V., & Bianchi, S. M. (1994). Married mothers' work patterns: The job-family compromise. *Monthly Labor Review, 117*(6), 24–30.

Heck, R. K. Z. (1992). The effects of children on the major dimensions of home-based employment. *Journal of Family and Economic Issues, 13,* 315–342.

Heck, R. K. Z., Owen, A. J., & Rowe, B. R. (1995). *Home-based employment and family life.* Westport, CT: Auburn House.

Heck, R. K. Z., Saltford, N., Rowe, B. R., & Owen, A. J. (1992). The utilization of child care by households engaged in home-based employment. *Journal of Family and Economic Issues, 13,* 213–237.

Heck, R. K. Z., & Walker, R. (1993). Family-owned home businesses: Their employees and unpaid helpers. *Family Business Review, 6,* 397–415.

Heilman, M. E. (1995). Sex stereotypes and their effects in the workplace: What we know and what we don't know. *Journal of Social Behavior and Personality, 10,* 3–26.

Hersch, J. (1991). Male-female differences in hourly wages: The role of human capital, working conditions, and housework. *Industrial and Labor Relations Review, 44,* 746–759.

Hisrich, R. D. (1989). Women entrepreneurs: Problems and prescriptions for success in the future. In O. Hagan, C. Rivchun, & D. Sexton (Eds.), *Women-owned businesses* (pp. 3–32). New York: Praeger.

Hochschild, A. (1989). *Second shift: Working parents and the revolution at home.* New York: Viking.

Horvath, F. W. (1986). Work at home: New findings from the current population survey. *Monthly Labor Review, 109*(11), 31–35.

Hukill, C. (1990). Homework. *Monthly Labor Review, 113*(5), 53–54.

Jacobsen, J. P. (1994). Trends in work force sex segregation, 1960–1990. *Social Science Quarterly, 75,* 204–211.

Jacobsen, J. P., & Levin, L. M. (1995). Effects of intermittent labor force attachment on women's earnings. *Monthly Labor Review, 118*(8), 14–19.

Kalleberg, A. L., & Leicht, K. T. (1991). Gender and organizational performance: Determinants of small business survival and success. *Academy of Management Journal, 34,* 136–161.

Kalleberg, A. L., & Rosenfeld, R. A. (1990). Work in the family and in the labor market: A cross-national, reciprocal analysis. *Journal of Marriage and the Family, 52,* 331–346.

Kanter, R. (1977). *Work and family in the United States: A critical review and agenda for research and policy.* New York: Russell Sage Foundation.

Kilbourne, B., England, P., & Beron, K. (1994). Effects of individual, occupational, and industrial characteristics on earnings: Intersections of race and gender. *Social Forces, 72,* 1149–1176.

King, M. C. (1992). Occupation segregation by race and sex, 1940–88. *Monthly Labor Review, 115*(4), 30–37.

Kodras, J. E., & Padavic, I. (1993). Economic restructuring and women's sectoral employment in the 1970s: A spatial investigation across 380 U.S. labor market areas. *Social Science Quarterly, 74,* 1–27.

Korenman, S., & Neumark, D. (1991). Does marriage really make men more productive? *Journal of Human Resources, 26,* 282–307.

Kraut, R. E. (1988). Homework: What is it and who does it? In K. E. Christensen (Ed.), *The new era of home-based work: Directions and policies* (pp. 30–48). Boulder, CO: Westview.

Kraut, R. E. (1989). Telecommuting: The trade-offs of home work. *Journal of Communication, 39*(3), 19–47.

Kraut, R. E., & Grambsch, P. (1987). Home-based white collar employment: Lessons from the 1980 census. *Social Forces, 66,* 410–426.

Lambert, S. J. (1990). Processes linking work and family: A critical review and research agenda. *Human Relations, 43,* 239–257.

Lozano, B. (1989). *The invisible work force: Transforming American business with outside and home-based workers.* New York: Free Press.

Marini, M. M. (1989). Sex differences in earnings in the United States. *Annual Review of Sociology, 15,* 343–380.

Markham, W. T. (1987). Sex, relocation, and occupational advancement: The 'real cruncher' for women. In A. H. Stromberg, L. Larwood, & B. A. Gutek (Eds.), *Women and work* (pp. 207–232). Beverly Hills, CA: Sage.

Martins-Crane, M. D., Beyerlein, M. M., & Johnson, D. A. (1995). Adjusting models of gender and work to new work environments. *Journal of Social Behavior and Personality, 10,* 27–50.

Miller, J., & Garrison, H. H. (1982). Sex roles: The division of labor at home and in the workplace. *Annual Review of Sociology, 8,* 237–262.

Mincer, J. & Ofek, H. (1982). Interrupted work careers: Depreciation and restoration of human capital. *Journal of Human Resources, 17,* 3–24.

Mintz, S., & Kellogg, S. (1988*). Domestic revolutions: A social history of American family life.* New York: Free.

Montalto, C. P., Olson, P. D., & Stafford, K. (1995). *At home, but worlds apart: Gender influence on home-based business income.* Unpublished manuscript, The Ohio State University, Department of Consumer and Textile Science.

Oaxaca, R. (1973). Male-female wage differentials in urban labor markets. *International Economic Review, 14,* 693–709.

O'Farrell, B., & Harlan, S. (1982). Craftworkers and clerks: The effect of male co-worker's hostility on women's satisfaction with non-traditional jobs. *Social Problems, 29,* 252–265.

Olson, P. (1990). The persistence of occupational segregation: A critique of its theoretical underpinnings. *Journal of Economic Issues, 24,* 161–171.

Olson, P. D. (1994). *Home-based business in rural America—defining and predicting success.* Unpublished master's thesis, The Ohio State University, Columbus.

Olson, P. D., Fox, J. J., & Stafford, K. (1995*).* Are women installing their own glass ceilings? *Family Economics and Resource Management Biennial, 1,* 163–170.

O'Neill, J., & Polachek, S. (1993). Why the gender gap in wages narrowed in the 1980s. *Journal of Labor Economics, 11,* 205–228.

Parcel, T. L., & Mueller, C. W. (1989). Temporal change in occupational earnings attainment, 1970–1980. *American Sociological Review, 54,* 622–634.

Pleck, J. H. (1985). *Working wives/working husbands.* Beverly Hills, CA: Sage.

Pratt, J. H. (1993). *Myths and realities of working at home: Characteristics of home-based business owners and telecommuters* (U.S. Small Business Administration, Office of Advocacy Contract SBA-647-OA-91). Washington, DC: U.S. Government Printing Office.

Reskin, B. F., & Roos, P. A. (1990). *Job queues, gender queues.* Philadelphia: Temple University Press.

Robinson, J. P., & Bostrom, A. (1994). The overestimated workweek? What time diary measures suggest. *Monthly Labor Review, 117*(8), 11–19.

Rowe, B. R., & Bentley, M. (1992). The impact of the family on home-based work. *Journal of Family and Economic Issues, 13,* 279–297.

Rowe, B. R., Haynes, G. W., & Bentley, M. (1994). Economic outcomes in family-owned home businesses. *Family Business Review, 6,* 383–396.

Sandell, S., & Shapiro, D. (1978). An exchange: The theory of human capital and the earnings of women, a re-examination of the evidence. *Journal of Human Resources, 13*, 103–117.

Sanik, M. M., & Mauldin, T. (1986). Single- versus two-parent families: A comparison of mother's time. *Family Relations, 35*, 53–56.

Shamir, B. (1992). Home: The perfect workplace? In S. Zedeck (Ed.), *Work, families, and organizations* (pp. 272–311). San Francisco: Jossey-Bass.

Shelton, B. A., & Firestone, J. (1989). Household labor time and the gender gap in earnings. *Gender and Society, 3*, 105–112.

Silver, H. (1989). The demand for homework: Evidence from the U.S. Census. In E. Boris & C. R. Daniels (Eds.), *Homework: Historical and contemporary perspectives on paid labor at home* (pp. 103–129). Urbana: University of Illinois Press.

Sloane, L. (1993, February 6). When a home also shelters a business. *New York Times*, p. 26.

Smith, J. P., & Ward, M. (1989). Women in the labor market and in the family. *Journal of Economic Perspectives, 3*, 9–23.

Sorensen, E. (1989). Measuring the effect of occupational sex and race composition on earnings. In R. T. Michael, H. I. Hartman, & B. O'Farrell (Eds.), *Pay equity: Empirical inquiries* (pp. 49–69). Washington, DC: National Academy Press.

Spitze, G. (1988). The data on women's labor force participation. In A. H. Stromberg & S. Harkess (Eds.), *Women working: Theories and facts in perspective* (2nd ed., pp. 42–60). Mountain View, CA: Mayfield.

Stafford, K., Winter, M., Duncan, K. A., & Genalo, M. A. (1992). Studying at-home income generation: Issues and methods. *Journal of Family and Economic Issues, 13*, 139–158.

Stevenson, M. H. (1988). Some economic approaches to the persistence of wage differences between men and women. In A. H. Stromberg & S. Harkess (Eds.), *Women working: Theories and facts in perspective* (2nd ed., pp. 87–100). Mountain View, CA: Mayfield.

Stroh, L. K., Brett, J. M., & Reilly, A. H. (1996). Family structure, glass ceiling, and traditional explanations for the differential rate of turnover of female and male managers. *Journal of Vocational Behavior, 49*, 99–118.

Taylor, P. A., Gwartney-Gibbs, P. A., & Farley, R. (1986). Changes in the structure of earnings by race, sex and industrial sector, 1960–1980. In R. V. Robinson (Ed.), *Research in social stratification and mobility* (Vol. 5, pp. 105–138). Greenwich, CT: JAI.

Thompson, L., & Walker, A. J. (1989). Gender in families: Women and men in marriage, work, and parenthood. *Journal of Marriage and the Family, 51*, 845–871.

Treiman, D. J., & Hartmann, H. I. (1981). *Women, work, and wages*. Washington, DC: National Academy Press.

U.S. Bureau of the Census. (1991). *Census of population and housing, 1990*. Summary tape file 3, United States [Machine-readable data file]. Washington, DC: U.S. Bureau of the Census (Producer and distributor).

U.S. Department of Commerce. Office of Federal Statistical Policy and Standards (1980). *Standard occupational classification manual*. Washington, DC: U.S. Government Printing Office.

Walker, R., & Haynes, G. (1995). Economic outcomes: The gender factor. *Proceedings of the International Family Business Programs Association Annual Conference* (pp. 94–101), Nashville, TN.

Ward, K. B., & Mueller, C. W. (1985). Sex differences in earnings: The influence of industrial sector, authority hierarchy, and human capital variables. *Work and Occupations, 12,* 437–463.

Witkowski, K. M., & Leicht, K. T. (1995). The effects of gender segregation, labor force participation, and family roles on the earnings of young adult workers. *Work and Occupations, 22,* 48–72.

Wolfgram, T. H. (1984). Working at home: The growth of cottage industry. *Futurist, 18* (3), 31–34.

Chapter 4

Home-Based Employment: Relating Gender and Household Structure to Management and Child Care

*Holly Hunts, Sharon M. Danes, Deborah C. Haynes,
and Ramona K. Z. Heck*

INTRODUCTION

For many Americans the home-worker has a female face. Perhaps this image comes from the second edition of *Women Working Home*, which was considered to be the "bible of home-based businesses" (Behr & Lazar, 1983). Also, the most prominent national events publicizing female home-workers were the court fights in the early 1980s with the U.S. Department of Labor debating whether home-based employees should be allowed to work in their homes as a variance to the Fair Labor Standards Act (Boris, 1987). These court battles for home knitters in New England and women sewing embroidery on sweatshirts in Iowa were landmark cases that received public attention. Both were led by and for women.

Despite the popular public impression that home-workers are women, well planned and executed studies show that both men and women engage in home-based employment, and men are slightly more likely to be involved in home-based employment (Heck, Owen, & Rowe, 1995; Pratt, 1993). Little is known, however, about the motivations for engaging in home-based employment. Possibilities include the following:

- Profit maximizing reasons such as optimally using paid-work and home space to reduce the cost of both enterprises; using a home address for employment even though the actual work is done at a different site, such as selling insurance on the road or working on a construction site; or using a home environment because the home is the best place to produce the work, such as in home-based child care
- Health or personal reasons such as having an illness (physical or mental) which makes working elsewhere less preferable, more difficult, or impossible
- Utility maximizing reasons motivated by the desire to care for family members

(children, disabled, or elderly) jointly with profit maximizing reasons including earning money, getting experience, or maintaining professional status and skills in a field of work

Profit maximization, the first motive, does not appear to be gender-related; both genders would desire profit-maximization and engage in home-based employment if it clearly offered greater profit than working in another setting. The second motive, health or personal reasons, would not likely be linked to gender differences because both men and women could find home-based employment more successful than working in a different location. However, the third reason, combining utility and profit maximization because of demands from both the household and the workplace, could certainly arise from differences in gender norms. The work of the home has been in the domain of women's roles for centuries. Although men have worked at home, the traditional role of the man has been as the breadwinner for the family. The breadwinner role took place primarily at the home farm in an agrarian economy and has since moved into the urban environment, dissociating paid-work from the home for the vast majority of men. For women, however, the role of paid-worker has become accepted in the United States as an additional role since the 1960s. Each of these roles, homemaker and paid-worker, is important in maximizing individual and family well-being.

The work of the home lies in the transformation of raw materials into finished consumable products (such as fed families and clean clothes) and in provision of the social-psychological supports necessary for mental well-being (such as loved children and a cherished spouse). The work in the marketplace provides the money to purchase raw materials for desired outcomes in the family. Families have moved from home production of many commodities such as food, home furnishings, and clothing to the purchase of these commodities in the marketplace. Therefore, the goal of families in the last century has changed from household production to household consumption, with the making and spending of money consuming the time and energy of the household members. The only areas in which the marketplace has not been able to replace household production at a level at least as good or better than the household produced product has been in the physical, social, and psychological care of family members. However, pieces of the care, such as child care, have developed as market services. Caring and arranging for care for children and other family members remain important jobs of families, arguably the most important jobs. Whereas food, clothing, and housing services can all be purchased at an acceptable level in the marketplace, the total care of family members is an area in which the household still has a comparative advantage over the marketplace.

Culture, public policies, and workplace policies have shifted in the last century to accommodate the notion of women's being employed outside the home in the United States and in other developed and developing countries around the world. However, family culture has not as completely adopted the idea that the marketplace or male family members can do an adequate job of nurturing family members. The care of family members has been and remains in the domain of women (Higgins, Duxbury, & Lee, 1995; Loscocco & Robinson, 1991). Because of this, women experience the roles of parent, spouse, and paid-worker differently than do men (Coverman, 1989; Higgins et al., 1995; Weigel, Weigel, Berger, Cook, & DelCampo, 1995).

Because of the societal expectations of women (and women's expectations of themselves), both to engage in paid-work and to be the main provider of household work, it is possible that conceptions of gender do influence the motivation for and styles in which women versus men engage in home-based employment. The purpose of this chapter is first to describe the men and women who choose home-based employment, focusing on the structure of the households in which the home-worker resides. The second section provides an in-depth analysis of the household manager and determines whether the management style of men and women household managers is different by gender. A third analysis focuses on the child-care choices of the households with home-workers. The purpose of this analysis is to determine whether the motivation to do home-based work for pay or profit is different for men and women. Some authors (Horvath, 1986; Olson, 1983; Pratt, 1984, 1993) have indicated that women select home-based employment so that they can combine child care with paid work. It is possible that the motive of female home-workers is to jointly produce child care and paid-work, whereas men primarily engage in home-based employment because it offers more income to the household than other work choices. Both factors of gender and household structure are used extensively within the chapter to study various aspects of the interface between employment and household systems.

The new information presented in this chapter about employment and family comes from the analysis of data gathered in an extensive research study of households in which at least one member was a home-worker. The next section describes this survey.

METHODS AND SAMPLE

Overview of the Survey

The data collected in a nine-state research survey, *At-Home Income Generation: Impact on Management, Productivity, and Stability in Rural/Urban Families*, provide an excellent and unique capacity to examine gender differences and similarities among the employment and family roles in home-worker households. The nine states surveyed were Hawaii, Iowa, Michigan, Missouri, New York, Ohio, Pennsylvania, Utah, and Vermont. The survey was conducted by telephone; interviewers spoke to the household manager, that is, the person in the household who engaged in tasks such as preparing most of the meals, scheduling family activities, and overseeing child care, if children were present in the household. The household manager was believed by the researchers to know about the employment/family interface for that household. Because the household manager was interviewed, he/she answered questions about the home-worker, even if the household manager and the home-worker were different persons in the household. For each household, only one home-worker (if there were more than one) was selected as the worker for whom data were collected. The primary home-worker was designated as the person who spent the greatest number of hours in home-based employment. An exception was made when the household manager met the minimum criteria (of 312 hours worked at home per year) but did not spend the highest number of total hours in home-based employment. In such cases the household manager was considered the home-worker (Winter & Stafford, 1995).

A total of 899 households with at least one home-worker were surveyed. Although most of the households comprised family members related by birth, adoption, and/or marriage, some of the households (11.8%) were non-family households. Therefore, the term *household* will be used in this chapter to represent the sample precisely, even though the majority of households were family households.

Home-based employment (the person involved is called a *home-worker* in this chapter) was defined as working for pay at home or from the home at least 6 hours per week throughout the year or, in the case of seasonal work, for a minimum of 312 hours annually. Individuals were included in the sample if they had been engaged in the activity for at least 12 months prior to the interview and had no other office or base for their employment. Some of the home-workers owned their own businesses and some were employed by others but completed the work in the home. Farmers who raised crops or livestock and sold them to brokers were excluded. Farmers who sold directly to the public or performed "value-added" activities were included. For further information about this survey, an excellent description of the sample design and questionnaire development can be found in Winter and Stafford (1995).

This nine-state survey was used because it allowed an exploration of the uniqueness of home-based employment. In conditions of outside employment, paid-work and family are often considered separate domains, but with home-based employment the overlap of spatial boundaries between these two systems dictates a different kind of investigation. The investigation of home-based employment allows for a focus on the household manager when appropriate, the home-worker when appropriate; it also accommodates a focus on dual-role holding (one person's holding both the household manager role and the home-worker role). Before delving into the in-depth analysis of the gender issues reported in this chapter, it is important first to examine the overall characteristics of the sample examined in the study.

Table 4.1
Demographic Characteristics of Home-Workers by Gender ($N = 899$)

Characteristics	Women ($n = 377$)			Men ($n = 522$)		
	n	%	Mean	n	%	Mean
Age			42.5			44.3
Under 30	46	12.1		43	8.3	
30–39	146	38.8		175	33.4	
40–49	91	24.3		125	23.9	
50–59	55	14.5		111	21.2	
60 and over	39	10.3		69	13.2	
Education (years)			13.9			13.9
Elementary or some high school	20	5.2		34	6.5	
High school diploma	124	32.9		171	32.7	
Some college	122	32.5		146	28.0	
College degree	67	17.8		116	22.2	
Some graduate school	44	11.6		55	10.6	
Married	316	83.7		445	85.2	
Number of children			1.3			1.0
None	148	39.2		248	47.6	
1	56	14.8		103	19.8	
2	106	28.0		106	20.2	
3 or more	67	18.0		65	12.4	
Child under 6 years	111	29.3		129	24.8	
Home ownership	321	85.1		464	88.9	
Years in community			20.2			19.6
0–5	80	21.2		101	19.3	
6–10	59	15.7		90	17.2	
11–20	88	23.2		141	27.0	
Over 20	150	39.9		190	36.5	
Place of residence						
Town or city > 2,500	193	51.1		292	56.0	
Town or city < 2,500	78	20.7		96	18.4	
Rural non-farm	74	19.6		103	19.8	
Farm	32	8.6		31	5.9	

Note: The data reported in this chapter were weighted to represent the populations of the nine states studied. See Winter and Stafford (1995) for more information.

Descriptive Statistics for the Sample

One of the variables of interest in this study was gender and its association with different aspects of home-based employment. Therefore, the first set of descriptive statistics (Table 4.1) examined the demographic characteristics of the home-workers in the sample disaggregated by gender. The age and education levels of men and women were quite similar. The women were just slightly younger than the men were. A slightly larger proportion of men than women had completed a college degree. A majority of the sample was married.

Households with female home-workers had more children than those households with male home-workers. Slightly more households with male home-workers had only one child. Households with female home-workers had two or more children more often than households in which the home-workers were men. More households with female home-workers had a child younger than 6 years of age than households with male home-workers.

More households with male home-workers owned their homes. The distribution of the length of time these home-workers lived in the community was about the same. Slightly over one-half of both male and female home-workers lived in communities with a population greater than 2,500.

The characteristics of home-workers were somewhat different if analyzed descriptively by gender, but some differences could also be seen by household structure. In Table 4.2, household structure is divided into four categories: non-family, single-parent, full-nest, and adult-only. Households categorized as non-family included single-person households and instances of unrelated adults sharing housing. Single-parent households included unmarried household managers living with one or more children. Full-nest households contained a married household manager, living with her or his spouse, with one or more children age 18 or younger in the household. Adult-only households were those in which the household manager was married and living with his or her spouse but had no children under age 18 present in the household. The labels given the four types of households were comparable to those in Ahrentzen's 1990 study of 104 home-based workers.

Of all households in the sample, the largest categories were those with male home-workers in full-nest and adult-only household types, and with female home-workers in full-nest households (see Table 4.2). The majority of the male single-parents (89.3%) had one child. The number of children in female single-parent families ranged between one and four, although 80.4% had either one or two children. The majority of home-workers in full-nest households, whether men or women, had one to three children, although the range extended to seven children for women and up to nine children for men.

About one-half of the sample across household structure types lived in communities of more than 2,500. For male home-workers in non-family and adult-only households the percentage increased to roughly 60%. The oldest home-workers were women in non-family households and men in adult-only households. The youngest home-workers (men and women) were found in full-nest households. The education level was approximately the same across categories. The home-workers living in their community the least amount of time were women in the single-parent household category and men in full-nest households. The descriptive statistics indicated some variation by gender and household structure of home-workers. Over 50% of home-workers had children, with the accompanying demands of both household and employment.

Table 4.2
Characteristics of Home-Workers by Household Structure Type and Gender of the Home-Worker (N = 899)

Characteristics	Non-Family		Single-Parent		Full-Nest		Adult-Only	
	Women	Men	Women	Men	Women	Men	Women	Men
Percent of sample	4.5	6.7	2.0	1.3	23.5	29.1	12.0	20.9
Number of children								
1 child	--	--	43.4	89.3	22.8	35.5	--	--
2 children	--	--	37.0	2.1	46.8	40.2	--	--
3 children	--	--	11.4	--	21.0	20.6	--	--
4 children	--	--	8.2	--	6.1	2.8	--	--
5 children	--	--	--	8.6	0.1	0.8	--	--
6 children	--	--	--	--	1.5	--	--	--
7 children	--	--	--	--	1.7	--	--	--
8 children	--	--	--	--	--	0.1	--	--
9 children	--	--	--	--	--	0.1	--	--
Total	--	--	100.0	100.0	100.0	100.0	--	--
Location of residence								
Town or city > 2,500	49.6	62.3	56.8	53.1	53.4	51.8	46.3	59.9
Town or city < 2,500	28.9	15.8	20.0	46.5	15.5	19.9	28.0	15.3
Rural non-farm	6.1	17.7	23.2	0.4	22.4	22.5	18.6	18.0
Farm	15.4	4.3	--	--	8.7	5.8	7.1	6.8
Total	100.0	100.1	100.0	100.0	100.0	100.0	100.0	100.0
Mean								
Age	52.1	42.1	44.2	45.0	36.7	39.2	50.1	52.2
Education	14.0	15.0	13.8	15.6	13.9	14.0	13.7	13.3
Years in community	27.8	19.7	14.2	27.6	16.7	15.6	25.2	24.5

In this chapter, the terms *home-worker, household manager* and *dual-role holder* are used. The home-worker, as defined previously, is the person in the household who works for pay or profit at home. One worker was selected from each of the 899 households. Of these households, 377 women and 522 men were the home-worker on whom the data about home-based employment were collected. Each of the 899 households had an identified household manager (778 women and 121 men), that is, the person who managed the meals, child care, and so forth, for the household. The household manager was the person inter-viewed in each household. Of the households surveyed, 482 people (368 women and 114 men) held the dual roles of household manager and home-worker. In the 208 households with children under the age of 5 years, 204 contained dual-role holders. See Figure 4.1 for the distribution of the sample.

These data are first used in this chapter to describe the dual roles of men and women in household work and home-based employment. The following analysis will discuss how home-workers manage multiple roles.

MANAGING MULTIPLE ROLES

Background on Multiple Roles

Work and family conflict occurs when an individual has to perform multi-ple roles that all require time, energy, and commitment (Greenhaus & Beutell, 1985; Higgins et al., 1995; Weigel et al., 1995). Although role overload and role conflict are central to explain work and family conflict, it is important to note that social stigma had the strongest effect on stress level in a study by Weigel et al. (1995). This finding indicated that the perceptions of others and the possible guilt generated from not performing adequately in all roles are in-fluential factors in explaining the level of stress experienced from paid-work and family conflict.

The literature presents two major explanations for the relationship of role involvement and the stress people experience from holding multiple roles. The first is the conflict hypothesis; the other is the enhancement hypothesis (Marks, 1977). The conflict hypothesis implies that the more roles one accumulates, the greater the probability of exhausting one's supply of time and energy and of confronting conflicting obligations. In direct contradiction to the conflict hy-pothesis, the enhancement hypothesis states that multiple role involvement can be energy generating; it assumes that people find energy for activities to which they are highly committed and they often feel more energetic after doing those activities.

Despite the outward appearance of contradiction in these two hypotheses, the independence of these two dimensions has been questioned in recent years. A debate has developed about whether they are part of a continuum, with en-hancement and conflict as the anchors of the continuum, or whether it is the relative balance between conflict and enhancement that is the crucial aspect of

Figure 4.1 Distribution of Sample

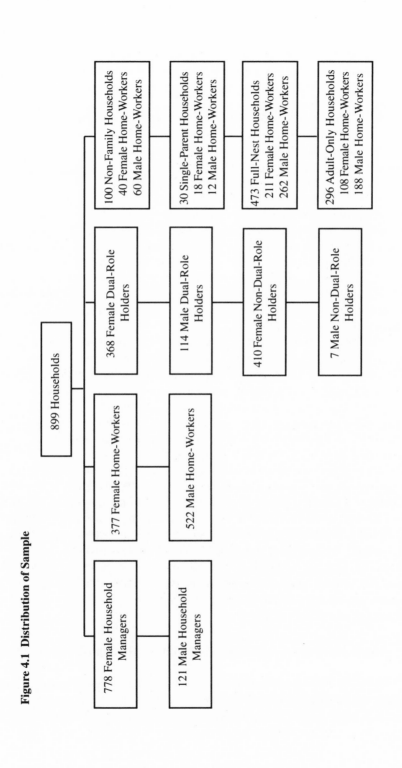

role perceptions (Tiedje et al., 1990). A determining factor in whether people feel drained or energized by given activities (in balance or out of balance) is their commitment to the roles they hold (Marks, 1979; O'Neil & Greenberger, 1994), and the varying commitment levels can create a buffering effect among the roles within their role system.

Role quality and commitment as well as gender and marital status are critical in explaining the buffering effect among roles. Role context considers not only the number of role involvements but their nature and circumstance as well. This approach is especially pertinent to women's lives (Danes & McTavish, 1997; Moen, Dempster-McClain, & Williams, 1989; O'Neil & Greenberger, 1994). Multiple-role involvement can benefit women by providing them with more than one arena in which to obtain role-related rewards (Barnett, 1994). Women who report high levels of job-role, partner-role, or parent-role quality report low levels of psychological stress symptoms (Barnett & Baruch, 1985; Barnett & Marshall, 1991, Tiedje et al., 1990). Barnett, Marshall, and Singer (1992) found that among single women and women without children, as job-role quality declined, levels of psychological distress increased; among partnered women and women with children, change in job-role quality was unrelated to change in psychological distress.

This brief summary of the factors that impact how people manage their multiple roles indicates that gender, marital status, and children in the family affect the amount of stress people experience from holding multiple roles. In households with a home-worker, boundaries between family and employment roles often become less clear. However, men and women involved in home-based employment might have varying degrees of multiple roles. All of the households in the sample reported in this chapter had someone in the role of home-worker. Another role that must be assumed by someone in the household was that of household manager. The household manager would be the person in the household who organizes, manages, and oversees the work of the household. Although all members would do some of the work of the household, the household manager coordinated the household operations to produce some standard of functioning. In this study, household managers were interviewed about the work of managing the household and the paid-work of the home-worker. Some of the household managers held both the roles of household manager and home-worker (dual-role holders), and some household managers were not the home-worker but reported on the work of the person who was living in the household who was engaged in home-based employment.

The Home-Worker Role Combined with the Household Manager Role

Table 4.3 delineates the entire sample of household managers within home-worker households and the sub-sample of those who hold the household manager and home-worker roles (dual-role holders). The table breaks down these groups by gender and household type.

As the table shows, household managers were more likely to be women than to be men. In this study of 899 households, there were 778 women and 121 men who were household managers. The greatest number of men who were household managers fell in the non-family household category, and the greatest number of women who were household managers belonged to the full-nest household structure. Of the 121 male household managers in the survey, 7 (5.8%) reported being a household manager only. The other 114 (94.2%) were dual-role holders. Of the 778 female household managers in the sample, 410 (52.7%) reported being a household manager only. The other 368 (47.3%) were dual-role holders. The men and women who reported they were both household managers and home-workers were the dual-role holders in the analysis that follows.[1]

Table 4.3
Household Managers and Dual-Role Holders by Gender and Household Type

| | Household Managers (n = 899) | | | | Dual-Role Holders (n = 482) | | | |
| | Women | | Men | | Women | | Men | |
Household Type	n	%	n	%	n	%	n	%
Non-family	42	4.7	59	6.6	37	7.9	58	12.0
Single-parent	18	2.0	12	1.3	17	3.5	12	2.5
Full-nest	448	49.8	25	2.8	208	43.1	21	4.3
Adult-only	270	30.0	25	2.8	106	22.0	23	4.7
Total	778	86.5	121	13.5	368	76.5	114	23.5

Background on the Home-Worker as Parent and Provider

In terms of home-based employment, the presence of children in the household can put more pressure on the home-worker to provide money resources to the family. However, the presence of children also demands more time and energy of the home-worker as parent. Married men and single women particularly feel the pressure to perform in both the provider and parent roles (Loscocco & Leicht, 1993); when they are compared to married women, family responsibilities motivate them to generate greater earnings. With changing economic times and the accompanying changes in social and economic roles of both genders, more intra-gender variation in the fulfillment of the provider and parental roles is possible within households.

Women are at a relative economic disadvantage compared to men (Loscocco & Robinson, 1991). Even among a successful group of small business owners, women generated lower sales volumes and derived less income than their male counterparts. Women's businesses tended to be smaller and to be concentrated in less profitable businesses (Loscocco, Robinson, Hall, & Allen, 1991). Several authors stated that it was the tremendous amount of household work done by women, including small business owners, that contributed to their economic disadvantage relative to men (Hisrich, 1989; Longstreth, Stafford, & Mauldin, 1987). Shelton and Firestone (1989) estimated conservatively that 8% of the gender gap in earnings was a direct result of women's greater burden of household management activities.

The Home-Worker as Parent and Provider

One motivation to engage in home-based employment is to earn income to pay living expenses for those in the household. If children are present in the home, the income must pay not only for the living expenses of the worker but also for part or all of the expenses of his or her dependents. The following analysis examines home-workers as providers for the household members.

Table 4.4 identifies some of the characteristics of home-based employment for men and women within the sample under consideration in this chapter. The table shows that about three-fourths of men and women were business owners as opposed to wage workers. The annual net home-based employment income was about three times more for men who were home-workers than for women who were home-workers; men earned a mean net annual home-based employment income of $24,603 and women earned $8,466. This table also shows that one explanation for the relatively lower income for women is that they had been in the home-based employment less time than men and that they spent fewer hours per week in the work than did men.

Table 4.5 indicates female home-workers earned less in every household structure type than male home-workers; in fact, the highest home-based income category for women (non-family, $14,009) was $5,183 less than the lowest income category for home-workers who were men (non-family, $19,192). Women who were home-workers in single-parent ($7,975) and full-nest households ($6,663) earned an average of $11,259 and $20,156 less, respectively, on average than the men who were home-workers in similar household structures ($19,234 and $26,819, respectively). These were the two household structure types in which children were a component and in which a woman was likely to have at least some responsibility for other individuals. In household types in which men and women had similar responsibilities (that is, they only cared for themselves) there were differences of $5,183 (non-family households, $14,009 vs. $19,192) and $13,587 (adult-only households, $10,007 vs. $23,594) between the home-based employment incomes of women and men. More than one-third of men in the non-family and full-nest family household types had other employment in addition to their home-based employment. Approximately 45% of the women who were single-parent had other employment, as might be expected because of their low earnings from home-based employment.

Table 4.4
Characteristics of Home-Based Employment by Gender

Characteristic	Women ($n = 377$)			Men ($n = 522$)		
	n	%	Mean	n	%	Mean
Ownership status						
Business worker	279	74.1		391	74.9	
Wage worker	98	25.9		131	25.1	
Net annual home-based						
employment income	377		$8,466	522		$24,603
Home-based						
employment hours (annual)	377		1,469	522		2,073
Home-based						
employment hours (per week)						
Less than 20	179	47.4		145	27.8	
20–29	57	15.1		29	5.5	
30–39	41	10.8		58	11.2	
40 or more	100	26.7		290	55.5	
Duration of home-based						
employment						
Less than 5 years	176	46.7		175	33.5	
5–9 years	88	23.3		126	24.1	
10–14 years	59	15.7		85	16.3	
15 years or more	54	14.3		136	26.1	
Seasonality						
Yes	46	12.1		76	14.6	
No	331	87.9		446	85.4	
Other employment						
Yes	79	21.1		156	29.8	
No	298	78.9		366	70.2	

Table 4.5 also presents several aspects of the gender gap in earnings by household structure type. One aspect was the marked difference in the types of occupations chosen by women and men (regardless of household type). For example, women were more likely to be in the "crafts/artisans" category as men were regardless of household type and at least three times as likely to be providing clerical/administrative support.

Another aspect of a gender difference by household structure was in the variance in occupations by household type. About one-half of women who were home-workers in non-family household structures were in marketing and sales, whereas men in similar households were primarily split among managerial/professional/technical, marketing and sales, and mechanical and transportation. In single-parent family households women were mainly craftspersons and artisans or workers in service occupations, whereas men were in manage-

Table 4.5

Characteristics of Home-Based Employment by Household Structure Type and Gender (N = 899)

Characteristics	Non-Family		Single-Parent		Full-Nest		Adult-Only	
	Women	Men	Women	Men	Women	Men	Women	Men
Occupation (percentage)								
Managerial/prof./tech.	9.0	26.9	--	58.8	9.0	11.8	3.9	14.1
Marketing and sales	46.6	22.0	5.6	40.4	23.7	24.5	25.0	21.0
Clerical/ad. support	5.0	--	--	--	12.0	2.7	11.2	3.3
Mechanical and trans.	5.9	26.3	2.0	0.4	1.2	19.5	1.8	23.5
Crafts and artisans	6.3	11.4	36.0	--	15.5	7.8	23.6	5.5
Managers	6.0	2.2	8.8	--	3.0	4.1	3.5	2.6
Services	18.8	--	29.0	--	33.4	0.1	23.2	0.2
Contracting	--	11.2	16.0	0.4	0.6	22.9	0.4	26.1
Ag. products and sales	2.5	--	2.5	--	1.7	1.7	7.4	3.6
Total	100.1	100.0	99.9	100.0	100.1	100.1	100.0	99.9
Means								
Length of home-based employment (yrs.)	9.5	12.2	6.6	6.7	6.2	7.8	10.0	13.5
Other employment (%)	14.7	36.7	45.1	19.0	21.1	34.6	19.5	21.5
Number of earners	1.2	1.0	1.1	1.0	2.0	1.7	1.9	2.0
Total household income	$28,434	$38,186	$27,670	$26,579	$39,543	$49,151	$38,084	$44,775
Home-based employment income	$14,009	$19,192	$7,975	$19,234	$6,663	$26,819	$10,007	$23,594

rial/professional/technical fields or marketing and sales. In full-nest family households, the largest occupation category for women was services and for men, contracting (with marketing and sales a close second). For adult-only family households, marketing and sales, crafts and artisans, and services were the largest occupation categories for women; contracting, mechanical and transportation, and marketing and sales were the largest occupational categories for men. The number of hours worked annually in home-based employment can also explain differences in income. Many women did home-based employment part-time, whereas more than half the men worked 40 hours a week or more (see Table 4.4).

An additional difference was that 46.7% of the women had been working in home-based employment for less than 5 years compared to 33.5% of the men (see Table 4.4). Being in home-based employment longer might lead to higher income levels either because wages would increase over time or because it takes a few years for the business to get established and make a profit. Nearly 30% of the men reported "other employment" compared to 21% of the women (see Table 4.4).

In summary, men worked longer hours, earned more money, and had been involved in home-based employment longer than women. Women were more likely to be engaged in service occupations than were men. The next section will examine the household management component of the home-worker's role performance.

BACKGROUND ON THE FUNCTION AND PROCESS OF HOUSEHOLD MANAGEMENT

Household management is a set of goal-directed activities that use existing or obtainable resources to meet individual and family demands. A woman, in most cases, is the main administrator of the chores of the household, including the care of children. The woman's job as administrator means that she determines what needs to be done, by whom, and when (Karsten, 1994). Women tend to utilize management strategies of planning and organizing more than do men (Bird, Bird, & Scruggs, 1983). Bem (1987) argued that planning and organizing take more mental energy than physically performing tasks. He might shop for groceries, but she probably made the list. He might pick up their child from an after-school activity and take her to the afternoon sitter's home, but she probably registered her and arranged for after-school child care.

Flexibility and control over one's schedule are characteristics identified in a study by Skinner (1980) as those that help make a dual-career life-style more manageable. Dual-career couples bought time in a variety of ways, such as paying for child care in order to have time to manage the household work. This result should be viewed in the context of the classic economic question of income versus substitution effects. That is, do parents purchase child care because they do not have time available for their children as a result of work demands (substituting a service for market time), or do they purchase child care because they can afford to (income effect) given their additional income from employment? In either case it seems clear that effective managerial behavior increases the likelihood of achieving desired outcomes and poor managerial behavior diminishes the likelihood of achieving desired results.

The basic idea behind the consideration of management is to investigate how pragmatic an individual is at defining goals and then reaching them efficiently. At one extreme, an individual might set a specific goal and then plan sequenced actions to reach that goal. The person who plans well will pay careful attention to the resources available and the level of satisfaction she or he wants to reach. As this individual moves toward the goal, he or she pays careful attention to how things are proceeding and then changes either the amount of resources, the process of using those resources, or the goal itself to make sure that the final product is a desirable one. This individual will also evaluate at the end of the process to understand better how this goal might influence future decisions. On the other extreme, some individuals might not set defined goals, work on plans, or evaluate the goal at the end of the process. The study reported in this chapter examined the functions of the household manager to determine whether male household managers (the majority of whom also held the role of home-worker) managed in the same way as female household managers (of whom about one-half were also home-workers). Analysis was also conducted of only those men and women who were dual-role holders, including by household type.

The Dual Roles of Home-Worker and Household Manager

Table 4.6 lists the specific questions asked of household managers to measure their household management processes. The household management questions represented the major concepts of the Deacon and Firebaugh (1988) family management model. The leading question was "Which number on a 5 point scale (1 = not at all; 3 = somewhat; 5 = exactly) describes how much the statement is like you?" The four main categories of managing household work were (a) setting work goals (demands), (b) planning the work (planning), (c) implementing the work (implementing), and (d) assessing the work once completed (output).

Differences in how men and women approached household management were tested, and results are reported in Table 4.7. Statistically significant differences between the genders were found for 7 of the 10 management items. Men set goals more often, contrary to the Bird, Bird, and Scruggs (1983) findings. Men set standards, clarified what was needed, assessed resource needs, checked, and adjusted more than did women. Women were more concerned with the timing of action than men.

Further investigation looked at gender differences in household management among dual-role holders and found four differences in management patterns (see

Table 4.8). However, the differences between men and women for timing of action and adjusting under the implementation of work category were not statistically significant, nor was there a statistically significant difference between women and men on setting standards.

Table 4.6
Description of Family Management Items

Management Concept	Questionnaire Item
Input	
Demands	
Goals (setting)	Each week you decide some way you can improve your life.[a]
Throughput	
Planning	
Standard setting	Before starting a job, you have a firm idea about how to judge the outcome.
Demand clarification	When planning a job, you think the plan through so that your goal is clear before you actually begin doing the job.
Resource assessment	Before you begin a job, you figure out how much of your time, money, and energy that you can devote to this particular task.
Action sequencing	You think about when to do a job, and not just how much time it will take.
Implementing	
Actuating	When there is a chore to be done at home, you wait until the last minute.[b]
Controlling	
Checking	As you work, you check whether things are going as you want them to.
Adjusting	When things are not going well, you figure out another way to do it.
Output	
Demand responses	When a job is done, you think about how well you like the results.
Resource changes	You are pleased if the work just gets done; you do not spend time thinking about how effectively it was done.[b]

Note: Questions were not asked in the order listed.
[a] Each question was asked of all household managers in reference to their family life with an emphasis on unpaid family work. The leading question was "Which number (1 = not at all; 3 = somewhat; 5 = exactly) describes how much the statement is like you?"
[b] This question was reverse coded in all analyses.

Table 4.7
Differences in Household Management for Household Managers by Gender

Management Concept	Women (n = 778)		Men (n = 121)		t-value	t-test Probability
	Mean	Standard Deviation	Mean	Standard Deviation		
Setting goals for the work	3.22	1.47	3.53	1.32	-2.36	0.020*
Planning for the work						
Setting standards	3.92	1.04	4.13	0.99	-2.15	0.033*
Clarifying what is needed	3.89	1.21	4.25	0.96	-3.76	0.000***
Assessing resource needs	3.51	1.25	3.93	1.02	-4.06	0.000***
Sequencing actions	3.50	1.28	3.34	1.39	1.18	0.238
Implementing the work						
Timing of action (actuating)	3.33	1.39	3.09	1.43	1.74	0.084*
Checking	4.02	1.08	4.26	1.02	-2.42	0.017**
Adjusting	4.17	1.04	4.41	0.82	-2.85	0.005***
Assessing work completed (output)						
Establishing goal achievement (demand responses)	4.42	0.99	4.32	0.92	1.18	0.240
Evaluating effectiveness (resource changes)	3.56	1.37	3.70	1.40	-1.02	0.311

aEach question is asked in this manner: "Which number (1 = not at all; 3 = somewhat; 5 = exactly) describes how much the statement is like you?" The specific statements are identified in Table 4.6.
*Statistical significance at .05; **statistical significance at .01; ***statistical significance at .001.

96

Table 4.8
Household Management of Dual-Role Holders by Gender

Management Concept	Women (n = 368)		Men (n = 114)		t-value	t-test Probability
	Mean	Standard Deviation	Mean	Standard Deviation		
Setting goals for the work	3.21	1.52	3.52	1.30	-2.14	0.033*
Planning for the work						
Setting standards	3.94	0.99	4.13	0.98	-1.85	0.066
Clarifying what is needed	3.98	1.17	4.26	0.95	-2.60	0.010**
Assessing resource needs	3.56	1.29	3.97	0.98	-3.61	0.000***
Sequencing actions	3.49	1.35	3.35	1.42	0.93	0.355
Implementing the work						
Timing of action	3.23	1.42	3.11	1.42	0.75	0.451
Checking	4.01	1.13	4.26	1.03	-2.20	0.029**
Adjusting	4.30	0.98	4.41	0.83	-1.15	0.251
Assessing work completed (output)						
Establishing goal achievement (demand responses)	4.44	0.95	4.32	0.94	1.13	0.260
Evaluating effectiveness (resource changes)	3.49	1.45	3.74	1.41	-0.96	0.338

*Statistical significance at .05; **statistical significance at .01; ***statistical significance at .001.

Table 4.9 disaggregates the management patterns of dual-role holders to determine if there were gender differences within household types. Men did more goal setting within the single-parent and full-nest families compared to women. They also scored higher on clarifying what is needed to accomplish the goal. Men in the non-family and full-nest family households did more assessing of resource needs than did women in those household structures. Women in the adult-only family households did fewer chores at the last minute (timing of action) than did men. Men did more checking than did women in the full-nest families. Women in the single-parent family households did both measures of assessing how the work is completed more than did men. Men, on the other hand, did more evaluating of the effectiveness of their work in non-family households than did women. Women in full-nest families also differed from men in establishing goal achievement.

Management patterns differed by gender for dual-role holders in this study. Of the statistically significant differences found between the genders on the various aspects of household management, in many cases it was the men who were performing in a way that would indicate more efficient management. These differences seen between the genders raise the question, Is it true that men are more proficient at management, or are the measurement instruments simply more reflective of how men manage and less reflective of how women manage?

Previous studies on household management might help clarify these somewhat perplexing results. Karsten (1994) stated, as indicated earlier, that women do not just do the job, but rather determine what is to be done, by whom, and when. Unlike men, women less often have the luxury to plan and do one job at a time. As the main administrator of the household, women manage a multitude of interconnected tasks in a constant, steady stream in a way that has to be flexible because of the ever-changing needs of family members. Men tend to do one task at a time in an analytical, intentional manner, as was presented in the questions asked. Women tend to utilize more strategies of planning and organizing than do men (Bird et al., 1983), but with more fluidity based on constantly changing parameters in an attempt to balance the demands of multiple roles. Thus, women's strategies might be less conscious to them and possibly are not as concrete as identified in the questions asked.

As primary managers of household work, many women sacrifice leisure time or time with their spouses in order to discharge capably both their employment and home responsibilities (Danes & Keskinen, 1990; Stafford, 1980). If women choose home-based employment as a way to balance employment and family, it is perhaps an indication of a commitment to both spheres, and it seems to preclude the intense commitment descriptive of the successful small business owner (Christensen, 1988; Goffee & Scase, 1985).

Additional study is necessary to discover how households with children manage the employment-family conflicts that they face. Single parents share some of the same sources of employment-family conflict as do their dual-income counterparts (Burden, 1986; Duxbury, Higgins, & Lee, 1994). Both are concerned with issues of role overload from the total volume of activities in-

Table 4.9

Household Management Practices by Household Type and Gender for Dual-Role Holders ($n = 482$)

Management Concepts	Non-Family		Single-Parent		Full-Nest		Adult-Only	
	Women	Men	Women	Men	Women	Men	Women	Men
Setting goals for the work	3.01	3.21	3.91	4.80*	3.13	3.69*	3.32	3.46
Planning for the work								
Setting standards	4.24	4.23	3.67	4.18	3.85	4.11	4.04	3.90
Clarifying what is needed	4.04	4.31	3.70	4.67*	3.96	4.42*	4.04	3.78
Assessing resource needs	3.35	4.05*	3.41	3.34	3.67	4.32*	3.43	3.76
Sequencing actions	3.69	3.38	3.39	3.25	3.39	3.39	3.61	3.29
Implementing the work								
Timing of action	3.18	3.22	2.99	3.57	3.25	3.16	3.24*	2.56
Checking	4.18	4.36	4.24	4.66	3.98	4.39*	3.97	3.66
Adjusting	4.46	4.36	4.24	4.65	4.34	4.50	4.18	4.34
Assessing work completed (output)								
Establishing goal achievement (demand responses)	4.58	4.56	4.59*	3.77	4.39*	4.02	4.47	4.29
Evaluating effectiveness (resource changes)	3.21	4.00*	4.02*	2.93	3.63	3.76	3.56	3.45

*Statistical significance at .05.

volved in paid-work and family life, and both must coordinate family activities with employment demands. However, two important differences exist between the two groups. First, single parents face an economic imperative to work for pay, and for single parents, the employment role is central to their identity (Belle, 1990; Burden, 1986; Norton & Glick, 1986; Tebbets, 1982). In either case, however, when very young children are present, the demands are higher. The next section focuses on how the presence of children, especially young children, affects the employment and family interface for home-workers. In particular, the section examines how families juggle the role of child-care provider with the role of the home-worker.

CHILD CARE FOR YOUNG CHILDREN: A CORE ISSUE IN ROLE MANAGEMENT

Background on Child Care Choices

Deciding about child care for families with young children is a key aspect of balancing paid-work and family. Young children simply require that their parents spend at least some time with them. Of course, many parents believe that it is not only a demand, but a desirable activity to spend a great deal of time with their children in teaching and nurturing them. Moen (1992) suggested that families could choose to manage their employment demands and child-care needs in one of four ways:

- One spouse remains out of the labor market for a certain amount of time.
- The number of hours worked is reduced (i.e., from full-time to part-time employment).
- Shift work is chosen to allow parents jointly to coordinate child care.
- Less time-consuming occupations are chosen to allow for less traveling, fewer evening meetings, or a flexible schedule which allows time for such activities as physician appointments.

An option under the fourth choice is to combine paid-work and child-care obligations directly by choosing to do one's paid-work at home while watching the children. Across all of the alternatives, flexibility and control over the parents' own paid-work schedules are the common thread.

Ordinarily, employees are unable to choose their own work schedule for a given job; instead they must choose a job with a given work schedule. This work schedule can be more or less accommodating to the demands of children than other schedules. Hayghe (1988) found that about 43% of all employers maintained flextime policies and an equal proportion had flexible leave arrangements. In 1989, unpaid maternity leave was available to 37% of full-time workers in medium and large private establishments, and unpaid paternity leave being available to only 18% of the full-time workers. These leave plans allowed an average of 20 weeks off for unpaid parental leave (Hyland, 1990). Shuster (1994) found that fathers consistently expressed their dissatisfaction with employers' personnel policies that limited their family time. Although relevant to household members with "outside employment," these statistics are less meaningful to those people who work full-time at their home-based employment. Home-based employees might have more opportunity to set their own schedule, be it flexible or more rigid, and to arrange their own amount of parental leave time, be it extended or virtually non-existent.

Clearly, the decisions about child care and labor force participation (either home-based or outside employment) are interconnected for families with young children. These two decisions were examined by Folk and Beller (1991) using the National Survey of Families and Households. These authors were particularly interested in what they called the joint decision of part-time versus full-time labor force participation and the type of child care chosen. They collapsed child care into non-market (parents, relatives, baby sitters) and market (family day care, center based care) types. Their findings indicated that child-care types and level of employment were decisions that were, in fact, made jointly.

Another study (Peterson & Gerson, 1992) found that not only did employment per se have an effect on child-care choice but the "corporate climate" within that employment might also have an influence. For example, the percentage of women in the husband's occupation and his occupation's freedom from supervision were found to be significant predictors of the husband's increased responsibility toward child care. That is, the more women he worked with and the more freedom he had from supervision at work, the more his child-care responsibility increased (Peterson & Gerson, 1992). Hence, it appears that corporate climate (with whom one works and the sort of supervision one has) is an important factor in how men view their child-care responsibilities. How families who have one or more parents involved in home-based employment choose to manage their child-care needs is an important question because those families essentially set their own corporate climate for how children should interface with the workplace.

Some families might specifically choose to engage in home-based employment to avoid placing their children in child care while maintaining an income flow that is high enough for the family to maintain financial security. They might choose to combine home-based employment and care of their own children for monetary reasons (no child-care expenses) and/or for value-laden reasons (caring for one's own child). However, home-based employment might not always be compatible with child care. Heck, Saltford, Rowe, and Owen (1992) found that of those families who had a home-worker and who reported needing child care, 38% chose to hire child care. Their results indicated that some home-workers were unable (or unwilling) to engage in child care and home-based employment simultaneously. The question remains whether or not men and women view the decision to engage in child care differently. The data from the survey being reported here give insights on how the pattern of child care was chosen depending on whether the man or the woman was the home-worker on whom data were collected within the household surveyed. It should be noted that in some households both the man and woman could have been home-workers, but this possibility was not considered in the analysis.

Gender Differences in How Home-Based Employment Is Combined with Child Care

The study of the home-workers in nine states provided data allowing the investigation of whether or not the gender of the home-worker influenced the household's child-care choices. Although the survey did not include a direct question asking whether the sex of the home-worker made a difference in child-care choices, the question can be answered in the context of the study. The survey revealed that some home-workers did purchase outside child care, but were families more or less likely to choose outside child care depending on whether the home-worker was a man or a woman? The literature on how gender influences the child-care choice is not consistent. Heck et al. (1992) found that gender was not a significant variable in determining whether outside care for all children (including school-aged children) was purchased by home-workers. However, some other authors suggested that men and women do view the child-care choice differently (Brayfield, 1995; Peterson & Gerson, 1992; Shuster, 1994).

The father's (husband's) contribution to the child-care choice is a point of interest in the literature. A study examining the determinants of responsibility for child-care arrangements among dual-earner couples found that husbands took on more responsibility when the demands on the household increased (i.e., more children, longer paid work hours for the wife) (Peterson & Gerson, 1992). Shuster (1994) found that the feelings of mothers and fathers about child care were correlated with different factors. Fathers' feelings about the child care being provided for their infants was significantly correlated to objective quality measures of the child care, their perceived support at their paid-work site, and their own desire for the infant's mother to be working in the labor force. Conversely, mothers' feelings were not positively correlated with any of those measures except their own desire to be working for pay.

Brayfield (1995) reported that fathers were more likely to care for their young (preschool) children if they worked evenings and/or nights, or if the mother worked evenings and nights. This result indicated that parents who work opposing shifts seem to be more likely to engage in "split-shift" parenting. Brayfield also found traditional demographic variables to be important in explaining whether fathers cared for their young children. Overall, men were found to be less likely to be the primary care givers for very young children than for school-aged children. Brayfield (1995) suggested that this stems from the requirements of caring for young children and their conflict with traditional male roles (i.e., men should not change diapers, give baths, etc.). Men's willingness to care for children at a certain age will likely affect the decision of whether to purchase child care or not. Of course, there can be other reasons why men are not willing to care for children, such as career goals or income.

Haynes (1996), too, found that fathers were more likely to provide regularly scheduled primary care for children if the father and the mother worked at different times of the day. The parents were offsetting their work hours to cover child care better. Additionally, the study showed that fathers who had some education about children and who had involvement with children as part of their occupations were more likely to provide regular care for their own children. Finally, fathers were more likely to provide care giving if the child was the father's biological child. Even with the growing number of fathers involved in regular child care, the Haynes and Brayfield studies showed that in 1990, only about 35% of all fathers assumed regular child-care responsibilities for children 5 years and under. Providing regular child care is still a role that many fathers are reluctant to assume for social and economic reasons.

Table 4.10 gives further empirical support to the literature in this area; it indicates whether households with home-workers and with at least one child under 5 years of age chose to use outside child care or to care for their children themselves. The table also indicates how this child-care choice varied by the gender of the home-worker. A higher proportion of households with one child under age 5 years and with male home-workers (54%) chose to purchase outside care compared to households with one child under age 5 but with female home-workers (47.7%). The difference becomes much more striking when there were two or more children under 5 years of age in the home. As the table shows, 52.1% of such households with male home-workers versus 13.7% of such households with female home-workers chose to purchase outside child care. This is clear support for the premise that women are indeed making more of a noticeable effort to combine home-based employment with their family responsibilities than are men who are participating in home-based employment.

Regression analysis provided a better method for examining gender differences in choosing to care for one's own child or in choosing to purchase market care. Regression analysis allowed examination of whether and how particular factors such as age or education differently affected the choice of child care. Because the interest in this part of the study was in families with young children who needed child care, the sample for the regression analysis (as well as the information presented in Table 4.10) was limited to households with children under the age of 5 years (a high percentage of 5 year old children attend kindergarten, so age 5 was used as the cut-off). In each case, the adult interviewed was both a home-worker and a household manager, that is, a dual-role holder. When the total sample of 899 respondents was narrowed to include only those dual-role holders who had children under the age of 5 years in the home, the total number of observations was reduced to 204. Of these, 89 were households in which the home-worker was a woman and in 115 cases the home-worker was a man. Many factors were entered into the regression equation, including worker characteristics (age, education, marital status), household characteristics (years in community, homeowners, number of children under age 5, other household in-

Gender and Home-Based Employment

come), work characteristics (business owners, managerial/professional/technical, other employment, home-based employment income, home-based employment hours spent outside home, duration, seasonality), and location characteristics (state of residence and size of town/city). Each of these factors had support from the literature indicating that the factors were important in the choice of child care. Because the variable of interest was dichotomous ("yes" indicated that the household bought outside child care and "no" indicated the household did not buy outside child care), a special form of regression known as logistic regression was used. Similarly to ordinary least squares regression results, each variable in a logistic regression can be interpreted as having either a positive effect or a negative effect on the decision to purchase child care. In logistic regression, the positive or negative effect is the effect of the variable on the likelihood of the dependent variable's being "yes" (purchasing outside child care).

Table 4.10
Use of Child Care by Gender of Home-Worker in Households with Children Under 5 Years Old ($n = 208$)

Gender of Worker and Number of Children	Percent Using Outside Child Care
Woman	
1 child under 5 years old	47.7%
2 children under 5 years old	13.7%
Man	
1 child under 5 years old	54.0%
2 children under 5 years old	52.1%

All of the statistically significant factors (those with an alpha of .05 or less) resulting from the logistic regression analysis are noted in Table 4.11 (non-significant factors are not listed). Positive significant results indicate that those factors were found to increase the likelihood of the purchase of outside child care. Households with women who were home-workers were more likely to purchase child care for young children if the women either had a college degree or had attended graduate school, were engaged in managerial/professional/technical home-based employment, had other types of employment besides their home-based employment, worked a greater number of hours in their home-based employment outside the home environment, and lived in a community of fewer than 2,500 people. Negative significant results found to decrease the likelihood of the purchase of outside child care included women who were business owners rather than wage earners, and those households in Iowa, New York, Pennsylvania, and Utah compared to households in Hawaii (the state used for comparisons).

The results of the logistic regression told a different story for households which included a man as the home-worker than it did when a woman was the home-worker. Many of the factors found to be significant in the analysis for households with female home-workers were not significant in the analysis for households with male home-workers. For example, female home-worker households with women who had a college education or had attended at least some graduate school were found to be more likely than other female home-worker households to purchase outside child care, yet these two education variables had no statistically significant effect for men.

Table 4.11
Factors Significant in Predicting the Purchase of Child Care for Young Children by Gender of the Home-Worker

Variable	Women	Men
Worker characteristics		
College	positive[a]	
Graduate school	positive	
Household characteristics		
Number of children under 5		negative[b]
Other household income		positive
Work characteristics		
Business owners	negative	
Managerial/professional/technical	positive	positive
Other employment	positive	negative
Home-based employment income		negative
Home-based hours outside home	positive	
Location characteristics		
Iowa	negative	
Missouri		positive
New York	negative	
Pennsylvania	negative	
Utah	negative	
Vermont		positive
Town < 2,500	positive	

[a]A positive relationship indicates that having that characteristic increases the likelihood that they will purchase outside child care.
[b]A negative relationship indicates that having that characteristic decreases the likelihood that they will purchase outside child care.

Another difference was that as the number of children under age 5 in the family increased, the likelihood of purchasing outside child care decreased in those households with male home-workers. No effect was found for this variable when women were the home-workers. Other household income (such as the wages of a spouse or dividends from investments) was another example of differences. Increases in other household income were found to have a positive effect for male home-worker households, increasing the likelihood that the household would purchase outside child care. No effect was found for households with female home-workers.

Unlike the results for the female home-worker households, which showed that being a business owner had a negative effect on the purchase of outside child care, no effect was found for male home-worker families. Only working in a managerial/professional/technical occupation had similar effects for both male and female home-worker households. This indicated that in both cases, the home-worker's having a managerial/professional/technical position increased the likelihood of the purchase of outside child care. The amount of money earned through the home-based employment was found to have a negative effect on the purchase of outside child care when men were the home-workers. That is, as the amount of money earned increased, the likelihood of purchasing outside child care decreased. Home-based employment income had no statistically significant effect for female home-worker households. Positive, significant results were found for households with male home-workers living in Missouri and Vermont compared to those living in Hawaii. Curiously, although four of the eight states entered in the regression were found to be significant for female home-worker households, Missouri and Vermont were not among them.

Discussion of the Findings on Child Care Choices for Home-Workers

In thinking through why such differences in child-care choices between households with men and women home-workers were evident in the results, the following ideas are offered. First, education seemed to be more of a factor for female home-worker households than for male home-worker households. Perhaps women with a higher level of education were more cognizant of the value of their time as workers (as compared to less educated women) and, therefore, were less willing to compromise their paid-work time by simultaneously caring for their children. For households with men engaged in home-based employment, education was not a significant factor. Perhaps this suggests that men were socialized early in life to value their time as workers, whereas women only acquired this idea through formal education.

For households with men as the home-workers the number of children under the age of 5 years was a negative factor in purchasing outside care. One might suppose that as the number of children under the age of 5 increases, one should expect to find a positive effect (find an increase in the likelihood of purchasing outside child care) for all households with home-based employment. This assumes that simultaneously working for pay at home and caring for multiple children becomes less and less feasible the more children there are added to the equation, so that the purchase of outside child care becomes more likely. However, in households with female home-workers, no statistically significant effect was found, and for households with male home-workers, the opposite of what was expected was found. For male home-worker households, the more children under the age of 5 years who resided in the household, the less likely they were to purchase outside child care. One explanation is that this reflected the cost of paying for outside child care for multiple children. As the number of children increased, the cost of outside care might have become prohibitive, and so fathers (and/or mothers) were willing to care for their children themselves. But why did the same effect not hold true for female home-worker households? One might theorize that for these households, the decision to care for their own children (as opposed to purchasing outside care) was more closely tied to their individual values than the number of children per se. In other words, in these households mothers perhaps stayed at home to work and simultaneously raise their children, and it did not matter whether they were raising one child or a dozen: the point was to be at home with the children.

The result regarding household income was curious. Why did other household income have a positive effect on the likelihood of purchasing outside child care when men were the home-workers and no effect when women were the home-workers? On the one hand, it could be expected that child care was something that home-workers would like to have purchased, if they could afford to, because it would have given them more time to concentrate on their home-based employment (so a positive effect would be expected). On the other hand, it could be expected that child care was something that home-workers would have liked to do themselves. Thus funds from other household income sources might have been used to reduce the pressure for the home-based employment to generate as much income, and thus have made simultaneous parental care/home-based employment more feasible (negative effect). In short, other household income could have been the income source that made outside care feasible (so a positive effect would be expected), but it might also have been the income source that allowed parents to keep their children at home (so a negative effect would be expected).

In the logistic regression, other household income was only found to be a factor for households with male home-workers and it had a positive effect. That is, for male home-worker households, an increase in other household income led to a higher likelihood of choosing to purchase child care. The non-significant result for female home-worker households might suggest that the decision to combine home-based employment and child care for women was not so much an economic decision as a parenting decision.

Another enlightening result was the finding that households with business owned by women were less likely to purchase outside child care than in cases in which women did home-based employment for someone else. This result might suggest that women who owned a business have the freedom to combine employment and family more fully. This result supports several of the findings of studies described earlier, which seem to show that women who owned home-based businesses were not driven purely by profits; instead a balance of paid-work and child-care responsibilities seemed to be more prevalent. For households in which men owned a business, the effect was not significant.

The findings also showed that for households with men or women engaged in managerial, professional, or technical home-based occupations, there was a significant, positive effect on the choice of purchasing outside child care. It could be that the demands of managerial/professional/technical home-based employment were such that the simultaneous care of children was impossible, or it could be that the role of simultaneously being "mother" or "father" and "professional" simply did not go hand-in-hand compared to other occupations.

There was a positive effect of "other employment" on purchasing child care when a woman who was a home-worker did this other employment. This result might be indicative that women needed child care specifically for that "other employment." For households with men who were the home-workers, however, other employment had a negative effect, suggesting that perhaps their spouse watched the children as the men did other employment.

Home-based employment income had a negative effect on the likelihood of purchasing outside child care for male home-worker households (a non-statistically significant effect for female home-worker households). As the income from the home-based employment increased, households with male home-workers were less likely to purchase outside child care. This finding supports the idea that with increased funds, men felt less compelled to devote all of their time and energy to their paid-work, so they could spend some time and energy looking after the children. That choosing whether or not they should purchase outside child care was not significant for female home-worker households seems to be building the case that such households were not as influenced by economic/income factors as were households in which men were engaging in home-based employment in.

For female home-worker households, the number of hours of home-based employment done outside the home was found to have a positive effect on their likelihood of purchasing outside child care. This result makes intuitive sense. The more the mother was away from home on business, the less feasible caring for her children simultaneously became. Intriguingly, that variable was not found to be statistically significant for male home-worker households, but men did work more hours on average than women.

State regulations regarding child care (influencing quality and cost), cultural norms, statewide child-care programs, and/or other geographic influences could be expected to have played a role in the likelihood of parents' purchasing outside child care. For this reason, all of the nine states in the survey were compared to determine whether any one had particular child-care standards that would make that state a good one for use as the comparison state. Compared to the other states, Hawaii had more rigorous restrictions on the age at which children were permitted to enter a child care center, the amount of outside space required for children in family day-care homes, and the maximum group size in family day-care homes. All of these factors might have influenced the cost/quality and overall desirability of purchasing outside child care (Hayes, Palmer, & Zaslow, 1990). For these reasons, Hawaii was chosen as the comparison state (also known as an omitted variable). The results of the regression analysis showed that households with women who were home-workers living in Iowa, New York, Pennsylvania, and Utah were all less likely to place their children in outside child care than were similar households living in Hawaii. This result could be indicative that Hawaii was providing higher quality child care (through stricter regulations), thus making female home-worker households in Hawaii more likely to place their children in child care than their counterparts in other states.

Households with male home-workers in Missouri and Vermont were more likely to place their children in child care, compared to their counterparts in Hawaii. Although the relationship between cost and quality of child care is far from perfect, it does seem true that, on average, higher levels of regulation do cause higher prices. Under this assumption, male home-worker households in Missouri and Vermont perhaps were more willing to pay the assumed lower cost of child care in their states compared to similar households in Hawaii who presumably faced higher costs. It is worth noting that although six of the eight state variables entered into the regression analysis were found to be statistically significant, none of them was significant for both male and female home-worker households. And for those that were significant, there were a negative effect for households with women who were home-workers and a positive effect for households with men who were home-workers. These results pointed to gender differences in terms of what happened concerning child care when a women or man worked at home for pay.

Finally, in small towns (less than 2,500 population), households with female home-workers were more likely to choose outside child care than were households with female home-workers living in communities greater than 2,500 (the variable of comparison). This finding was somewhat surprising. It could be assumed that households would have been less able to find outside care in such small communities let alone purchase it. However, perhaps this result showed that in small towns households with female home-workers had confidence in the outside care giver they chose because of familiarity and/or because of the "watchdog" effect of living in a community where most people knew one another. In some rural communities there could have been a greater availability of relatives that might also explain this result.

SUMMARY AND CONCLUSIONS

This chapter examines multiple facets of gender differences within families in which there is a home-worker: that is, someone who works for pay or profit with the work site her or his home. Overwhelmingly, the results show significant and important differences in home-based employment as experienced by men and women. Household management and child-care choices appear to be linked in many important ways to the gender of the household manager and home-worker, and to the household structure.

Major differences are found in the net annual home-based employment income levels generated by women (an average of $8,466) and men ($24,603). When examined within household structure, even more dramatic results are found. In "family" environments with children under age 18 years, women have significant home-based employment income gaps: $11,200 in single-parent family household types, $13,600 in adult-only family types, and a large $20,100 gap in full-nest family households. However, in non-family households in which men and women only had themselves to care for, the gap between income for home-based employment for men and women is about $5,200. These results indicate that women's smaller earnings from home-based employment might indeed be related to family responsibilities.

Gender differences are also found in the "dedication" to the home-based employment. Female home-workers are less likely to be engaged in "other employment" and furthermore spend fewer (604 hours a year or about 12 hours per week less) hours engaged in the home-based employment than are their male counterparts. Men are also found to be engaged in more stable, long-term home-based employment (14.4% of women were involved in the same home-based employment for over 15 years compared to 26.1% of men involved in the same home-based employment for 15 years or longer).

The occupational choices within the home-based employment are also different for men and women. Across almost all household types women are more likely to be in clerical/administrative support and services, and in non-family households, marketing and sales, whereas men are more likely to be in contracting and managerial/professional/technical occupations.

Examining household management helps in determining how pragmatic individuals are at defining goals and then reaching them efficiently. Striking differences in the management styles are found for the men compared to the women who hold the role of household manager. Men show significantly more "efficient" behavior, including setting goals for work, setting standards, clarifying what is needed, assessing resource needs, checking, and adjusting, when compared to women. Women show more timing of action behavior than do men, however. These differences could be due, in part, to the instrument used to measure efficiency. Men and women are also found to be different in their management styles when they act as dual-role holders.

Examining the data for dual-role holders provides information about possible motivations for working for pay in the home. Of the 482 dual-role holders, 114 (23.7%) are men and 368 (76.3%) are women. However, in the households in which women are home-workers, they are dual-role holders in 97.6% (368 out of the 377) of these households. In the households with male home-workers, in contrast, 21.8% (114 of the 522) of the men are dual-role holders. In this sample of home-workers, women are much more likely to have two roles—home-worker and household manager. Although no information was directly gathered to indicate the total number of roles held by the men and women, this survey does indicate that women are being called on to carry two important functions of the family. It is probable that women are trying to produce paid-work and family care jointly through their home-based employment. Stress or role conflict between these two roles could be a problem for the dual-role holder. This study reveals that women are more at risk for such stress or role conflict given that they are more often dual-role holders.

Marked differences are also found in the child-care choice arena. Households with male home-workers, in general, are more likely to purchase outside child care. Households with male home-workers with one child under the age of 5 years are more likely (54%) to purchase outside child care than households with female home-workers (47.7%) with one child under the age of 5. When there are two children under the age of 5, the difference becomes greater; in households with male home-workers, 52.1% hire outside child care versus the 13.7% of households with female home-workers.

The regression analysis reveals that there are different factors driving these choices in child care. Households with male home-workers are influenced to hire outside child care by having other household income, if the home-worker is in a managerial/professional/technical occupation, and if they live in either Missouri or Vermont. These households are influenced not to hire outside child care by the number of children under the age of 5, the home-worker's having other employment, and the amount of home-based employment income. Conversely, households in which there are female home-workers are influenced to purchase outside child care by the worker's level of education, managerial/ professional/technical occupation, other employment, number of home-based employment hours spent outside the home, and residence in a town with a population of fewer than 2,500. Households with female home-workers are influenced not to purchase outside child care by the home-worker's being a business owner and by living in Iowa, New York, Pennsylvania, and Utah. The only factors having similar effects on the child-care choice of households with male home-workers and those with female home-workers, are whether the home-worker is in a managerial/professional/technical occupation and whether the home-worker is engaged in other employment.

RESEARCH IMPLICATIONS AND THE NEED
FOR FURTHER RESEARCH

The overriding goal of research, such as that described in this chapter, is to help find practical solutions to the problems faced by real people. In this study the focus is to examine gender differences in the vitality and management of both the paid-work sphere and the family sphere for households engaged in home-based employment. Many notable gender differences are detected.

As stated at the beginning of the chapter, the motivation for home-based employment for women might be a desire to maximize utility and maximize profits through simultaneously doing household production, especially child care, and doing work for pay. This chapter shows some indications of how this motivation is played out. Women are earning less money as home-workers partially because they work fewer hours. Perhaps this is intentional, but it might be that combining employment and family in the home-based setting results in women's achieving less than desired in the work-for-pay side of the venture. Households with female home-workers are less likely than households with male home-workers to purchase outside child care, again indicating that household production is a major factor in women's choosing employment in the home setting. A research issue that remains unexamined is whether or not women are satisfied with the household production/work-for-pay situation in which they are involved. It could be that women see any income as better than none, but it could also be that expectations for merging paid-work and family are frustrated when family takes more time and attention than anticipated.

In comparing the motivations of men and women for engaging in home-based employment, results in this chapter suggest that female motivations would be to maximize utility through household production with profit maximization as a secondary activity. This is suggested because women spend less time in home-based employment, are less goal oriented (as measured by the home-management instrument), purchase less outside child care, and earn less income from the home-based employment. Men appear to be doing the opposite, focusing primarily on profit maximization and secondarily maximizing utility through household production while working at home. Further research is needed on the initial motivation for men and women when they embark upon home-based employment.

Many men and women in this sample are doing both jobs of household production and home-based employment as part of their daily activities. Their choice to do so might lie partially in the fact that fairly rigid work environments are offered in the mainstream employment pool. The world of paid-work outside the home usually demands more rigid hours for the work, less flexibility in the location of the work, and less tolerance of the presence of children in the workplace. Governmental and business policies for the workplace are driven by tradition, societal expectations, and real demands for rigid separation of work and family that are related to safety, control, liability, and production issues. However, it could be that the rigid workplace rules are causing households to engage in efforts to combine paid-work and family through ventures such as home-based employment even when the workplace could change to accommodate employment and family issues without harm to productivity. Innovative solutions to this problem could include the following:

- Job sharing
- More part-time employment that also provides a career track and benefits
- Flex-time
- Defining of jobs or parts of jobs which could be accomplished at home
- Electronic travel versus physical travel
- Day-care on site
- Sick child care
- Stable shift work

• More help for families to accomplish the work of the household (through services such as meal preparation, laundry services, and errand services which could
be offered either for profit or not-for-profit)

Although some work sites have incorporated these family-friendly innovations, many more are needed to help families accomplish their household responsibilities in addition to allowing more work productivity, income, and stability than home-based employment provides. Further, societal expectations of
men and women also need to change in order to even the load of role responsibility for the home and for paid-work between men and women. Until home and
paid-work roles are more evenly valued for men and women, flexibility to adapt
and accommodate each role will be hampered.

Some home-workers might see their work as the best accommodation possible for combining employment and family because of barriers in the workplace. However, many business and government policies discourage successful
home-based employment for those who prefer home-based employment to other
work opportunities. Zoning ordinances, high amounts of tax regulation, busi-
ness-licensing codes, lack of up-to-date telephone services, and myriad other
barriers make working at home less lucrative and workable. Many possible
home-based business ideas that would include joint production, such as caring
for one's own child while caring for other children or making dinner for a
neighbor family for pay while making dinner for one's own family, are less possible because of licensing requirements and other laws and regulations forcing
investments in the business that are much larger than can be supported by the
business revenue.

Optimally, families who choose to work at home for the purpose of combining paid-work and family more seamlessly should have good choices available for those roles, supported by society, business, and government. Families
also need help in having a work world adapt to family needs without resorting
to home-based employment as one of the few solutions available to allow combining employment and family in a satisfactory manner.

A final implication of the research reported in this chapter is that much
more must be known about the dual management of households and home-based
employment. Apparently women and men do not manage the household using
the same management models, terms, or processes. Although women apparently
set fewer goals and define standards less often than men, they are still accom-
plishing a great deal in a given period. Perhaps the household management
model used by women is more reactionary when goals are less self-devised than
when they are presented to women in the form of demands, either from family
or from customers or bosses of the home-based employment. Women manage,
no doubt, but apparently not in the language of household management as was
presented in the study. More needs to be understood about gender differences in
management and the way management is measured and reported.

It is important to recognize these gender differences and to incorporate them
into educational and informational materials marketed toward home-based em-

ployment. Clearly, when the income generation, dedication level, occupational choice, household management styles, and child-care choices all reveal significant gender differences, it is obvious that households with home-workers are not a homogeneous group.

The chapter highlights the fact that lessons can be learned from both genders. For example, this study gives further empirical support to the well-documented fact that men earn more money than do women, even in home-based employment. As another example, it is clear that household management styles, occupation types within home-based employment, and number of hours dedicated to the home-based employment differ between men and women. With further research it might be possible to determine which (or what combination) of these determines the earnings differences.

Finally, as couples or home-based employment partners strive to make cross-gender relationships thrive, they can find useful research results that compare and contrast the genders. This study has proved fruitful, and it has only begun to examine the differences in the ways in which gender and household structure affect home-based employment.

NOTE

1. It is possible that the household managers who were not home-workers had other employment. However, for the purposes of this chapter, only those people who were household managers and home-workers were considered to be dual-role holders.

REFERENCES

Ahrentzen, S. B. (1990). Managing conflict by managing boundaries: How professional home workers cope with multiple roles at home. *Environment and Behavior, 22,* 723–752.

Barnett, R. (1994). Home-to-work spillover revisited: A study of full-time employed women in dual-earner couples. *Journal of Marriage and the Family, 56,* 647–656.

Barnett, R. C., & Baruch, G. K. (1985). Women's involvement in multiple roles and psychological distress. *Journal of Personality and Social Psychology, 49,* 135–145.

Barnett, R. C., & Marshall, N. L. (1991). The relationship between women's work and family roles and subjective well-being and psychological distress. In M. Frankenhaeuser, U. Lundber, & M. Chesney (Eds.), *Women, work and health: Stress and opportunity* (pp. 111–136). New York: Plenum.

Barnett, R. C., Marshall, N. L., & Singer, J. D. (1992). Job experiences over time, multiple roles, and women's mental health: A longitudinal study. *Journal of Personality and Social Psychology, 62,* 634–644.

Behr, M., & Lazar, W. (Eds.). (1983). *Women working home: The homebased business guide and directory.* Edison, NJ: WWH Press.

Belle, D. (1990). Poverty and women's mental health. *American Psychologist, 45,* 385–389.

Bem, D. (1987, Fall). *A consumer's guide to dual career marriages.* ILR Report, pp. 10–12.

Bird, G. A., Bird, G. W., & Scruggs, M. (1983). Role management strategies used by husbands and wives in two-earner families. *Home Economics Research Journal, 12,* 63–70.

Boris, E. (1987). Homework and women's rights: The case of Vermont knitters, 1980–1985. *Signs, 13,* 98–120.

Brayfield, A. (1995). The impact of employment schedules on fathers' caring for their children. *Journal of Marriage and the Family, 57,* 321–330.

Burden, D. (1986). Single parents and the work setting: The impact of multiple job and homelife responsibilities. *Family Relations, 35,* 37–43.

Christensen, K. E. (1988). *The new era of home-based work: Directions and policies.* Boulder, CO: Westview.

Coverman, S. (1989). Role overload, role conflict, and stress: Addressing consequences of multiple role demands. *Social Forces, 67,* 965–982.

Danes, S. M., & Keskinen, S. M. (1990). The extent of off-farm employment and its impact on farm women. *Human Services in the Rural Environment, 14,* 10–14.

Danes, S. M., & McTavish, D. G. (1997). Role involvement of farm women. *Journal of Family and Economic Issues, 18,* 69–89.

Deacon, R. E., & Firebaugh, F. M. (1988). *Family resource management principles and application* (2nd Ed.). Boston: Allyn & Bacon.

Duxbury, L., Higgins, C., & Lee, C. (1994). Work-family conflict: A comparison by gender, family type, and perceived control. *Journal of Family Issues, 15,* 449–466.

Folk, K. F., & Beller, A. H. (1991). *Joint choice of child care and labor supply by mothers of preschool children.* Working paper, University of Illinois, Division of Consumer Sciences.

Goffee, R., & Scase, R. (1985). *Women in charge: The experience of female entrepreneurs.* London: George Allen & Unwin.

Greenhaus, J., & Beutell, N. (1985). Sources of conflict between work and family roles. *Academy of Management Review, 10,* 76–88.

Hayes, C. D., Palmer, J. L., & Zaslow, M. J. (Eds.). (1990). *Who cares for America's children? Child care policy for the 1990s.* Washington, DC: National Academy Press.

Hayghe, H. (1988). Employers and child care: What roles do they play? *Monthly Labor Review, 111* (9), 38–44.

Haynes, D. C. (1996). The determinants of fathers' time spent in child care. *Family Economics and Resource Management Biennial, 2,* 51–58.

Heck, R. K. Z., Own, A. J., & Rowe, B. R. (Eds.). (1995). *Home-based employment and family life.* Westport, CT: Auburn House.

Heck, R. K. Z., Saltford, N. C., Rowe, B., & Owen, A. J. (1992). The utilization of child care by households engaged in home-based employment. *Journal of Family and Economic Issues, 13,* 213–237.

Higgins, C., Duxbury, L., & Lee, C. (1995). Impact of life-cycle stage and gender on the ability to balance work and family responsibilities. In G. L. Bowen & J. F. Pittman (Eds.), *The work and family interface: Toward a contextual effects perspective* (pp. 313–322). Minneapolis, MN: National Council on Family Relations.

Hisrich, R. D. (1989). Women entrepreneurs: Problems and prescriptions for success in the future. In O. Hagan, C. Rivchun, & D. Sexton (Eds.), *Women-owned businesses* (pp. 3–32). New York: Praeger.

Horvath, F. W. (1986). Work at home: New findings from the current population survey. *Monthly Labor Review, 109* (11), 31–35.

Hyland, S. L. (1990). Helping employees with family care. *Monthly Labor Review, 113*(9), 22–26.

Karsten, M. F. (1994). *Management and gender: Issues and attitudes.* Westport, CT: Praeger.

Longstreth, M., Stafford, K., & Mauldin, T. (1987). Self-employed women and their families: Time use and socioeconomic characteristics. *Journal of Small Business Management, 25,* 30–37.

Loscocco, K. A., & Leicht, K. T. (1993). Gender, work-family linkages, and economic success among small business owners. *Journal of Marriage and the Family, 55,* 875–887.

Loscocco, K. A., & Robinson, J. (1991). Barriers to women's small-business success in the United States. *Gender and Society, 5,* 511–532.

Loscocco, K. A., Robinson, J., Hall, R. H., & Allen, J. K. (1991). Gender and small business success: An inquiry into women's relative disadvantage. *Social Forces, 70,* 65–85.

Marks, S. R. (1977). Multiple roles and role strain: Some notes on human energy, time, and commitment. *American Sociological Review, 42,* 921–936.

Marks, S. R. (1979). Culture, human energy, and self-actualization: A sociological offering to humanistic psychology. *Journal of Humanistic Psychology, 19* (3), 27–42.

Moen, P. (1992). *Women's two roles: A contemporary dilemma.* Westport, CT: Auburn House.

Moen, P., Dempster-McClain, D., & Williams, R. M., Jr. (1989). Social integration and longevity: An event history analysis of women's roles and resilience. *American Sociological Review, 54,* 635–647.

Norton, A., & Glick, P. (1986). One parent families: A social and economic profile. *Family Relations, 38,* 390–395.

Olson, M. H. (1983). *Overview of work-at-home trends in the United States* (CRIS Working Paper No. 57). New York: New York University, Center for Research on Information Systems.

O'Neil, R., & Greenberger, E. (1994). Patterns of commitment to work and parenting: Implications for role strain. *Journal of Marriage and the Family, 56,* 101–118.

Peterson, R. R., & Gerson, K. (1992). Determinants of responsibility for child care arrangements among dual-earner couples. *Journal of Marriage and the Family, 54,* 527–536.

Pratt, J. H. (1984). Home teleworking: A study of its pioneers. *Technological Forecasting and Social Change, 25,* 1–14.

Pratt, J. H. (1993). *Myths and realities of working at home: Characteristics of home-based business owners and telecommuters* (U.S. Small Business Administration, Office of Advocacy Contract SBA-6647-OA-91). Washington, DC: U.S. Government Printing Office.

Shelton, B. A., & Firestone, J. (1989). Household labor time and the gender gap in earnings. *Gender and Society, 3,* 105–112.

Shuster, C. (1994). First-time fathers' expectations and experiences using child care and integrating parenting and employment. *Early Education and Development, 5*, 261–276.

Skinner, D. A. (1980). Dual-career family stress and coping: A literature review. *Family Relations, 29*, 473–480.

Stafford, F. P. (1980). Women's use of time converging with men's. *Monthly Labor Review, 103* (1), 57–59.

Tebbets, R. (1982). Work: Its meaning for women's lives. In D. Belle (Ed.), *Lives in stress: Women and depression*. Beverly Hills, CA: Sage.

Tiedje, L. B., Wortman, C. B., Downey, G., Emmons, C., Biernat, M., & Lang, E. (1990). Women with multiple roles: Role-compatibility perceptions, satisfaction, and mental health. *Journal of Marriage and the Family, 52*, 63–72.

Weigel, D. J., Weigel, R. R., Berger, P. S., Cook, A. S., & DelCampo, R. (1995). Work-family conflict and the quality of family life: Specifying linking mechanisms. *Family and Consumer Sciences Research Journal, 24*, 5–28.

Winter, M., & Stafford, K. (1995). Research methods including sample design and questionnaire development. In R. K. Z. Heck, A. J. Owen, & B. R. Rowe (Eds.), *Home-based employment and family life* (pp. 229–240). Westport, CT: Auburn House.

Chapter 5

A Gender Comparison of Business Management Practices of Home-Based Business Owners

Cynthia R. Jasper, Karen P. Goebel, Kathryn Stafford, and Ramona K. Z. Heck

INTRODUCTION

Seeking the flexibility of working from home, many American workers have left the confines of a conventional workplace for the challenges of home-based employment, either self-employment or business ownership (Edwards & Field-Hendrey, 1996). The number of home-based businesses has expanded for both men and women as a result of factors such as limited job opportunities, dependent care responsibilities, lower capital expenses, entrepreneurial ambitions, secondary income generation, and self-determination (Bates, 1998; Blakely, 1997; Edwards & Field-Hendrey, 1996; Stern, 1996; Verespej, 1998). Decades ago, innovations in industry and transportation allowed men and women to work away from the home. Today, innovations in electronic technology have enabled men and women to organize, manage, and promote businesses from the home (Soldressen, Fiorito, & He, 1998).

Recent statistics support the observation that home-based businesses developed by women are increasing faster than any other segment of business start-ups (Stern, 1996; Tigges & Green, 1994). The impact of home-based businesses is reflected in a report by the New York based marketing research firm LINK Resources, which stated that home-based businesses increased from 14.9 million in 1988 to 27.1 million in 1996. Conventional wisdom suggests that men and women often approach business management practices differently. One would expect these differences to be particularly evident in home-based businesses because management of businesses traditionally has been considered in the man's realm, whereas management of the home has been in the woman's domain.

This examination of home-based businesses explores specifically the similarities and differences in how men and women set goals, plan, and implement management strategies for their businesses. The management styles of men and women for both family work and home-based business work are compared. Differences between male and female managers in their methods of advertising and promoting as well as distributing products and services are examined. Also considered are the types of professional services used and whether these services vary according to the gender of managers who own their own businesses. Because no previous studies have specifically examined the issues reported in this study, research on the relationship between gender and entrepreneurship or business ownership is reviewed. Although entrepreneurship is similar to business ownership, the terms have distinct meanings and should not be used interchangeably. They are reviewed together because of the limited amount of research in this area.

REVIEW OF LITERATURE

Gender Differences in Entrepreneurship and Business Ownership

As women's participation in the labor force has grown in recent years, the number of female business owners and managers also has increased significantly (Bowen & Hisrich, 1986; Coleman & Carsky, 1997; Gaskill et al., 1996; Karsten, 1994; O'Hare & Larson, 1991; Olson & Currie, 1992; Scherer, Brodzinski, & Wiebe, 1990; Scott, 1986; Stevenson, 1986). Businesses owned by women—mostly retail, wholesale, finance, insurance, and service—have received attention by researchers (Hisrich & Brush, 1984; O'Hare & Larson, 1991).

Many studies since the mid-1970s have investigated the motivations and characteristics of women who become business owners and managers (Bowen & Hisrich, 1986; Stevenson, 1986). Other studies have focused on entrepreneurs or business owners in general. Currently, national attention is being given to entrepreneurship and home-based and microbusinesses. Entrepreneurial efforts differ from business ownership in that entrepreneurial ventures frequently involve more risk associated with innovation. Business ownership is more likely to be characterized by stability and an established way of doing business. Assuming the risk of a business venture can be an individual's response to changes in the welfare system, shifts in traditional sources of employment, and technological changes in the workplace (Amott & Matthaei, 1996; Bauer & Braun, 1997).

Women choose business ownership to gain economic independence, flexibility, personal challenge, and satisfaction (Birley, 1989; Olson & Currie, 1992; Power, 1995; Scott, 1986; Stevenson, 1986). Additionally, Cromie (1987) indicated that women go into business because of dissatisfaction with their current job or career and society's expectation that they give primary care to their family. This latter expectation supports the idea that women can combine family and paid-work by launching a business based in the home. In contrast, men go into business because of dissatisfaction with their current job and a desire to own their own business.

Since the early 1980s, research models such as the socialization influence model have been developed to explain why more women have become business owners. According to this model, gender differences in social learning and cultural background influence preferences for careers. Traditionally, men have been more likely than women to prefer business careers such as accounting and manufacturing, whereas women have tended to aspire to service careers such as nursing and teaching. The theory contends that these differences have lessened as more women have become business owners and thus have served as role models for other women (Scherer et al., 1990).

Earlier studies of entrepreneurship frequently examined issues related to gender differences. To determine the similarities and differences between female entrepreneurs and their male counterparts, researchers examined demographic factors (Hisrich & Brush, 1984; Scott, 1986; Stevenson, 1986), personality traits (Chaganti, 1986; Olson & Currie, 1992; Stevenson, 1986), and business skills (Nelson, 1987). Several of these studies were based on surveys that yielded similar results about the demographic characteristics of women who own businesses. Female entrepreneurs are likely to have attended college and, on average, have more education than their male counterparts. However, few have formal business training (Bowen & Hisrich, 1986; Hisrich & Brush, 1984; O'Hare & Larson, 1991; Scott, 1986; Stevenson, 1986).

Female owners typically have had careers in education, mid-level management, administration, and clerical fields (Bowen & Hisrich, 1986; Scott, 1986). They value any previous management experience as well as business education and training (Nelson, 1987; Scherer et al., 1990; Scott 1986; Stevenson, 1986). Although they are likely to have supportive husbands or parents (Bowen & Hisrich, 1986; Hisrich & Brush, 1984; Stevenson, 1986), their marriages tend to be less stable than those of male entrepreneurs (Birley, 1989; Stevenson, 1986).

Gender Differences in Management

Some researchers have maintained that psychological differences cause differences between male and female entrepreneurs in management strategies and decision-making processes (Chaganti, 1986; Karsten, 1994). However, other researchers have shown that personality traits and values do not significantly affect business management and decision making (Olson & Currie, 1992; Scherer et al., 1990; Stevenson, 1986). These researchers concluded that more significant differences exist between women who own businesses and women in general than between female and male entrepreneurs (Stevenson, 1986). Olson and Currie (1992) found no relationship between gender and strategic planning. However, women in their survey were more likely than men to stress quality, service, and price as their marketing strategies (Olson & Currie, 1992).

Other researchers who studied operational strategies found common patterns of management among women who own businesses (Gaskill et al., 1996; Nelson, 1987). Compared with their male counterparts, female entrepreneurs identified themselves as more people oriented (Chaganti, 1986; Hisrich & Brush, 1984; Scott, 1986) and more open to new ideas and product innovations (Hisrich & Brush, 1984; Olson & Currie, 1992). Nelson (1987) indicated that female entrepreneurs who lacked education and experience in business tended to seek more information about business management than did male entrepreneurs. In an early analysis of the nine-state data set also analyzed in the study reported here, Zuiker, Stafford, Heck, and Winter (1995b) found that the management styles of men were similar in business and home environments. The management responses of women, however, were domain-specific. In other words, women did not manage their businesses in the same way they managed their families.

In two studies that focused specifically on female entrepreneurs, Hisrich and Brush (1984) found that the lack of financial knowledge and skills in areas such as budget preparation and tax planning was the greatest obstacle to women's success in business (Nelson, 1987). The information sources female business owners used most frequently were business executives and family members. They also gained information from accountants, attorneys, and bankers. Although this information could be costly, most female entrepreneurs concluded that it was useful (Nelson, 1987). Related to the lack of financial knowledge was the difficulty women often experienced in obtaining credit for business needs (Scott, 1986; Stevenson, 1986). Although both male and female business owners could have financial and personnel problems, balancing business and family needs was a more common difficulty for women (Olson & Currie, 1992; Scott, 1986; Stevenson, 1986).

Using the nine-state data set to study home-based business owners, Heck, Rowe, and Owen (1995) discovered that women spent more time (85% of their work time) than men doing their business in the home, a practice which could have created additional managerial problems for women. Lack of time was often a problem for female business owners, who had to manage the home as well as the business. Women commonly reduced the time spent on personal activities, family functions, and household responsibilities when they were busy with paid-work activities (Power, 1995).

A small business firm's performance depends on planning and decision making (Gaskill, Van Auken, & Manning, 1993). Although few gender differences in the retail field have been found in operational planning, especially personnel and financial planning, significant differences have been observed in inventory planning and marketing, such as in planning merchandise assortment. Men have tended to be more analytical in their decisions regarding inventory control, whereas women have been more creative in planning merchandise assortments. In addition, men have been more likely to consider economic changes and financial issues in marketing strategies, whereas women have tended to be more sensitive to sales, advertising, and customer service (Gaskill et al., 1996). Gaskill and colleagues (1996) also found that in the retail field women were more likely than men to introduce new products or services and focus on special market segments. Women also put more emphasis on customer service and maintained larger inventories. However, no significant differences were apparent in cost leadership strategies; that lack of difference supported the finding that both female and male business owners perceived that maintaining efficiency in business operations was vital to success (Gaskill et al., 1996).

Gender differences in management practices do not necessarily mean women have been at a disadvantage in the business world (Gaskill et al., 1996). In their analysis of longitudinal data, Kallenberg and Leicht (1991) concluded that businesses owned by women were no more likely to fail than were those owned by men.

Other researchers have analyzed the limitations of studies on gender differences among business owners (Stevenson, 1986, 1990) and recommended improved research methods (Moore, 1990). Previous to Stevenson's studies, men's activities represented one behavior pattern that denied the whole range of women's experiences. This bias served to perpetuate entrepreneurial stereotypes. Stevenson (1986, 1990) indicated studies that use concepts appropriate for the male-dominated business world might not contribute to an understanding of female entrepreneurs. In comparing men and women who owned businesses, she concluded that "research should be formulated in such a way that the entrepreneurial activity of women can be analyzed within the context of their whole lives" (Stevenson, 1986, p. 36). In her 1990 study, Stevenson challenged researchers to use the experiences of women rather than of men as the starting point for inquiry on female entrepreneurship.

METHODS OF COLLECTING DATA

This study was based on data from the nine-state research project on home-based employment, which was defined as working for pay at home or from the home at least 6 hours per week throughout the year or, in the case of seasonal work, a minimum of 312 hours annually (Stafford, Winter, Duncan, & Genalo, 1992). Households were included in the sample if a member had been engaged in home-based employment for at least 12 months prior to the interview and had no other office from which he or she conducted work. Survey data were gathered in two stages. A stratified (rural/urban) random sample of almost 19,000 households was used in the first stage. Households in the sample were contacted by telephone to ascertain whether anyone in the household worked at or from the home for income.

In the second stage, households with home-based employment were called and the household manager was interviewed for 30 minutes (Stafford et al., 1992). These 899 households were located in Hawaii, Iowa, Michigan, Missouri, New York, Ohio, Pennsylvania, Utah, and Vermont. The data were weighted by the relative population of the respective state and rural/urban proportion of the state (Stafford et al., 1992).

A subsample of households engaged in home-based businesses ($n = 670$) was used for the analyses reported in this chapter. Of the 670 home-based business owners, 353 (83 men and 270 women) answered both the business management and home management questions.

The Deacon and Firebaugh (1988) model provided a basis for this study. Respondents answered questions related to business management that paralleled household management questions enabling a comparison of management practices in the two domains.

ANALYSIS AND FINDINGS

Business Management Practices of Home-Based Business Owners

A number of management concepts were examined in this study: setting goals, setting standards, clarifying demand, assessing resources, sequencing actions, actuating, checking, adjusting, responding to demand, and changing resources (Heck, Winter, & Stafford, 1992). The owners were asked to respond to each of 10 statements on a scale of 1 to 5, representing the degree to which the statement described them. The statements about business management practices were as follows[1]:

1. Each week you decide how much work you will do. (Setting goals)
2. Before starting a job, you have a firm idea about how to judge the outcome. (Setting standards)
3. When planning a job, you think the plan through so that your goal is clear before you actually begin doing the job. (Clarifying demand)
4. Before starting a particular job, you figure out what you need, like tools, supplies, and time. (Assessing resources)
5. Although you are flexible, you make work schedules. (Sequencing action)
6. When there is work to be done, you wait until the last minute. (Actuating) (This item was reverse coded so that a higher score indicated not waiting until the last minute.)
7. As you work, you check whether things are going as planned. (Checking)
8. You change how you are doing a task when the results are not as planned. (Adjusting)
9. When you finish a job, you think about whether the results meet your standards as well as your client's or employer's. (Responding to demand)
10. When finished, you ask whether people and equipment have been used to the best advantage. (Changing resources)

Similarities and Differences in Business Management Practices of Men and Women

Table 5.1 shows the frequency of responses to home-based employment management items for female and male home-based business owners. Table 5.2 shows the means and standard deviations, based on a 5-point scale.

Table 5.1

Percentage of Responses to Business Management Items (n = 353)

Management Concepts	Women (n = 270)					Men (n = 83)				
	Not at all		Somewhat		Exactly	Not at all		Somewhat		Exactly
	1	2	3	4	5	1	2	3	4	5
Setting goals	24.6	6.2	26.9	10.2	32.1	25.2	4.9	19.1	11.2	39.5
Setting standards	3.4	0.4	20.1	33.2	42.9	3.5	0.1	14.1	27.8	54.5
Clarifying demand	5.0	1.5	20.3	20.7	52.5	1.4	0.0	19.4	18.8	60.3
Assessing resources	1.2	2.8	11.7	13.4	70.9	0.0	7.0	5.3	21.3	66.3
Sequencing action	7.6	3.6	24.3	23.3	41.2	9.6	5.9	16.2	19.6	48.7
Actuating	8.3	4.5	27.9	16.1	43.1	1.0	3.0	33.9	17.9	44.1
Checking	1.6	3.5	27.9	21.4	45.7	2.3	0.1	23.0	27.9	46.7
Adjusting	1.8	2.6	17.3	20.8	57.5	4.5	1.3	17.6	28.8	47.7
Responding to demand	2.0	0.4	6.3	19.6	71.7	1.6	1.5	4.3	21.2	71.4
Changing resources	11.1	4.5	23.8	27.3	33.3	9.5	5.2	21.7	25.2	38.4
Total mean of scale	40.24					41.09				
Alpha for additive scales	.73					.77				
Standardized item alpha	.74					.80				

Note: Each statement was coded to describe how much the statement is like the respondent.

Table 5.2
Means and Standard Deviations for Business Management Items (*n* = 353)

Management Concepts	Women (*n* = 270)		Men (*n* = 83)		*t*-test	
	M	SD	M	SD	*t*-value	*p*
Setting goals	3.19	1.55	3.35	1.63	-.79	0.433
Setting standards	4.12	.97	4.30	.97	-1.47	0.144
Clarifying demand	4.14	1.10	4.37	.89	-1.89	0.061*
Assessing resources	4.50	.90	4.47	.89	.27	0.787
Sequencing action	3.87	1.21	3.92	1.33	-.32	0.748
Actuating	3.81	1.27	4.01	1.00	-1.49	0.138
Checking	4.06	1.01	4.17	.95	-.87	0.387
Adjusting	4.30	.97	4.14	1.05	1.22	0.227
Responding to demand	4.59	.80	4.59	.79	-.07	0.943
Changing resources	3.67	1.29	3.78	1.28	-.67	0.503
Total scale	40.24	6.06	41.09	6.31	-1.08	0.283

*p < .10.

Setting Goals. When home-based business owners were asked whether they decide each week how much work they will do, the responses of women were more varied than those of men. About one-third (32.1%) of the women reported they plan the work they will do each week, slightly over one-fourth (26.9%) have a general idea, and about one-fourth (24.6%) do not plan ahead. The men tended to be more planning oriented: almost two-fifths (39.5%) plan the amount of work they will do each week.

Despite these differences, the means and standard deviations for men and women were similar for goal setting. The means of both were slightly over 3 ("somewhat"), with standard deviations of 1.55 and 1.63 for women and men, respectively. These results indicated that in most cases some time is spent planning the week's activities. No significant differences were found between the genders when comparing means and standard deviations regarding weekly goal setting related to the amount of work.

Setting Standards. Both women and men reported they plan their jobs with a clear understanding of their standards for acceptable work. Over one-half of the men (54.5%), compared with slightly over two-fifths of the women (42.9%), reported they clearly define their intentions before starting to work. Only a small percentage of home-based business owners (3.4% of women and 3.5% of men) reported they are ambiguous about their expected results. The means and the standard deviations were similar for women and men. Both means were over 4, suggesting that most respondents clearly know their standards before beginning a job. Differences between the genders were not significant.

Clarifying Demand. When asked whether they have a firm idea as to how to judge the outcome before beginning a job, 60% of the men and 53% of the women responded affirmatively. A small percentage of both genders stated they do not have a firm idea as to how the job will turn out. More women (5.0%) than men (1.4%) reported they are uncertain about the outcome. The mean for men was higher (4.37 for men vs. 4.14 for women), with a smaller standard deviation (0.89 for men vs. 1.10 for women), which indicated men are more likely than women to project the outcome before starting to work. The difference between women's and men's responses to "When planning a job, you think the plan through so that your goal is clear before you actually begin doing the job" was significant at the 0.06 level. This was the only significant difference found for the variables presented in Table 5.2.

Assessing Resources. Even though a large majority of both genders reported they figure out their needs (tools, supplies, time, etc.) before beginning a job, slightly more women (70.9%) than men (66.3%) plan for their needs before beginning a job. The means of both genders were high (4.50 for women and 4.47 for men), implying that most respondents believe they know what they need before starting a particular job. The difference in results was not significant.

Sequencing Action. Men and women responded similarly when asked whether they make work schedules. Slightly over two-fifths of the women (41.2%) and close to one-half of the men (48.7%) indicated they work with a schedule. A small percentage of respondents indicated that they do not develop a schedule; men (9.6%) were more likely than women (7.6%) to skip this process. Curiously, for both genders, more respondents reported they are likely to skip this task than any of the other planning tasks. Men had a slightly higher mean (3.92) than women (3.87) and a higher standard deviation (1.33 for men vs. 1.21 for women), implying men were more likely to make work schedules. However, the difference in results was not significant.

Actuating. When it comes to doing the work, two-fifths of each gender (43.1% of women and 44.1% of men) reported they usually do not wait until the last minute. Approximately one-third (27.9% of women and 33.9% of men) responded that they sometimes do not wait until the last minute. The men had a higher mean (4.01 vs. 3.81 for women) and a smaller standard deviation in their response to this item, yet the difference between the genders was not significant.

Checking. Similar behavior patterns were seen for both genders in checking the job as it progresses. Slightly under one-half of both genders (45.7% of women and 46.7% of men) reported they check to see that things are going as planned as they work. Even though both genders had means over 4, implying they are likely to check whether things are going as planned as they work, the men's mean was higher with a lower standard deviation. Nevertheless, the difference in results was not significant.

Adjusting. A majority of the respondents reported changing how they do a task when they are not receiving the expected results. However, more women

(57.5%) than men (47.7%) reported they make changes. High means for both genders indicated the respondents' willingness to make changes when results of their work are not as planned. Women had a higher mean (4.30 vs. 4.14 for men) with a lower standard deviation, yet the difference between the genders was not significant.

Responding to Demand. When asked whether the results of a job meet the standards of the respondent and the client or employer, men and women had a similar breakdown in responses. About 72% of women and 71% of men reported the standards are met. Under 10% of the men and women (6.3% of women and 4.3% of men) said they are met somewhat, and only a small percentage (2.0% for women and 1.6% for men) responded that the standards are not met. The mean for the men (4.59) was the same as that for women (4.59); also the genders had similar standard deviations in their scores on the item "When you finish a job, you think about whether the results meet your standards as well as your client's or employer's." The difference between the results was not significant.

Changing Resources. Slightly over 33% of women and 38% of men indicated that when they are finished with a job, they question whether people and equipment have been used to the best advantage. Women and men had similar means (3.67 and 3.78, respectively), with slight differences in standard deviation in their reports of utilizing resources (people and equipment) to the best advantage for the job. Therefore, the difference between the genders was not significant.

Factors Influencing Women's and Men's Management of the Business

Five management styles, based on ideas presented in Eisenhardt (1985), were delineated. The managing style describes those whose main concern is achieving goals. The leading style is indicative of individuals who plan work around setting goals. The sensing style characterizes those who manage work according to the way they feel about the activity. The evaluating type monitors work progress, often checking the results and observing other individuals' reactions to the results. The doing/action style is used by those who are most action oriented. In other words, they begin the work with a minimum of planning and goal setting. Results of factor analysis suggested that four of the five styles were utilized by the 353 owners in the management of their businesses (see Table 5.3).

Two of these management styles, managing and leading, were shared by men and women home-based business owners. A group of women used the sensing style of management, whereas a group of men were more likely to use the evaluating style of management. Neither men nor women used the doing/action style.

Table 5.3
Factor Loadings for Business Management Items (*n* = 353)

Management Concepts	Women (*n* = 270)			Men (*n* = 83)		
	Managing	Leading	Sensing	Managing	Evaluating	Leading
Setting goals	0.07	**0.73**	0.01	-0.28	0.28	**0.68**
Setting standards	**0.74**	0.03	-0.03	**0.79**	0.14	0.13
Clarifying demand	**0.54**	0.47	0.25	**0.85**	0.10	0.23
Assessing resources	**0.74**	0.10	0.33	**0.71**	0.32	-0.20
Sequencing action	0.26	0.69	0.03	0.33	-0.12	0.72
Actuating	**0.50**	0.43	-0.12	0.14	0.35	0.22
Checking	0.41	0.05	**0.56**	0.14	0.34	**0.74**
Adjusting	0.04	0.00	**0.80**	**0.58**	**0.60**	0.17
Responding to demand	0.01	0.15	**0.69**	0.07	**0.87**	0.01
Changing resources	-0.07	0.63	0.37	0.38	**0.58**	0.34
Eigenvalues	3.05	1.35	1.09	3.75	1.45	1.03
Percentage of variation explained	30.5%	13.5%	10.9%	37.5%	15.4%	10.3%

Note: Factor loadings higher than .5 for each management concept are in boldface. Definitions for management concepts are taken from Deacon and Firebaugh (1988).

Services Used by Home-Based Business Owners

Home-based business owners were asked what types of services they used, for example, accounting, legal, banking, and copying services. They were also asked whether they utilized services made available by their suppliers or the post office. They were asked how far these services were located from their home in minutes traveled. Table 5.4 presents the percentage, by gender, of the 670 home-based business owners who commonly used each of these services. Although no significant difference was found between genders, a higher percentage of men in the sample used accounting, legal, copying, supplier, and banking services. As would be expected, all respondents used the services provided by the post office for their businesses.

Of particular interest was the finding that 62% of the men used accounting services, whereas only 41% of the women relied on such services. Additionally, the results showed that men were more likely to use legal services than were women (38% and 23%, respectively). Close to half of all respondents (45% of women and 53% of men) reported they employed copying services. A high percentage of both men and women reported the use of banking services (94% and 85%, respectively).

Table 5.4
Percentage of Home-Based Business Owners Using Business Services ($n = 670$)

Service	Percentage Using Service		Mean Travel Time From Home (minutes)	
	Women	Men	Women	Men
Accounting	41	62	17	17
Legal	23	38	17	17
Copying	45	53	9	13
Suppliers	88	97	19	21
Banking	85	94	11	9
Post office	100	100	8	7

Table 5.4 also includes the mean travel time to commute to receive these services. No significant difference was observed between the genders. However, on average, men reported they spent a few more minutes traveling to copying services and suppliers than did women. Women reported they spent 2 minutes more in travel to banking and 1 minute more in travel to the post office than did men.

Methods for Advertising and Promoting Products and Services

Table 5.5 presents the strategies used by the 670 home-based business own-ers to advertise and promote products and services to potential customers. The percentages do not add to 100% because one owner might use several promotion strategies. The methods fall into seven categories: (a) newspapers (advertisers, shoppers, community calendar); (b) yellow pages; (c) direct mail (postcards, brochures); (d) catalogs or trade journals (magazines, books); (e) word of mouth, referrals; (f) flyers or ads in bulletins; and (g) other ways.

Similar percentages were observed for female and male entrepreneurs in us-ing referrals (94% for both), newspapers (30% of women vs. 29% of men), and other methods (16% of women vs. 17% of men). For both genders, the top choice for attracting customers was referrals, followed by newspapers. A higher percentage of men advertised in yellow pages and flyers or ads in bulletins than did women. However, women were almost twice as likely as men to use mail-ings and were slightly more likely to use catalogs to get their information known.

Table 5.5
Percentage of Home-Based Business Owners Using
Advertising Methods (n = 670)

Advertising Method	Percentage Using Method	
	Women	Men
Newspapers	30	29
Yellow pages	15	20
Direct mail	19	10
Catalogs	11	9
Referrals	94	94
Flyers or ads in bulletins	10	15
Other	16	17

Methods Used to Distribute Goods to Customers

Home-based business owners were asked what methods they use to sell their goods (see Table 5.6). First, they were asked whether they sold their prod-ucts wholesale or retail. Second, they were asked about specific outlets, that is, whether they sold their goods (a) on consignment; (b) through mail order ads or catalogs; (c) at bazaars, craft fairs, trade shows, flea markets, farmer's markets, antique shows, or guns shows; (d) through sales representatives; (e) through wholesalers; (f) at retail stores or galleries; (g) to consumers who go to their home; (h) to customers who do not go to their home; or (i) in some other way.

Methods used by male and female home-based business owners to sell their goods were compared. Results showed that women (22%) were more likely to use direct marketing such as bazaars, fairs, and shows than were men (10%). In addition, more women (14%) than men (7%) reported the use of retail stores and galleries. With respect to consignment to retail stores, slightly more women reported the use of this sales channel than did men (14% for women and 12% for men). Women also indicated they were more likely to use mail order (9% of women vs. 6% of men). Distribution methods in which men reported a leading percentage were sales representatives (15% of men vs. 4% of women) and wholesalers (8% of men vs. 0.6% of women).

Table 5.6
Percentage of Home-Based Business Owners Using Distribution Methods ($n = 670$)

| | Percentage Using Method | |
Distribution Method	Women	Men
Consignment in retail stores	14	12
Mail order	9	6
Bazaars, fairs, or shows	22	10
Sales representatives	4	15
Wholesalers	0.6	8
Retail stores or galleries	14	7
To customers who go to home	43	42
To customers who do not go to home	14	16
Other	4	1

Having the customer go to the home was the most frequently used of the nine distribution methods for both men (42%) and women (43%). Sending goods directly to the consumer was used by 14% of the women and 16% of the men.

CONCLUSION AND IMPLICATIONS

Given the importance of home-based businesses to the national economy and the recent increase in the number of these businesses, this chapter examines how men and women who own home-based businesses manage business and family. Management practices and styles regarding the management of both the business and the family are compared on the basis of gender. Also, gender differences in advertising and promoting as well as distributing home-based products and services are examined.

The Deacon and Firebaugh (1988) model of management designed for the family did not match up as well as would be desired for investigating women's management of home-based businesses. A major reason for selecting this model was that women often choose to start their own business in order to remain in the home, and the assumption was that much of the management style that they used in running the household would naturally be utilized in operating the home-based business. The study reported in this chapter shows differences in the frequency of responses to home-based business management items for female and male home-based business owners. The men in the study rely on the evaluating style more than do the women. Yet women more frequently utilize sensing in their business management. The findings also indicate differences between men and women when setting goals: men tended to be more planning oriented. Women function differently when it comes to home-based employment, perhaps because they are continually dovetailing family and employment responsibilities.

These results support the findings of an earlier study by Zuiker, Stafford, Heck, and Winter (1995a). The authors commented, "Perhaps the frameworks that dominate family resource management today are not gender neutral. Perhaps they are male models" (p. 98). The scales used in the study reported here also might measure the management styles of men better than those of women.

This study finds that women tend to use the sensing style more than do men. This finding might relate to the work by Cromie (1987), who noted that one reason women began a business was to combine paid-work with care for their families. He also noted that women were more likely to remain in female service industries, which might be reflected in the types of distribution methods they were most likely to utilize. Cromie stressed that men were more likely than women to begin a business as a result of job dissatisfaction or the desire to own their own business. This difference could be reflected in the finding reported in this chapter that men are more likely than women to use the doing/action method of managing their home-based business.

In addition to management styles of the business and the family, differences between men and women business owners regarding advertising and promoting and distributing products and services are examined. Although the respondents were not asked why they selected particular services, some decisions were likely affected by gender. Men might typically begin a business with more financial backing and incentives because traditionally loans and financial assistance are easier for them to secure. Men might then plan to use their time and energy expanding the business and leave the detailed operations to others. Women, on the other hand, might be more likely to start with a one-person operation. Because their cash flow could be more limited, women might assume the responsibilities of record keeping, banking, and so on. Having experienced running a household, women might also apply much of their household management expertise to their own businesses. Finding ways to cut costs, such as doing part of the work themselves or substituting supplies that can do double duty, are other possibilities. This concept that gender differences affect use of services seems to be supported because both tend to use the post office, a service that neither gender could provide, equally. Educators and direct service providers might need to acknowledge, as they prepare materials and workshops for potential or current home-based business owners, differences in the management styles of men and women. Researchers need to ask what influences the management styles of women and explore those influences to have a better understanding of why gender differences could be more than just psychological differences.

NOTES

This chapter reports results from the Cooperative Regional Research Project NE-167, *At-Home Income Generation: Impact on Management, Productivity, and Stability in Rural and Urban Families*, supported by Cooperative States Research Service; U.S. Department of Agriculture; and the Experiment Stations at the University of Hawaii, Iowa State University, Lincoln University (Missouri), Michigan State University, Cornell University (New York), The Ohio State University, Pennsylvania State University, Utah State University, and the University of Vermont.

1. See Heck, Winter, and Stafford (1992) for the items used for the measurement of household management as well as the terms used to describe each management concept, which differ in some respects from the terms used in this chapter.

REFERENCES

Amott, T., & Matthaei, J. (1996). *Race, gender, and work: A multi-cultural economic history of women in the United States*. Boston: South End Press.

Bates, S. (1998). Following their homing instinct. *Nation's Business, 86* (6), 75–76.

Bauer, J. W., & Braun, B. S. (1997). Leadership perspectives: Responding knowledgeably to welfare reform. *Family Economics and Resource Management Biennial, 2*, 71–74.

Birley, S. (1989). Female entrepreneurs: Are they really different? *Journal of Small Business Management, 27* (1), 32–37.

Blakely, S. (1997). Finding coverage for small offices. *Nation's Business, 85* (6), 30–34.

Bowen, D. D., & Hisrich, R. D. (1986). The female entrepreneur: A career development perspective. *Academy of Management Review, 11* (2), 393–407.

Chaganti, R. (1986). Management in women-owned enterprises. *Journal of Small Business Management, 24* (4), 18–29.

Coleman, S., & Carsky, M. (1997). Women-owned businesses, access to capital, and family support. *IFBPA Family Business Annual, 3*, 63–75.

Cromie, S. (1987). Motivations of aspiring male and female entrepreneurs. *Journal of Occupational Behaviour, 8*, 251–262.

Deacon, R. E., & Firebaugh, F. M. (1988). *Family resource management: Principles and applications* (2nd ed.). Boston: Allyn & Bacon.

Edwards, L. N., & Field-Hendrey, E. (1996, November). Home-based workers: Data from the 1990 Census of Population. *Monthly Labor Review, 119* (11), 26–34.

Eisenhardt, K. M. (1985). Control: Organizational and economic approaches. *Management Science, 31* (2), 134–149.

Gaskill, L. R., Jasper, C., Bastow-Shoop, H., Jolly, L., Kean, R., Leistritz, L., & Stern-quist, B. (1996). Operational planning and competitive strategies of male and female retailers. *The International Review of Retail, Distribution, and Consumer Research, 6* (1), 76–95.

Gaskill, L. R., Van Auken, H. E., & Manning, R. A. (1993). A factor analytic study of the perceived causes of small business failure. *Journal of Small Business Management, 34* (1), 18–31.

Heck, R. K. Z., Rowe, B. R., & Owen, A. J. (1995). What we know and do not know about the "home" and the "work" and the implications of both. In R. K. Z. Heck, A. J. Owen, and B. R. Rowe (Eds.), *Home-based employment and family life* (pp. 193–228). Westport, CT: Auburn House.

Heck, R. K. Z., Winter, M., & Stafford, K. (1992). Managing work and family in home-based employment. *Journal of Family and Economic Issues, 13,* 187–212.

Hisrich, R. D., & Brush, C. (1984). The woman entrepreneur: Management skills and business problems. *Journal of Small Business Management, 22* (1), 30–37.

Kallenberg, A. L., & Leicht, K. (1991). Gender and organizational performance: Determinants of small business survival and success. *Academy of Management Journal, 34* (1), 136–161.

Karsten, M. F. (1994). *Management and gender: Issues and attitudes*. Westport, CT: Praeger.

Moore, D. P. (1990). An examination of present research on the female entrepreneur: Suggested research strategies for the 1990s. *Journal of Business Ethics, 9* (4/5), 275–281.

Nelson, G. W. (1987). Information needs of female entrepreneurs. *Journal of Small Business Management, 25* (3), 38–44.

O'Hare, W., & Larson, J. (1991). Women in business. *American Demographics, 13* (7), 34–38.

Olson, S. F., & Currie, H. M. (1992). Female entrepreneurs: Personal value systems and business strategies in a male-dominated industry. *Journal of Small Business Management, 30* (1), 49–57.

Power, M. (1995). Home is where the work is. *Human Ecology Forum, 23* (1), 8–11.

Scherer, R. F., Brodzinski, J. D., & Wiebe, F. A. (1990). Entrepreneur career selection and gender: A socialization approach. *Journal of Small Business Management, 28* (1), 37–44.

Scott, C. E. (1986). Why more women are becoming entrepreneurs. *Journal of Small Business Management, 22* (4), 37–44.

Soldressen, L., Fiorito, S. S., & He, Y. (1998, April). An exploration into home-based businesses: Data from textile artists. *Journal of Small Business Management, 36* (2), 33–34.

Stafford, K., Winter, M., Duncan, K. A., & Genalo, M. A. (1992). Studying at-home income generation: Issues and methods. *Journal of Family and Economic Issues, 13,* 139–158.

Stern, G. M. (1996). Home-run firms increasingly a hit. *Nation's Business, 84* (6), 49.

Stevenson, L. A. (1986). Against all odds: The entrepreneurship of women. *Journal of Small Business Management, 24* (4), 30–36.

Stevenson, L. A. (1990). Some methodology problems associated with researching women entrepreneurs. *Journal of Business Ethics, 9* (4/5), 439–446.

Tigges, L. M., & Green, G. P. (1994, October). Does small business ownership offer opportunities for women in rural areas? *Community, 216,* 1–2.

Verespej, M. A. (1998). Just note the difference. *Industry Week, 247* (15), 16.

Zuiker, V. S., Stafford, K., Heck, R. H. Z., & Winter, M. (1995a). Home-based work: Differences in management across domains. *Family Economics and Resource Management Biennial, 1,* 97–98.

Zuiker, V. S., Stafford, K., Heck, R. H. Z., & Winter, M. (1995b). Home-based work: Gender differences in management of family management. *Proceedings of the 24th Annual Conference of the Eastern Family Economics and Resource Management Association,* 30–42.

Chapter 6

Home-Based Employment and Work-Family Conflict: A Canadian Study

Rosemary S. L. Mills, Karen A. Duncan, and D. Jill Amyot

INTRODUCTION

Coping with the challenges of raising a family in the 1990s was difficult for most couples. Coping with all of the stressors associated with getting and keeping a paid job, added to the challenges of doing a good job of parenting, can prove to be a balancing act that even the most resilient can find stressful. As greater numbers of women are participating in the labor force and remaining there throughout the childbearing years (Fast & Skrypnek, 1994; La Novara, 1993), the difficulty of balancing paid-work and family responsibilities raises important questions for family researchers. The phenomena of role overload and role conflict are well documented in the literature. Employed women, particularly those with children, have the most to do and the least time in which to do it (Alvi, 1994; Lewis & Cooper, 1988). They are more likely than other women to report role-related tensions (Kelly & Voydanoff, 1985) and spillover between their employment and family roles (Crouter, 1984). As a group, employed women with children have been reported to be at a greater risk of poor mental health than have other employed women (McLanahan & Adams, 1987).

The term work-family conflict is most often used to describe the role-related tension that employed women experience. As a type of stress, work-family conflict has been linked to increased health risks; increased use of cigarettes and alcohol; anxiety and depression; less effective parenting; and decreased life satisfaction (Frone, Barnes, & Farrell, 1994; Greenhaus & Beutell, 1985; Kelly & Voydanoff, 1985; MacEwen & Barling, 1991, 1994; Pleck, 1985; Pleck, Staines, & Lang, 1980; Voydanoff, 1987). Stone and Lero (1994) noted that work-family conflict is both widespread and multidimensional. At the societal level, attention has increasingly been focused on the role of the workplace in reducing work-family conflict for dual-earner families. Society has made considerable progress in establishing "family-responsive" policies for the workplace. Large corporations have become increasingly involved in their employees' non-work lives by developing and testing such initiatives as employee assistance programs, on-site day-care, parental leave, flextime, and flexiplace, to name a few (Guzzo, Nelson, & Noonan, 1992; Stone & Lero, 1994). Employees are also expressing interest in alternative arrangements (Alvi, 1994).

According to recent statistics, one alternative arrangement that is steadily gaining in popularity is home-based employment. Depending upon how broadly it is defined, an estimated 10% to 23% of Canadian households are engaged in some form of home-based employment (Orser & Foster, 1992). With the so-phistication of home office technology, telecommunications to link homes to offices, and computerization of the majority of office functions, many office workers and professionals can be released from the confines of the standard nine to five business day in a conventional office. However, the majority of home-workers are not the telecommuters depicted in the popular press, that is, paid workers linked to central offices by computers and telecommunications equip-ment (Shamir, 1992). Masuo, Walker, and Furry (1992) reported that the home-worker was more frequently an older male maintenance contractor, truck driver, or office cleaner.

Home-based employment has been offered by the popular press as a panacea for dual-earner couples attempting to manage the multiple demands of job and family. It has often been claimed that by eliminating the daily commute be-tween home and office, workers can spend more time with their families, and parents with young children might eliminate the need for outside day-care alto-gether. The assumption has been that work-family conflict will be significantly reduced and responsibilities juggled more efficiently.

Family research, however, has only recently begun to examine this assump-tion (Carsky, Dolan, & Free, 1991; Christensen, 1985; Heck, Saltford, Rowe, & Owen, 1992; Loker & Scannell, 1992; Rowe & Bentley, 1992). As Kraut (1988) has observed:

> We have little information about the texture of the lives of those who work from home and the ways working from home differs from working in a conventional loca-tion. For example, we know little about the interaction between the family and the work spheres and the manner in which accommodations between them are made. (p. 47)

In order to gain more insight into the impact of this alternative to tradi-tional work force participation on families, more information is required about how couples with children cope in this arrangement. Does home-based employ-ment help to ease the day-to-day juggling of employment and family responsi-bilities? Does it decrease employment-family tension and conflict? The answers to such questions have policy implications. Difficulty in balancing family and employment demands has been associated with increased absenteeism, poor mo-rale, and low worker loyalty (Alvi, 1994). Thus, if home-based employment can help families balance their responsibilities, it might be "good business" for business in particular and society in general to support it.

The purpose of this study is to examine the effect of home-based employment on the work-family conflict experienced by families with young children. Specifically, the focus is on the work-family conflict of women in dual-earner families who use child care for their young children. Because parenting demands are high when children are young, families with young children are at the greatest risk of experiencing work-family conflict, and the impact of "family-responsive" policies is likely to be the most dramatic in these families.

LITERATURE REVIEW ON WORK-FAMILY CONFLICT

Work-Family Conflict

The definition of work-family conflict proposed by Kahn, Wolfe, Quinn, Snoek, and Rosenthal (1964) has been widely accepted in the family literature (e.g., Greenhaus & Beutell, 1985; Kopelman, Greenhaus, & Connolly, 1983; Voydanoff, 1988). According to this definition, *work-family conflict* is the interrole conflict that can be experienced by an individual when the role pressures from the employment and family domains are incompatible or conflicting. A role is "a set of activities and relations expected of a person occupying a particular position in society, and of others, in relation to that person" (Bronfenbrenner, 1979).

Variously referred to as job-family role strain (Bohen & Viveros-Long, 1981; Keith & Schafer, 1980; Kelly & Voydanoff, 1985), interrole conflict (Kopelman et al., 1983), interference (Duxbury, Higgins, & Thomas, 1996), work-family interference (Moen & Dempster-McClain, 1987), work-nonwork role conflict (Wiley, 1987), and role strain (Marks, 1977; O'Neil & Greenberger, 1994), it is typically measured by asking questions that gauge a subject's perception of overload within roles and conflict between roles (Guelzow, Bird, & Koball, 1991). Work-family conflict has also been measured by a subject's response to one question, "How much do your job and your family life interfere with each other?" (Moen & Dempster-McClain, 1987; Voydanoff, 1988). In some studies, the distinction has been made between family interference with employment and employment interference with family through two separate measures (Duxbury, Higgins, & Lee, 1994; Gutek, Searle, & Klepa, 1991; MacEwen & Barling, 1994). The prevalence of work-family conflict and two models of work-family conflict, the rational view and the gender view, are reviewed in the next sections.

In a synopsis of a Conference Board of Canada publication (1990) reporting the findings of a survey of 7,003 public- and private-sector employees, almost two-thirds of the employees indicated that the juggling of their various roles was at the very least "somewhat difficult to accomplish." Almost 80% reported that they experienced stress or anxiety as a result of having to manage both home and employment responsibilities, and over 25% reported that they felt "a lot" or "a moderate degree" of stress. A sizable portion of the sample reported that they were considering leaving their job because of family responsibilities (14.3%) or had done so in the past (11.6%). A 1992 study of over 14,000 Canadian private-sector employees (Higgins, Duxbury, & Lee, 1992) yielded similar findings. One-quarter of the respondents reported experiencing high levels of role overload, feeling that they had more to do than they could handle and feeling physically and emotionally drained. Emmons, Biernat, Tiedje, Lang, and Wortman (1990) documented that over 75% of their sample of professional women with preschool aged children reported experiencing conflicts between employment and family almost every day. The situation most frequently reported by women in their sample was having to rush their children to get ready in the morning so that they themselves would not be late for work.

At first glance, then, it appears easy to answer the question of whether there will be an appreciable difference in work-family conflict between the home-based and non-home-based employment groups. Why would mothers in home-based employment *not* find it easier to cope with their dual responsibilities than would women in traditional employment? They are able to take care of both roles in one location, reduce their commuting time between employment and home, eliminate the stressful morning routine, and perhaps take care of family emergencies when they arise. The answer seems obvious, but when one considers the potential for stress and strain associated with trying to be "at work" in the midst of family demands and "with family" in the midst of employment demands, it becomes less obvious. It could become even less obvious when one considers the multitude of variables that have been found to be associated with work-family conflict.

Rational and Gender Views of Work-Family Conflict

There are two implicit viewpoints concerning the phenomenon of work-family conflict: the rational view and the gender view (Gutek et al., 1991). According to the rational view, there is a direct correspondence between objective conditions and the perception of work-family conflict: the amount of conflict an individual perceives will be directly related to objective factors such as the number of hours spent performing employment or family responsibilities. Research from this perspective has focused on such objective conditions as time spent in paid-work and time spent in family-work; on employment characteristics such as job tension, work salience, work schedule, work flexibility, and autonomy; and on family characteristics such as number of children in the family and the age of the youngest child. In a comprehensive review of this literature, Amyot (1995) concluded that although objective conditions and employment and family characteristics have been found to affect work-family conflict, they have not fully explained the variance in reported work-family conflict of dual-earner couples.

Gender, on the other hand, appears to play a significant role in work-family conflict (e.g. Duxbury et al., 1994, Gutek et al., 1991). According to the gender view, the association between objective factors and work-family conflict is a matter of perception and differs for men and women. Specifically, this view holds that the amount of conflict an individual perceives will vary depending on whether the objective conditions under which employment and family roles are performed are consistent with gender-role expectations. This is the view taken in the present study.

From the perspective of gender roles, the amount of work-family conflict an individual perceives is assumed to depend, not on objective conditions associated with the performance of roles, but on the individual's perception of his or her gender-role identity. That is, the amount of conflict is dependent on the individual's concept of what he or she should be doing with regard to the performance of employment and family roles. There is considerable evidence in the literature to support the idea that traditional gender-role attitudes continue to affect employment and family roles for men and women.

The Effect of Traditional Gender Roles on Work Attitudes and Behavior. Several studies have reported negative outcomes for men and women who do not conform to the traditional gender-role stereotypes of the man going out to work and the woman looking after the children (Staines, Pottick, & Fudge, 1986). These findings are often referred to in the literature as a "breadwinner adequacy" issue for men and neglect of the maternal role for women (Bernard, 1981; Gronseth, 1972).

In a study of professional employed mothers and their husbands (Emmons et al., 1990), the majority of the women in the sample viewed their careers as having a positive effect on their marital roles. However, 40% of the women in this sample viewed their careers as having a negative effect on their parental roles, that is, as interfering with their relationships with their children. Bohen and Viveros-Long (1981) found similar patterns when they interviewed mothers and fathers about the general effects of employment on family life. Mothers not only tended to worry more than fathers about whether they were neglecting their children, but also tried to spend more good-quality time with their children in an effort to lessen their anxiety. In a similar vein, Mills, Pedersen, and Grusec (1989) found that women experienced more conflict than men when confronted with dilemmas in which they must choose between their own needs and those of someone else.

Gender and the Division of Household Labor. The psychological pressure women and men feel to conform to gender roles can also be observed in the division of labor in the home. Safilios-Rothschild (1971) introduced the notion of the woman's psychological investment in the domain of the home to explain why studies indicated that women did not appear to want men to perform the amount of housework that they were willing to perform. Women felt psychological pressure to conform to traditional concepts of gender roles, and to avoid the discomfort associated with deviation from this concept, women preferred to do household work themselves. Using data from the National Survey of Families and Households, South and Spitze (1994) found that the gap between women's and men's time in household work was greatest among married couples. These researchers concluded that men and women in married couple households were "doing gender"—creating gender in their everyday household activities by adopting a traditional division of household labor.

In their study of 14,549 private-sector Canadian employees, Higgins et al. (1992) found that women indicated that they had the primary responsibility for child care in 71.6% of the cases compared to 4.7% of the men. Further, results of Statistics Canada's 1990 General Social Survey showed that the division of labor in the household tended to follow traditional patterns in the majority of Canadian dual-earner families (Marshall, 1993). According to the data collected, women were likely to assume primary responsibility for housework (e.g., meal preparation and cleaning-up, house cleaning, laundry), and men were likely to assume primary responsibility for repairs, maintenance, and outside work.

It appears that traditional gender-role patterns are continuing to have an impact on dual-earner couples' attitudes and behavior regarding their roles within the home. Given the greater psychological investment in the home of women than men, one can speculate that home-based employment can provide greater opportunity for employed mothers to perform their family roles, thereby decreasing their perception of role overload. Alternatively, women's presence in the home can cause their husbands and children to do less, thereby increasing women's work loads and their perceptions of work-family conflict.

Employment-Family Boundary Permeability and Work-Family Conflict

More evidence is needed regarding the permeability of the employment-family boundary in order to predict whether fulfilling family and employment roles in one location will result in more or less work-family conflict for women with young children. Pleck (1977) suggested that the boundaries of men's and women's employment and family roles are asymmetrically permeable. Whereas family responsibilities are allowed to intrude upon women's employment, the employment role is allowed to intrude upon men's family roles. An examination of the research that has directly or indirectly tested this model has obvious relevance for predictions regarding the work-family conflict experienced by women when there is no employment site-home boundary, as there is in home-based employment.

Duxbury and Higgins (1991) found gender differences in the antecedents and consequences of work-family conflict in a sample of dual-career managers and professionals. Their results provided support for Pleck's (1977) hypothesis that wives would allow their family lives to intrude into their employment lives more, and men would allow their employment lives to intrude into their family lives more. Duxbury and Higgins suggested that women who are highly involved in their employment role could have greater work-family conflict, as a result of anxiety and guilt associated with not performing traditional roles. Men who are active in their family roles can also experience greater work-family conflict because of anxiety associated with a lower commitment to their jobs.

In an attempt to gain a better understanding of this permeability, some researchers have examined the effects that experiences in one sphere of life might have on behavior and experiences in other spheres (e.g., Greenberger & O'Neil, 1993; Marshall & Barnett, 1993). For example, in a study of dual-earner couples, Marshall and Barnett found that the predictors of work-family conflict were the same for women and men: there was more conflict when work load was greater, role experiences were more negative, and jobs were of higher status.

In a study of dual-earner couples with a preschool age child, there was some evidence of gender differences in the predictors of work-family conflict. Greenberger and O'Neil (1993) found that men were more committed to their employment role than women. Family role commitments also differed: men were more committed than women to their marital roles and women were more committed than men to their parenting roles. High employment commitment was a stronger predictor of work-family conflict in men than in women, whereas high time allocation to employment was a stronger predictor of work-family conflict in women than in men. High employment commitment can interfere with men's investment in family roles; long hours in employment can heighten women's concerns about their family roles.

Taken together, these studies suggest that the boundary between employment and family can be permeable for both women and men, but in different ways. It is not clear, however, whether home-based employment should have a negative or positive impact on women's work-family conflict. If, as suggested by Hall and Richter (1988), women are unable to separate their two roles psychologically while at home, they can experience role overload and conflict. It could be, however, that women experience greater synergy by being in the home and feeling that they are fulfilling their traditional family roles while retaining their other potentially rewarding role as paid-worker. This might help women cope with the tension arising from conflict between their employment and family responsibilities.

Home-Based Employment and Work-Family Conflict

Home-based employment (or being a home-worker) is growing in popularity and has been identified as a work arrangement that can help families respond to the competing demands of employment and family life. However, despite the widespread belief that a major motivation for women to engage in paid-work at home is that it allows them to care for their children (Beach, 1989; Horvath, 1986), there has been limited investigation into the relationship between home-based employment and the management of child care (Heck et al., 1992). The few existing studies (Ahrentzen, 1990; Christensen, 1988) showed that home-based employment does not necessarily eliminate the need for child care during working hours. Furthermore, in one analysis (Heck et al., 1992), female home-workers were found to use outside child care as frequently as were male home-workers. Heck et al. also found that the use of child-care services was more prevalent among home-workers who were younger, had higher incomes, and were parents of toddlers.

Much of what is known about the management of home-based employment and family life comes from studies originating in the Cooperative Regional Research Project (NE-167), *At-Home Income Generation: Impact on Management, Productivity, and Stability in Rural/Urban Families*. For example, Rowe and Bentley (1992) found that in full-nest families, men who were home-workers were more likely than women who were home-workers to have a distinct work space. In addition, male home-workers seldom experienced simultaneous activity of employment and family responsibilities and were less likely to have to adapt to family interruptions than their female counterparts. Women, on the other hand, adapted by curtailing hours or rescheduling work times. Loker and Scannell (1992) also reported gender differences in the division of labor in two-earner households in which one partner worked at home for pay. They determined that among these dual-earner families it was predominantly men who were the home-workers (97%) and of these only 11% were also the household manager, or the person most responsible for seeing that the household duties, including child care, were performed. This finding, that male home-workers were rarely also the partner responsible for seeing that household chores were performed, underscores the significance of the gendered division of labor and its relevance to the study of home-based employment.

Although family-responsive policies for the workplace, such as flexible schedules, have been examined in previous research (e.g., Bohen & Viveros-Long, 1981), decreases in women's work-family conflict as a result of these policies have not been found. Gender-role concepts have been provided as an explanation as to why these strategies do not serve to help those who could benefit most. The inequity in the division of household labor clearly indicates that the conventional concepts of gender roles have continued to influence role-sharing behavior in dual-earner couples. Gender differences in how men and women view their family and employment roles have been a consistent theme throughout the literature, among both conventional employment couples and those of whom one or both members do their paid-work at home. The evidence is not clear, however, as to whether home-based employment increases or decreases work-family conflict in women in dual-earner couples with children.

It is evident throughout the literature that researchers have attempted to link various family and employment characteristics and demands to the experience of work-family conflict. Results have been inconclusive and sometimes contradictory. There has been no consensus on the variables that decrease women's work-family conflict. Certain variables have been reported to be related more frequently than other variables, but the role of gender has also been significant. Clearly, examination of the effect of home-based employment on work-family conflict is warranted.

OBJECTIVES OF THE STUDY

On the basis of the literature reviewed, three objectives and three hypotheses were developed. The first objective was to determine whether women in home-based employment would, as a group, report lower levels of work-family conflict than their counterparts who work at their employment outside the home. It appears that, even today, many women in dual-earner couples with children are conventional in their gender-role concepts. There is no evidence that among these couples, female home-workers are any less traditional. In fact, one of the most frequently reported reasons women have given for doing paid-work at home has been care of family (Rowe & Bentley, 1992). Therefore, in keeping with the perspective taken here, it was speculated that home-based employment could contribute to women's sense of fulfilling their family roles and reduce their work-family conflict. If so, then among dual-earner couples with children, self-perceived work-family conflict would be lower in women who are engaged in home-based employment than in women who are employed outside the home (Hypothesis 1).

A second objective was to determine whether, in addition to the wife's workplace location, the husband's would also be related to women's work-family conflict. Women whose husbands do not "go out to work" might find this arrangement more conflictual than might those whose husbands have traditional workplace employment. As in previous studies in which men have had flexible schedules (Bohen & Viveros-Long, 1981), it is possible that men maintain their lower participation rates in housework despite being in the home. This, in turn, might cause conflict for their wives arising from a perception of inequity (Guelzow et al., 1991) and increase their wives' work-family conflict. Following from this reasoning, a second hypothesis was that women's self-perceived work-family conflict would covary with the husband's workplace location—among dual-earner couples with children, women's self-perceived work-family conflict would be lower when their husbands' workplace is outside the home than when it is in the home (Hypothesis 2).

A third objective was to determine how well the workplace locations of wife and of husband would predict the work-family conflict of women in dual-earner couples with children. As suggested, a number of employment and family characteristics are related to work-family conflict and can be closely associated with workplace location. In order to determine the unique contribution of workplace location, the degree to which this variable adds to the prediction of work-family conflict was assessed over and above the variance accounted for by certain employment and family characteristics commonly linked to role overload. Specifically, it was postulated that among dual-earner couples with children, the workplace location of the couple would be a significant predictor of women's self-perceived work-family conflict even after accounting for the variance due to other employment and family characteristics believed to be associated with work-family conflict (that is, total usual hours worked per week, age of youngest child, family size, and total family income).

METHOD

The hypotheses were tested using data collected for the 1988 Canadian National Child Care Study (NCCS), a cooperative research project of the National Day Care Research Network, and the federal government departments of Statistics Canada and Health and Welfare Canada. The household survey component, known as the 1988 National Child Care Survey, was conducted in September and October 1988 as a supplement to the September 1988 monthly Canadian Labour Force Survey (LFS).

Sample

Households were selected for inclusion in the LFS by means of a stratified, multi-stage cluster sampling technique. The LFS was administered and then the NCCS was done with households in which there were one or more children under the age of 13 years. The NCCS interview was conducted with the parent who was identified as most responsible for arranging child care for the family. The response rate was 84.3% of the selected households. Approximately 90% of the respondents were interviewed over the telephone; the remainder were interviewed in person. The length of the average interview was approximately three-quarters of an hour.

The sample consisted of 24,155 families with a total of 42,231 children under the age of 13 years. The majority of families were drawn from urban areas of 100,000 or more. Approximately 85% of the families could be considered two-parent families; on average they had one or two children. The interviewed parent (IP) was almost always female (95.5%). The mean age of the IP was 33.2 years and the mean age of the partner was 35.8 years. Only 34% of the IPs were unemployed and not looking for work, and almost all the partners of the IPs were employed full-time. Among all families in the study, the most common employment pattern was the dual-earner family (49.2%).

The NCCS was designed to provide descriptive information on the nature of current child-care needs, child care use patterns, cost of care, and parental preferences among child-care alternatives. It was also designed to provide information about the ways in which family, child care, and employment variables are interrelated (Lero, Pence, Shields, Brockman, & Goelman, 1992). The respondents who were home-based in their employment (i.e., home-workers) were classified as such if they answered, "none, works at home" to the question "What is the approximate distance from your home to your (main) place of work?" The respondents whose spouses were home-based in their employment answered, "none, works at home" to the question "What is the approximate distance from your home to his/her place of work?" According to Lero, Brockman, Pence, Goelman, and Johnson (1993), 9.1% of the employed parents with primary child-care responsibilities surveyed were home-workers (2,198 respondents); of these, 63.7% were self-employed and 36.3% were paid-workers.

Home-based self-employed individuals were owners and operators of small businesses, professionals in private practice, and various free-lance artists, tradespeople, private nurses, home-care providers, and service workers. Home-workers were employed within the private sector or by governments.

For the present study, the respondent had to be in a dual-earner couple in which both partners were employed full-time (at least 30 hours per week), and for whom there were data regarding the respondent's level of work-family conflict. A total of 4,743 women met these criteria; of these, 199 indicated that they were home-workers (9% of the total number of home-worker respondents in the NCCS) and 4,544 indicated that their workplaces were away from their homes. When the employment workplace of both the respondent and her husband were considered, the sample was further broken down into four groups according to the couple's workplace locations. The largest proportion of the women were in a non-home-based employment couple—that is, neither was a home-worker (93%, $n = 4,405$). The remainder of the women in the sample were either in a home-based employment couple in which both were home-workers (2%, $n = 95$), a couple in which the woman was a home-worker and her husband was not (2%, $n = 104$), or a couple in which the woman was not in home-based employment and her husband was a home-worker (3%, $n = 139$). The inequality of group size was taken into account in the statistical analysis.

Measure of Work-Family Conflict

Work-family conflict, or "work/family/child-care tension" as it is referred to in the NCCS, was measured by the IP's self-report response to the question "While things vary from day to day, overall, how much tension do you feel in juggling work, family and child care responsibilities?" Responses were rated on a 10-point scale ranging from "no tension" (1) to "a great deal of tension" (10). Higher scores reflected greater work-family conflict. There was no direct evidence for the reliability of the measure. There was, however, some evidence for the measure's concurrent validity. Specifically, it was strongly related to the NCCS respondents' preference to change their work schedule from full-time to part-time, which is considered an indirect measure of work-family conflict (D. Lero, personal communication, March 24, 1995).

The measure of work-family conflict was administered only to parents who hired child care. That is, only those respondents who responded "yes" to the question, "Does anyone other than you or your spouse look after any of your children (your child) while you are working?" were given the question concerning work-family conflict. Thus, by virtue of the staging of the questions, women in dual-earner couples with children who were cared for exclusively by a parent or parents were not represented in the NCCS sample. This staging limitation is the most serious drawback to using the NCCS data to answer the research questions. The fact that parents who provided exclusive care for their children were not asked about work-family conflict means that the research can-

not be generalized to these families. Work-family conflict in families who provide parental care for their children might be quite different from that in families
that use child care, and these differences cannot be addressed with the NCCS
data.

Measures of Demographic, Employment, and Family Characteristics

Two demographic characteristics were assessed: age of respondent and level
of education. Age of respondent was measured as five categories: 15–19 years,
20–24 years, 25–34 years, 35–44 years, and over 44 years. Education of respondent was classified into five categories: none to elementary, high school (some
or all), some post-secondary, post-secondary diploma, and university degree.

The NCCS included measures of several employment and family characteristics, some of which have been linked to women's role overload and role conflict (e.g., Keith & Schafer, 1980; Voydanoff, 1988): total usual hours worked
per week, occupational classification, age of youngest child, family size, and
family income. Total usual hours worked per week was computed using a question from the LFS in which respondents were asked, "How many hours per
week do you usually work at your main job?" The responses were coded from 1
to 50 hours, where 50 included 50 hours and over. Occupational classification
was measured using information from the LFS that asked the respondent to describe his or her main job or business. Responses were classified into one of
seven categories defined by Statistics Canada in the Standard Occupational
Classification: managerial and other professional; clerical; sales; service; primary
occupations; processing, machining, and fabricating; and construction, transportation, equipment, material handling, and other crafts. Age of youngest child
was computed using the date of birth of the youngest family member from the
Household Record Docket of the LFS, listing all household members in the
selected dwelling. The responses ranged from 0 to 12 years. Family size was
measured by a count of the respondent, the spouse, and the number of children
less than 16 years. Family income was measured by asking respondents to estimate their own and their spouse's 1987 total income from wages and salaries
before taxes or deductions, or net income from self-employment. The spouses'
incomes were then added to determine family income. The estimates were classified into the following six categories (Canadian dollars): 1 = $0–$10,000, 2 =
$10,001–$20,000, 3 = $20,001–$30,000, 4 = $30,001–$40,000, 5 =
$40,001–$50,000, 6 = $50,001 and over.

RESULTS

Differences Between Home-Based and Non-Home-Based Employed Women

The home-based and non-home-based employed women were examined with respect to several demographic, employment, and family characteristics.

Table 6.1
Demographic Characteristics of Women in Home-Based and Non-Home-Based Employment

	Home-Based Women (n = 199)		Non-Home-Based Women (n = 4,544)			
	n	%	n	%	df	χ^2
Age of respondent						
15–19 years	1	0.5	8	0.2	4	11.64*
20–24 years	5	2.5	260	5.7		
25–34 years	102	51.3	2,637	58.0		
35–44 years	88	44.2	1,557	34.3		
45 years and over	3	1.5	82	1.8		
Education of respondent						
None or elementary	4	2.0	170	3.7	4	n.s.
High school (some or all)	98	49.3	2,228	49.0		
Some post-secondary	26	13.1	400	8.8		
Post-secondary diploma	49	24.6	1,012	22.3		
University degree	22	11.1	734	16.2		

* $p < .02$; n.s. indicates not significant.

Demographic Characteristics. Table 6.1 summarizes the demographic characteristics of the sample by workplace location. With respect to the age of the respondent, the women in home-based employment were significantly older than were the women in non-home-based employment. There was a higher proportion of home-based (45.7%) than non-home-based (36.1%) women in the two older age categories. No significant differences were found between the two groups of women in education of the respondent. The sample was distributed in a similar manner over the five education levels, with approximately half of each group having attained at least some post-secondary education.

Employment Characteristics. A breakdown of the sample with respect to respondents' employment characteristics, as a function of workplace location, is given in Table 6.2. As noted earlier, the sample was restricted to those women who generally worked 30 hours or more per week in their employment. How-ever, there was a small group of individuals in the sample who, although they worked less than 30 hours at their main job, considered themselves employed full-time. This meant that the variable, total usual hours worked per week, was skewed and could not be analyzed parametrically. Instead, the variable was grouped into five categories, and a chi-square score was computed. The women who were home-workers were significantly less likely to work a standard 35- to 40-hour employment week than the non-home-based women, with the greatest proportion of female home-workers working at their jobs 45 or more hours (38.7%).

Table 6.2
Employment Characteristics of Women in Home-Based and
Non-Home-Based Employment

	Home-Based Women ($n = 199$)		Non-Home-Based Women ($n = 4,544$)			
	n	%	*n*	%	*df*	χ^2
Total usual hours worked						
< 30	19	9.6	79	1.7	4	281.42*
30–34	36	18.1	521	11.5		
35–39	17	8.5	1,668	36.7		
40–44	50	25.1	1,866	41.1		
45–50+	77	38.7	410	9.0		
Occupational category						
Managerial and other professional	23	11.6	1,706	37.5	6	660.61*
Clerical	37	18.6	1,441	31.7		
Sales	17	8.5	319	7.0		
Service	41	20.6	447	9.8		
Primary occupations	75	37.7	117	2.6		
Processing, machining, and fabricating	4	2.0	355	7.8		
Construction, transportation, equipment operating, material handling, other crafts	2	1.0	159	3.5		
Type of family						
Farm	84	42.2	141	3.1	1	645.28*
Non-farm	115	57.8	4,403	96.9		

*$p < .001$.

Women in home-based and non-home-based employment differed significantly with respect to occupational classification. A combined 58.3% of the home-based women were in occupations classified in the "service" or "primary occupations" categories; 69.2% of the non-home-based women were in occupations classified in either the "managerial and other professional" or "clerical" categories.

Because 37.7% of the home-based employment women were classified as being involved in a primary occupation (farming, fishing, hunting, forestry, or mining), a further comparison of the two groups was done to determine whether more women in home-based than in non-home-based employment were members of a farm family. For purposes of the NCCS, a farm family was one who lived in a rural area, in which either the respondent or the spouse was self-employed, and in which the occupation of either the respondent or the spouse was classified as farming or related to farming. As shown in Table 6.2, using chi-square, significantly more women in home-based than non-home-based employment (42.2% vs. 3.1%, respectively) were living in a farm family. A further breakdown of the respondents who were classified as working in the primary occupations revealed that 88% of the women in home-based employment in this category lived on a farm. Thus, it is possible that the majority of the women classified as working in primary occupations were involved in a farm-related occupation.

Family Characteristics. A breakdown of the home-based employment and non-home-based employment samples by age of youngest child, number of family members, and family income is shown in Table 6.3. Chi-square analysis revealed no significant differences between the home-workers and non-home-based women in age of youngest child. In both groups, the youngest child was 5 years or younger in the majority of families in the study. In contrast, a significant association existed between the two groups in family size. Although both groups tended to have small families (three to four members), women in home-based employment were more likely to have families of five members or more (29.6%) than women in non-home-based employment (18.5%). Total family income also differed significantly between the two groups. The families of the female home-workers tended to be concentrated in the lower income categories. Almost half of the female home-workers (48.3%) were in families whose total family income did not exceed $30,000; by contrast, approximately 20% of the women in non-home-based employment were in this income category. Likewise, almost 40% of the families with non-home-based employed women reported 1987 incomes of $50,000 or greater, compared to 21% of the families in the other group.

Effect of Workplace Location on Work-Family Conflict

Hypothesis 1 stated that, among dual-earner couples with children, self-perceived work-family conflict would be lower in women who are engaged in home-based employment than in women who are employed outside the home. Hypothesis 2 proposed that, among dual-earner couples with children, women's self-perceived work-family conflict would be lower when their husbands' workplace is outside the home than when it is in the home.

Table 6.3
Family Characteristics of Women in Home-Based and
Non-Home-Based Employment

	Home-Based Women (n = 199)		Non-Home-Based Women (n = 4,544)			
	n	%	n	%	df	χ²
Age of youngest child						
0–2 years	71	35.7	1,561	34.4	3	n.s.
3–5 years	61	37.2	1,246	34.3		
6–9 years	44	22.1	1,157	25.5		
10–12 years	23	11.6	580	12.8		
Family size						
3–4 members	140	70.4	3,702	81.5	2	17.79*
5–6 members	56	28.1	822	18.1		
7–8 members	3	1.5	18	0.4		
9–11 members	0	0.0	2	0.04		
Family income						
$0–$10,000	19	9.6	67	1.5	5	137.88*
$10,001–$20,000	29	14.6	823	5.2		
$20,001–$30,000	48	24.1	592	13.0		
$30,001–$40,000	34	17.1	902	19.9		
$40,001–$50,000	27	13.6	939	20.7		
$50,001 and over	42	21.1	1,806	39.7		

* $p < .001$; n.s. indicates not significant.

Descriptive statistics for the variable of work-family conflict, as a function of wife and husband's workplace location, are shown in Table 6.4. The mean level of work-family conflict for the sample as a whole was 4.23 ($SD = 2.25$, $n = 4,743$); the scores ranged from 1 to 10. Although the distributions of work-family conflict in the four groups were somewhat skewed, the F test is robust against violations of normality. Thus, the hypotheses were tested by means of a two-way factorial analysis of variance, with the two independent variables wife's workplace location (home vs. non-home) and husband's workplace location (home vs. non-home). The design was disproportionately unbalanced, however: by far the largest proportion of the women (93%) were in a couple in which neither spouse was engaged in home-based employment. The analysis of such un-balanced data is problematic, in that effects of other factors contaminate differ-ences between the factor means. As a result, methods of partitioning the total sums of squares into the sums of squares for the different effects do not yield identical results, the sums of squares are not necessarily independent of one an-other, and the F ratios are not distributed exactly according to the F distribu-tion. As well, the power of the analysis is reduced, such that it is quite possible to find a nonsignificant effect even though an effect does exist.

Table 6.4
Descriptive Statistics for Work-Family Conflict as a Function of
Workplace Location

| Husband's Employment Location | Wife's Employment Location | | | | | |
| | Home-Based | | | Non-Home-Based | | |
	n	Mean	SD	*n*	Mean	SD
Home-based	95	4.17	2.4	139	4.32	2.0
Non-home-based	104	3.90	2.4	4,405	4.24	2.2

One solution to the problem is to adjust the means to remove the contami-nating effects. Various methods, each of which is appropriate to particular situa-tions, have been proposed. For models containing main effects and interactions, Yates's (1934) weighted squares of means analysis (sometimes referred to as Type III sums of squares) is often recommended (e.g., Milliken & Johnson, 1984; Searle, 1987). In this method, each effect is adjusted for all other effects; that is, for each factor the sums of squares is the estimate that would be ob-tained from a model in which that factor appeared last. However, when the im-balance is severe, as in the present case, the problem can remain (e.g., Shaw & Mitchell-Olds, 1993). An alternate solution is to impose balance on the data by discarding subjects from the larger cells.

In order to compare the results obtained by these two methods, two analy-ses were done. The first was a weighted squares of means analysis of variance using all the data; the second was an analysis of variance on a balanced subset of the data obtained by drawing a random sample of each of the three larger sub-groups of the sample, such that all cell sizes were 95.

The results of these analyses were quite similar (see Table 6.5). In both analyses, there were no significant main effects of wife or husband's workplace location, and no significant interaction. Neither Hypothesis 1 nor Hypothesis 2 was supported. However, women's workplace location did approach significance in the balanced design, as work-family conflict was lower among women in home-based than those in non-home-based employment.

The Predictive Power of Workplace Location

Hypothesis 3 stated that, among dual-earner couples with children, the workplace location of the couple would be a significant predictor of women's self-perceived work-family conflict even after accounting for the variance due to other employment and family characteristics believed to be associated with work-family conflict (that is, total usual hours worked per week, age of youngest child, family size, and total family income). To test this hypothesis, a hierarchical multiple regression analysis was performed in two steps. The following variables were entered in the first step of the equation: total usual hours worked, age of youngest child, family size, and total family income. Husband's workplace and wife's workplace locations were entered in the second step.

Table 6.5
Analyses of Variance for Work-Family Conflict

Source of Variation	df	MS	F	p
Weighted Squares of				
Mean Analysis ($n = 4,743$)				
Wife's work location (W)	1	8.71	1.73	0.35
Husband's work location (H)	1	4.44	0.88	0.19
W x H	1	1.17	0.23	0.63
Within group error	4,739	5.04		
Total	4,742			
Balanced Analysis of				
Variance ($n = 380$)				
Wife's work location (W)	1	14.80	2.69	0.10
Husband's work location (H)	1	0.00	0.00	0.98
W x H	1	7.39	1.34	0.25
Within group error	376	5.50		
Total	379			

The results of this analysis are summarized in Table 6.6. Only 2% of the variance in work-family conflict was explained by the entire model (F [4,743] = 0.95, n.s.). Couple's workplace location added nothing to the prediction of work-family conflict. Several employment and family characteristics, however, were found to be significantly predictive of work-family conflict, namely, the total usual hours worked, the age of the youngest child in the family, and total family income. Specifically, work-family conflict was associated with working long hours, presence of young children in the home, and higher family income.

DISCUSSION

The purpose of this study is to examine, from a gender perspective, the effect of home-based employment on the work-family conflict of women in dual-earner couples with children. On the basis of evidence indicating that gender-role concepts influence the way in which men and women fulfill their employment and family roles, it was reasoned that women might feel less tension between their paid-work roles and their traditional wife-mother roles when their husbands work outside the home. On the basis of this reasoning, it was predicted that women engaged in home-based employment would report lower levels of work-family conflict than non-home-based employed women, that women whose husbands go out to work would experience less work-family conflict than those whose husbands are home-based, and that the workplace location of both husband and wife would account for some of the variance in women's perceptions of their work-family conflict above that which could be attributed to objective variables associated with work-family conflict (total number of hours in paid-work, age of youngest child, family size, and total family income).

The analysis shows that there is no significant difference between the home-based employed women as a group and the non-home-based employed women as a group in their levels of work-family conflict in general and when controlling for location of husbands' work. The two groups do differ, however, on a number of employment, family, and demographic characteristics. In the analysis of predictive relationships, several employment and family variables are found to contribute to the prediction of work-family conflict, but workplace location is not a significant predictor.

Table 6.6
Summary of Hierarchical Regression Analysis for Variables Predicting Work-Family Conflict ($N = 4,743$)

Variable	β	SEβ	§
Step 1			
Total hours worked	0.02	0.01	0.04*
Age of youngest child	0.09	0.01	0.13*
Family size	0.03	0.04	0.01
Total family income	0.01	0.02	0.06*
Step 2			
Husband's workplace location	0.25	0.19	0.02
Wife's workplace location	0.20	0.19	0.02

Note: $R^2 = .02$ for Step 1; R^2 change = .00 for Step 2 (n.s.).
*$p < .05$.

Comparison of the Home-Based Employed and
Non-Home-Based Employed Women

Examination of the characteristics of the women in dual-earner couples with children who were in home-based employment and those who were not reveals that there are significant differences. Women who are in home-based employment and those who work outside the home are involved in significantly different occupations. The home-based employed women are largely in farm families (42.2%) and work in primary occupations (37.7%) or service occupations (20.6%). The women in non-home-based employment are more likely to work in occupations classified as managerial or professional (37.5%) or clerical (31.7%). Thus, the majority of home-based employed women are in occupations that would typically be considered blue-collar, whereas the non-home-based employed women are in occupations that would typically be considered white-collar.

The finding that women who are home-workers differ from other paid workers in their occupational classification is consistent with the findings of several U.S. studies from the 1980s, which indicated that the majority of home-workers are not telecommuters (Shamir, 1992). Whether this finding would be accurate today can only be speculated. It is possible, however, that a greater percentage of telecommuters made up the home-workers of the 1990s as a result of advances in technology and the introduction of family-responsive employment practices in the workplace.

The finding that a large proportion of the home-based employed women are in farm families is also somewhat consistent with earlier studies of home-workers. Stafford, Winter, Duncan, and Genalo (1992) reported that 7% of the NE-167 home-based employed sample lived on farms, even though ordinary farmers who grew crops or raised livestock for processing were excluded from the sample. Similarly, Kraut (1988), using 1980 U.S. census data that excluded farmers in the definition of home-based employment, reported that living in a more rural environment increases the odds of home-based employment. Whether this association would be as strong today depends in part on how much of the growth in the home-based employment sector has been in the telecommuting segment.

Female home-workers in the present study have lower family incomes than have the women in the non-home-based group. This result is consistent with Kraut's (1988) finding that full-time home-based workers earn 76% of the income earned by conventional workers. It might also be that a larger proportion of the female home-workers in the present study are self-employed rather than paid-workers. Lero et al. (1993) reported that there are almost twice as many home-based self-employed workers in the NCCS sample as there are home-based paid workers (5.8% vs. 3.3%). Stafford et al. (1992) reported that the self-employed home-based worker contributes significantly less to the total family income than does the home-worker who is a wage earner.

The finding that home-based employed women in the present study are significantly older than women who are employed outside the home is also consistent with the results of previous studies (Kraut, 1988; Masuo et al., 1992) which find that home-workers are generally older than 35 years. It could also be that many younger women have been eliminated from the present sample because they did not report that someone cares for their children other than the couple. Heck et al. (1992) reported that fewer child-care services are needed in home-based business situations, as women in these situations have more control over the flow of their work, which allows for a balancing of their employment and child-care roles.

The Effect of Workplace Location on Work-Family Conflict

The first and second objectives of this study are to determine the effect of wife and husband's workplace location on reported work-family conflict. It was predicted that, among dual-earner couples with children, self-perceived work-family conflict would be lower in women who are engaged in home-based employment than in women who are employed outside the home (Hypothesis 1) and be lower in women whose husbands are employed outside the home than in women whose husbands' workplace is at home (Hypothesis 2). Although work-family conflict is lower in couples of whom both were in home-based employment, the difference is not statistically significant. Husband's workplace location has a nonsignificant effect on women's self-perceived work-family conflict.

There can be several reasons for these nonsignificant effects. One is that workplace location has no effect on work-family conflict. Perhaps, as the rational view suggests, employment and family characteristics are the important factors in work-family conflict. Indeed, the results of the regression analysis in the present study suggest that numbers of hours worked, presence of a young child in the family, and family income play a more important role in work-family conflict than workplace location. For example, it appears that the amount of time spent at employment is a more significant source of stress for women than the conflict experienced in being employed outside the home.

Another possibility is that the influence of workplace location is evident only in women with highly traditional gender-role expectations. Gerson and Kraut (1988) found that women with home-based employment report greater job satisfaction and less role conflict and overload than do office workers, even though the home-based do more housework and child care. They also found that the home-based and non-home-based in their sample differ in their attitudes regarding gender roles. Non-home-based workers are more likely than home-workers to agree with statements supporting shared division of household labor, equal employment opportunities for men and women, and egalitarianism between men and women. In short, it appears that female home-workers are more traditional in their gender-role ideology than women with non-home-based employment.

A post hoc examination of mean work-family conflict scores for various subgroups of the women in this study reveal some differences based on occupation. Work-family conflict is significantly lower among female home-workers in clerical (t [1,476] = -2.56, p < .01) and service (t [486] = -2.37, p < .02) occupations compared to women in these same occupational categories who are non-home-based. Perhaps these workers are more traditional in their values than women in other occupations and, hence, feel less tension with their belief systems when they are employed at home. However, this explanation is speculative, as there is no information available in the data regarding women's gender-role expectations. Such information is required to assess this explanation directly.

Predictive Power of Workplace Location

The third objective of the study is to determine the unique contribution of workplace location to the prediction of work-family conflict. It was postulated that among dual-earner couples with children, the workplace location of the couple would be a significant predictor of women's self-perceived work-family conflict even after accounting for the variance due to other employment and family characteristics believed to be associated with work-family conflict. Support for this hypothesis is not found. Certain characteristics, however, are found to be associated with work-family conflict: total usual hours worked, age of youngest child, and total family income.

The finding that total hours worked predicts women's work-family conflict supports previous findings in the literature (Guelzow et al., 1991; Gutek et al., 1991; Voydanoff, 1988), indicating that spending longer hours in employment is associated with higher levels of work-family conflict. Having younger children in the home is also a strong predictor of work-family conflict. This finding is consistent with previous studies (Friedman, 1988; Kelly & Voydanoff, 1985). Although having younger children could involve more work for the family, especially for the mother, all the respondents in this study had to have someone look after their children while they were working for pay in order to be included in the sample. Thus, an alternative explanation for the relationship between age of youngest child and work-family conflict could be that women with young children who hire child-care help perceive greater work-family conflict because the feeling of conflict with conventional gender roles is particularly strong at this stage of the life cycle. Having a larger family (more children under the age of 13 years), on the other hand, does not predict women's work-family conflict when they are employed and hire child-care help. This could mean that women develop, with time, cognitive coping strategies to deal effectively with their dual roles. It might also be that, as the family grows, children need less direct care and supervision and older siblings become available to help with family responsibilities, and this helps to reduce work-family conflict. Clearly, research is required to examine changes in work-family conflict over the family life cycle. Gender-role expectations might have the most important function in the early stages when women are first faced with major identity dilemmas regarding their social roles (Rapoport & Rapoport, 1976).

Total family income is the third significant predictor of work-family conflict identified in the regression analysis. The direction of the relation is unexpected, as previous research links higher family income with higher levels of well-being and, consequently, lower levels of work-family conflict. In the present study, higher family income is associated with higher work-family conflict. One explanation could be that higher family income is associated with greater work intensity and responsibility that can result in increased opportunity for role strain and role conflict. It might also be that higher family income reflects the husband's greater employment effort and his decreased involvement in family responsibilities, which can, in turn, result in the wife's perception of marital inequity (Guelzow et al., 1991). Studies show that husbands who have demanding jobs and work long hours feel less compelled to help with the family-work (Sekaran, 1983). To understand how women's home-based employment affects their experience of work-family conflict, it is important to examine the effect that workplace location has on the division of domestic labor in the home, perceptions of marital equity, and parenting behavior.

SUMMARY AND IMPLICATIONS

Limitations of the Study

The main limitations of this research are a skewed sample distribution that can affect the analysis, problems with the staging of questions, and the use of self-report measures. Although the problem of the unbalanced respondent categories was addressed in the analysis, the other limitations are significant concerns. As previously noted, limitations imposed by the staging of the questions affect the composition of the sample. Those home-worker respondents who chose to look after their children while working and those couples who alternate shifts (off-shift) are excluded from this sample because, as a result of the design of the questionnaire, they were not asked about their work-family conflict. The findings, therefore, cannot be generalized to such families and these families should be included in future research. Similarly, none of the home-based employment respondents had the opportunity to answer the question about work flexibility. As a result, there are no data with which to address the question of whether work flexibility reduces women's work-family conflict in dual-earner couples in which there is home-based employment. In future research, detailed information about all aspects of the employment environment, including the respondent's satisfaction with the job and amount of support received from management and co-workers, should be collected in order to assess the specific contribution of the employment environment in the family conflict equation.

The study also relies entirely on self-reports of the respondents with regard to the constructs measured in this research. A recognized work-family conflict scale with several items would have been preferable as a measure of this construct. For example, Bohen and Viveros-Long's (1981) job-family role strain scale has been successfully adapted and used in a study of Canadian public- and private-sector employees (Duxbury & Higgins, 1991). Objective reports of respondents' employment environments and behavioral indices of respondents' stress also would strengthen the study.

Recommendations for Future Research

The present study provides only a glimpse of the way in which home-based employment affects dual-earner couples with children and is limited by a sample of families who all hire child-care help. Much research has yet to be done to assess how this alternative to traditional work force participation affects families, whether it does help to ease the day-to-day juggling of a couple's employment and family responsibilities, and whether men's and women's perceptions of work-family conflict differ. It would be valuable to know to what extent women use home-based employment as a strategy for coping with work-family conflict. A woman's shift to home-based employment can occur as a result of choice or of external forces. Longitudinal research in which work-family conflict is measured before and after the shift to home-based employment would help to shed light on this process.

Historically, gender has been provided as an explanation of why men and women's roles differ within employment and the family, and why many family-responsive strategies such as home-based employment do not always serve to help those who could benefit most. With the physical merging of the two spheres of employment and family, as in home-based employment, the role of gender and gender differences might be unique and especially important to the extent of work-family conflict in those households. Studies should be directed at determining how men and women cope with working at home for pay, whether couples with traditional values cope differently with this arrangement than do those with egalitarian values, and whether couples' values change in response to this employment arrangement. More information is also required with respect to the perception of work-family conflict and the influence of the objective conditions associated with role overload relative to the subjective influences of gender.

The 1990s offered new and expanding roles for women and men in employment and in the family. An appreciation of how the family will deal with these new realities that often raise conflict requires a fuller understanding of the dynamics of the changing labor force and the fundamental changes that will have to take place in societal attitudes regarding the roles of men and women.

Policy Implications of the Results

The results of this study do not support the hypothesized relationships between workplace location and work-family conflict in dual-earner Canadian families with young children who have hired child-care help. However, even though plausible explanations exist for the lack of significance of workplace location in this study, the fact that it is not significant in explaining work-family conflict does have practical implications. On the basis of the results of this study, there is no evidence that work-family conflict is lower for those who engage in home-based employment, even though one might expect this to be the case. In other words, this study does not support a view of home-based employment as a family-responsive policy—a workplace policy that would assist families in balancing their home and employment obligations. Workplace initiatives that promote home-based employment to employees as a means of decreasing conflict and to employers as a useful employee benefit are not supported by the results here. Data from the National Child Care Study provide little reason to believe that switching from non-home-based to home-based employment will result in lower work-family conflict for families.

Thus, in order to address the reality of role conflict in the lives of parents, there is a need to look beyond home-based employment for the answer. Although home-based employment might well be a viable solution for some families, it is not the universal answer to the work-family dilemma that it is often depicted as being in the popular press. In particular, it might not be an appropriate solution for families with young children who have hired child-care help, families for whom the stress of combining parental responsibilities with paid-work is often greatest. Parents who are considering home-based employment as the means to lessen their work-family conflict should do so with caution, as should those who are in advisory positions to these families.

REFERENCES

Ahrentzen, S. B. (1990). Managing conflict by managing boundaries: How professional homeworkers cope with multiple roles at home. *Environment and Behavior, 22,* 723–752.

Alvi, S. (1994). *The work and family challenge: Issues and options.* The Conference Board of Canada.

Amyot, D. J. (1995). *Work-family conflict and home-based work.* Unpublished master's thesis, University of Manitoba, Winnipeg.

Beach, B. A. (1989). *Integrating work and family life: The home-working family.* Albany: State University of New York Press.

Bernard, J. (1981). The good-provider role: Its rise and fall. *American Psychologist, 36,* 1–12.

Bohen, H. H., & Viveros-Long, A. (1981). *Balancing jobs and family life: Do flexible work schedules help?* Philadelphia: Temple University Press.

Bronfenbrenner, U. (1979). *The ecology of human development: Experiments by nature and design.* Cambridge, MA: Harvard University Press.

Carsky, M. L., Dolan, E. M., & Free, R. K. (1991). An integrated model of homebased work effects on family quality of life. *Journal of Business Research, 23,* 37–49.

Christensen, K. E. (1985). Women and home-based work. *Social Policy, 15* (3), 54–57.

Christensen, K. E. (Ed.) (1988). *The new era of home-based work: Directions and policies.* Boulder, CO: Westview.

Conference Board of Canada. (1990, December). *Work and family: Employment challenge of the '90's* (Report 59–90). Ottawa: Author.

Crouter, A. C. (1984). Spillover from family to work: The neglected side of the work-family interface. *Human Relations, 37,* 425–441.

Duxbury, L. E., & Higgins, C. A. (1991). Gender differences in work-family conflict. *Journal of Applied Psychology, 76,* 60–74.

Duxbury, L., Higgins, C., & Lee, C. (1994). Work-family conflict: A comparison by gender, family type, and perceived control. *Journal of Family Issues, 15,* 449–466.

Duxbury, L. E., Higgins, C. A., & Thomas, D. R. (1996). Work and family environments and the adoption of computer-supported supplemental work-at-home. *Journal of Vocational Behavior, 49,* 1–23.

Emmons, C., Biernat, M., Tiedje, L. B., Lang, E. L., & Wortman, C. B. (1990). Stress, support, and coping among women professionals with preschool children. In J. Eckenrode & S. Gore (Eds.), *Stress between work and family* (pp. 61–93). New York: Plenum.

Fast, J. E., & Skrypnek, B. J. (1994). Canadian women's labor force behavior: A forty year review. *Canadian Home Economics Journal, 44,* 171–177.

Friedman, D. E. (1988). Family-supportive policies: The corporate decision-making process. In F. E. Winfield (Ed.), *The work and family sourcebook* (pp. 101–116). New York: Panel.

Frone, M. R., Barnes, G. M., & Farrell, M. P. (1994). Relationship of work-family conflict to substance use among employed mothers: The role of negative affect. *Journal of Marriage and the Family, 56,* 1019–1030.

Gerson, J. M., & Kraut, R. E. (1988). Clerical work at home or in the office: The difference it makes. In K. E. Christensen (Ed.), *The new era of home based work: Directions and policies* (pp. 49–64). Boulder, CO: Westview.

Greenberger, E., & O'Neil, R. (1993). Spouse, parent, worker: Role commitments and role-related experiences in the construction of adults' well-being. *Developmental Psychology, 29,* 181–197.

Greenhaus, J. H., & Beutell, N. J. (1985). Sources of conflict between work and family roles. *Academy of Management Review, 10,* 76–88.

Gronseth, E. (1972). The breadwinner trap. In L. K. Howe (Ed.), *The future of the family* (pp. 175–191). New York: Simon & Schuster.

Guelzow, M. G., Bird, G. W., & Koball, E. H. (1991). An exploratory path analysis of the stress process for dual-career men and women. *Journal of Marriage and the Family, 53,* 151–164.

Gutek, B. A., Searle, S., & Klepa, L. (1991). Rational versus gender role explanations for work-family conflict. *Journal of Applied Psychology, 76,* 560–568.

Guzzo, R. A., Nelson, G. L., & Noonan, K. A. (1992). Commitment and employer involvement in employees' nonwork lives. In S. Zedeck (Ed.), *Work, families, and organizations* (pp. 236–271). San Francisco: Jossey-Bass.

Hall, D. T., & Richter, J. (1988). Balancing work life and home life: What can organizations do to help? *Academy of Management Executive, 11*, 213–223.

Heck, R. K. Z., Saltford, N. C., Rowe, B., & Owen, A. J. (1992). The utilization of childcare by households engaged in home-based employment. *Journal of Family and Economic Issues, 13*, 213–237.

Higgins, C., Duxbury, L., & Lee, C. (1992*). Balancing work and family: A study of Canadian private sector employees.* London, ON: University of Western Ontario.

Horvath, F. W. (1986). Work at home: New findings from the current population survey. *Monthly Labor Review, 109* (1), 31–35.

Kahn, R. L., Wolfe, D. M., Quinn, R. P., Snoek, J. D., & Rosenthal, R. A. (1964). *Organizational stress: Studies in role-conflict and ambiguity.* New York: John Wiley & Sons.

Keith, P. M., & Schafer, R. B. (1980). Role strain and depression in two-job families. *Family Relations, 29*, 483–488.

Kelly, R. F., & Voydanoff, P. (1985). Work/family role strain among employed parents. *Family Relations, 34*, 367–374.

Kopelman, R. E., Greenhaus, J. H., & Connolly, T. F. (1983). A model of work, family and interrole conflict: A construct validation study. *Organizational Behavior and Human Performance, 32*, 198–215.

Kraut, R. E. (1988). Homework: What is it and who does it? In K. E. Christensen (Ed.), *The new era of home-based work: Directions and policies* (pp. 30–48). Boulder, CO: Westview.

La Novara, P. (1993). *A portrait of families in Canada* (Statistics Canada Catalogue No. 89-523E). Ottawa: Minister of Industry, Science and Technology.

Lero, D. S., Brockman, L. M., Pence, A. R., Goelman, H., & Johnson, K. L. (1993, December). *Workplace benefits and flexibility: A perspective on parents' experiences* (Catalogue 89-530E). Ottawa: Statistics Canada.

Lero, D. S., Pence, A. R., Shields, M., Brockman, L. M., & Goelman, H. (1992, February). *Canadian National Child Care Study: Introductory report* (Catalogue 89–526E). Ottawa: Statistics Canada.

Lewis, S. N. C., & Cooper, C. L. (1988). Stress in dual-earner families. In B. A. Gutek, A. H. Stromber, & L. Larwood (Eds.), *Women and work* (Vol. 3, pp. 139–168). Newbury Park, CA: Sage.

Loker, S., & Scannell, E. (1992). Characteristics and practices of home-based workers. *Journal of Family and Economic Issues, 13*, 173–186.

MacEwen, K. E., & Barling, J. (1991). Effects of maternal employment experiences on children's behavior via mood, cognitive difficulties, and parenting behavior. *Journal of Marriage and the Family, 53*, 635–644.

MacEwen, K. E., & Barling, J. (1994). Daily consequences of work interference with family and family interference with work. *Work & Stress, 8*, 244–254.

Marks, S. R. (1977). Multiple roles and role strain: Some notes on human energy, time, and commitment. *American Sociological Review, 42*, 921–936.

Marshall, K. (1993, Autumn). Employed parents and the division of housework. *Perspectives on Labour and Income* (Statistics Canada Catalogue No. 75-001E), *5* (3), 23–30.

Marshall, N. L., & Barnett, R. C. (1993). Work-family strains and gains among two-earner couples. *Journal of Community Psychology, 21*, 64–78.

Masuo, D. M., Walker, R., & Furry, M. M. (1992). Home-based workers: Worker and work characteristics. *Journal of Family and Economic Issues, 13*, 245–262.

McLanahan, S., & Adams, J. (1987). Parenthood and psychological well-being. *Annual Review of Sociology, 13*, 237–257.

Milliken, G. A., & Johnson, D. E. (1984). *Analysis of messy data. Volume I: Designed experiments*. New York: Van Nostrand Reinhold.

Mills, R. S. L., Pedersen, J., & Grusec, J. E. (1989). Sex differences in reasoning and emotion about altruism. *Sex Roles, 20*, 603–621.

Moen, P., & Dempster-McClain, D. I. (1987). Employed parents: Role strain, work time, and preferences for working less. *Journal of Marriage and the Family, 49*, 579–590.

O'Neil, R., & Greenberger, E. (1994). Patterns of commitment to work and parenting: Implications for role strain. *Journal of Marriage and the Family, 56*, 101–118.

Orser, B., & Foster, M. (1992). *Home enterprise: Canadians and home-based work*. National Home-based Business Project Committee.

Pleck, J. H. (1977). The work-family role system. *Social Problems, 24*, 417–427.

Pleck, J. H. (1985). *Working wives/working husbands*. Beverly Hills, CA: Sage.

Pleck, J. H., Staines, G. L., & Lang, L. L. (1980). Conflicts between work and family life. *Monthly Labor Review, 103*, 29–32.

Rapoport, R., & Rapoport, R. N. (1976). *Dual-career families re-examined: New integrations of work and family*. New York: Harper & Row.

Rowe, B. R., & Bentley, M. T. (1992). The impact of family on home-based work. *Journal of Family and Economic Issues, 13*, 279–297.

Safilios-Rothschild, C. (1971). Towards the conceptualization and measurement of work commitment. *Human Relations, 24*, 489–493.

Searle, S. R. (1987). *Linear models for unbalanced data*. New York: John Wiley & Sons.

Sekaran, U. (1983). How husbands and wives in dual-career families perceive their family and work worlds. *Journal of Vocational Behavior, 22*, 288–302.

Shamir, B. (1992). Home: The perfect workplace? In S. Zedeck (Ed.), *Work, families, and organizations* (pp. 272–311). San Francisco: Jossey-Bass.

Shaw, R. G., & Mitchell-Olds, T. (1993). ANOVA for unbalanced data: An overview. *Ecology, 74*, 1638–1645.

South, S. J., & Spitze, G. (1994). Housework in marital and nonmarital households. *American Sociological Review, 59*, 327–347.

Stafford, K., Winter, M., Duncan, K. A., & Genalo, M. A. (1992). Studying at-home income generation: Issues and methods. *Journal of Family and Economic Issues, 13*, 139–158.

Staines, G. L., Pottick, K. J., & Fudge, D. A. (1986). Wives' employment and husbands' attitudes toward work and life. *Journal of Applied Psychology, 71*, 118–128.

Stone, L. O., & Lero, D. (1994). Factors in job-family tension, a perspective from the National Child Care Survey and the Total Work Accounts System. In L. O. Stone (Ed.), *Dimensions of job-family tension* (Statistics Canada Catalogue No. 89-540E). Ottawa: Minister of Industry Science and Technology.

Voydanoff, P. (1987). *Work and family life*. Newbury Park, CA: Sage.

Voydanoff, P. (1988). Work role characteristics, family structure demands, and work/family conflict. *Journal of Marriage and the Family, 50*, 749–761.

Wiley, D. L. (1987). The relationship between work/nonwork role conflict and job-related outcomes: Some unanticipated findings. *Journal of Management, 13*, 467–472.

Yates, F. (1934). The analysis of multiple classifications with unequal numbers in the different classes. *Journal of the American Statistical Association, 29*, 754–786.

Chapter 7

Industry and Self-Employment Analysis by Gender
Elizabeth S. Trent

INTRODUCTION

For a long time, multiple disciplines and workplace forums have appreciated the importance of gender as it relates to employment. Home-based employment provides a special option for women in the workplace. Some women have argued that home-based employment allows them to accommodate both their family and paid-work responsibilities in one place—at home. Others claim that working at home allows for more flexibility and job satisfaction than away from home employment. Additionally, demographers (U.S. Bureau of Census, 1996) have emphasized the increase in the number of women, especially women with children under age 6 years, who are both entering the labor force and remaining in the work force while mothering small children. Working at home can provide an option for some of these women who are balancing employment and family responsibilities.

When focusing on the location, flexibility, and job satisfaction issues that make home-based employment attractive to women, several concepts emerge that might be related to gender. The type of home-based employment, whether the home-worker owns a business (i.e., is self-employed) or works for someone else for wages, and the number and kinds of interruptions to the family might affect the proximity to family, flexibility of hours and work formats, and satisfaction with both the job and its relationship to family responsibilities. Investigating type, ownership, and interruptions to family can help produce better understanding of the similarities and differences between women and men who are employed in the home for pay.

Sex segregation at work occurs for many reasons. Societal norms and gender stereotypes shape perceptions about what type of work is appropriate for men and women. As a consequence, aspirations about what type of work to pursue become gender specific. Likewise, hiring and promotion decisions might be influenced by ideas concerning who is appropriate for a particular job, further perpetuating gender stereotypes. These jobs can even be within the same general occupational category. As a result of these social factors, men and women can be differentiated and thus "grouped" into dissimilar types of jobs or occupations.

Reskin and Padavic (1994) reported that sex segregation occurs within all standard occupational categories. They give the example that male bakers more than likely earn union wages making mass produced baked goods for large firms, whereas female bakers are more likely to earn low wages working in small retail bakeries. By considering bakers only from an occupational category perspective, the differences in jobs for different size firms might not be apparent and thus any gender differences within an occupation group will not be readily understood. Research on employees working in a centralized place away from home, the most common U.S. employment pattern, has implied differences within occupational groups can exist and similar gender specific patterns of job segregation might characterize home-based employment.

Heck, Owen, and Rowe (1995) reported that 75% of the home-workers in their study were self-employed and the remainder worked for wages. However, there was a significant difference between the percentages of women and men who were self-employed in that study. Loker and Scannell (1992) also found the effect of gender. Using cluster analysis defined by 17 variables, their results identified one cluster made up of exclusively self-employed who were 90% women. Considering gender along with self-employment by home-workers might provide new insights into home-based employment.

Interruptions during employment can be viewed as a negative aspect of home-based employment. On the other hand, working at home allows for family time in the middle of paid-work time, thus taking advantage of opportunities to teach, learn from, bond, or discipline in a regular, sustained time frame and environment. Likewise, employment related duties can bring interruptions to family activities. Women have been identified as more likely to be the household managers in families participating in home-based employment (Heck, Owen, & Rowe, 1995). Are women more likely than men to be interrupted by their home-based employment during family activities? Studying this question will further detail the gender issues involved in the choice of and satisfaction with home-based employment. One important aspect might be how male and female home-workers are similar or different in terms of the flexibility of home-based employment and family life, especially the intermingling of paid-work and family activities.

The purpose of the research reported in this chapter is to analyze differences related to gender and the choice of certain types of home-based employment by industry and business ownership. In addition, the gender relationship of interruptions to the family by home-based employment activities is studied. Data from a nine-state study of home-based employment are used (see Heck et al., 1995 for details concerning this study).

REVIEW OF LITERATURE

The literature is reviewed in four sections. First, the occupational segregation literature is presented to frame the study of gender in home-based employment on the basis of industry classifications. Then, the literature on selection of job type and self-employment is reviewed. Next, issues about defining and counting self-employment are reviewed. Finally, the prevalence of women in self-employment is discussed.

Gender and Occupational Segregation

Boris (1985) described the history of industrial home-work, arguing that there was a division of labor and wage differentials for women's home-work based on gender. Policymakers in the United States in the early 1930s tried to abolish home-work and institute what was considered a "normal" family life, that is, a male earner, a housewife, and children. Both organized labor and the Women's Bureau believed that the best way to improve the economic life of families was to have women working in a factory instead of at home if they needed to work for pay. However, the primary roles of women were being mothers and caring for their children. In addition, Boris (1985) noted that transferring paid-work from the home into factories did not remove the gender division within occupations.

Jacobsen (1994) used the Duncan Index to examine work force segregation for a 30-year period. The index is a common measure of occupational segregation. The index ranges from 0% indicating complete integration to 100% for complete segregation by gender. She evaluated census data and reported a decrease from 64% segregation in 1960 to 51% in 1990. However, she also reported that the index value falls to 31% when occupations are grouped into six categories and rises to 66% with the largest number of job categories. This research indicated that major groupings of jobs might mask gender segregation and imply integration.

Using the 1990 census for data analysis, Edwards and Field-Hendrey (1996) attempted to describe how male and female home-workers differed from other workers. To identify home-workers, these authors used the answers to the census question "How did this person usually get to work last week?" Those who responded, "Worked at home," and had earnings in 1989 that were consistent with their worker's status were included for analysis. Edwards and Field-Hendrey limited the sample of home-workers by age, including only those from 25 to 55 years old to encompass those who had finished their education and had not yet retired. They found that 59% of all home-workers were women, compared to only 46% of on-site workers. Also, 30% of married women with home-based employment had pre-school age children, whereas only 15% of on-site women workers had similar aged children. When Edwards and Field-Hendrey examined hourly earnings of workers, they found that home-based men earned 85% and home-based women earned 75% of the pay of their on-site counterparts. Earnings were especially low for workers in rural farm occupations. Omitting workers younger than age 25 and older than age 55 makes it difficult to compare these results to the results of other studies.

Walker and Heck (1995) analyzed the same nine-state data used by the study reported in this chapter to study female-dominated occupations, defined as those in which women made up 75% or more of the workers in their sample. Their results showed differences in net business income and hours worked by home-based business owners in female-dominated occupations compared to other occupations. In this sample, the net income for both men and women in female-dominated occupations was significantly lower than that for those working in non-female-dominated occupations. Men reported significantly fewer hours worked in female-dominated occupations than in other occupations. Number of hours worked by women was not significantly different in female- and male-dominated home-based businesses.

Standard evaluations of gender and employment are based upon occupational classifications such as the Standard Occupational Classification (SOC) system the United States government uses to classify work. Using this system, Heck, Walker, and Furry (1995) described how 1,591 responses to the question "What does the home worker do?" were classified into nine occupational categories. Using the same data set and cluster analysis with 17 clustering variables, Loker and Scannell (1992) showed that gender was important in the selection of occupation. They identified two clusters with dominant female membership, one distinguished for its total membership's being business owners and the other distinguished by its high percentage of wage workers. These results, including both wage workers and self-employed home-workers, indicated that grouping type of work by occupation did differentiate workers by gender. Unfortunately, standard occupational classifications did not take into account the industry in which the occupation was included. For example, a person working as an artisan by occupation could have been classified in the manufacturing, consumer services, or retail trade industry classification. Moreover, some industries were more likely to be male- or female-dominated; such dominance would have effects on income, business ownership, and number of hours worked, to name a few variables (Olson, Fox, & Stafford, 1995; Walker & Heck, 1995). For home-based employment, gender distinctions by industry might be different from those already identified by occupation.

Beck, Horan, and Tolbert (1980) studied the earnings discrimination of minorities including women. Their model measured the human capital variables of years of schooling and labor market experience. On the basis of results of a previous factor analysis, the economic sector was divided into two industrial characteristics, either core or periphery. These corresponded to the continuum of the market from fully competitive (core) to totally monopolistic (periphery). They concluded that the segmentation of the industrial structure intensifies the inequality between the genders and races, though there was greater gender than race discrimination when the human capital variables were held constant. Women earned substantially less than men did regardless of the sector. In addition, women had a greater likelihood of being employed in the periphery industrial sector, in which they earned less than in the core sector.

In evaluating gender wage gaps for self-employed workers, Olson et al. (1995) used the same nine-state data set used for the analysis reported in this chapter. They reported that men and women in home-based businesses earned different amounts of gross business income. Specifically, with respect to gross business income matched by occupational groups, these authors found that male home-based business owners in five of the nine occupational categories reported significantly higher incomes than did women in these same categories. Men in the clerical and administrative support, crafts/artisans, managers, services, and agricultural products categories earned on average more income than did women in these same occupations. A partial explanation was offered by Olson and colleagues—that women might be discriminating against themselves by setting their own prices for products or services lower than do men in the same occupations.

Selection of Job Type and Self-Employment

Little is written on choice of self-employment in home-based employment. However, the process of choosing a job, at home or away from home, has been analyzed by many.

Social heritage and cultural heritage often dictate job choice. Familial role models may guide a person to pursue one job rather than another. Many authors have indicated that having a parent who is self-employed increases the likelihood of self-employment (Bowen & Hisrich, 1986; Carroll & Mosakowski, 1987; Coleman & Carsky, 1997; Watkins & Watkins, 1984). Race and ethnic background can also influence career choice. In the United States, Koreans have higher rates of self-employment than do other immigrant groups (Fairlie & Meyer, 1996). Immigrants often view industrial home-work as a way to combine employment and family (Amott & Matthaei, 1996). Reskin and Padavic (1994) pointed out that gender dominance in certain jobs might persist in some cultures. They stated, for example, that women outnumber men as dentists and street cleaners in Russia whereas the reverse is true for these job types in the United States.

Parr and Neimeyer (1994) replicated research that examined how men and women differed in using occupational information and career relevance in choosing a vocation. These authors sampled undergraduate psychology students who were, on average, 19 years of age. Students who were closer to making a career decision, when asked to evaluate career relevance, were able to exclude career alternatives unacceptable to them more readily than were those who viewed their career as more distant. Men showed higher levels of vocational differentiation than did women in this sample. The authors could not explain the gender difference. However, this difference was perhaps related to traditional gender roles.

That is, career choice was more relevant for men as society expected men to be employed. Women, seemingly, had a choice about whether to be employed as well as about which occupation to choose. Therefore, it is important to study how men and women choose the type of home-based employment, their reasons, and their expectations.

Job paths today look different from the way they looked in the early 1980s. A modification of corporate structures in the 1990s began to demonstrate that employees were changing companies rather than climbing a corporate ladder. Downsizing often decreased corporate loyalty. These shifts might have accelerated the move to home-based employment or self-employment. Some researchers (Fairlie & Meyer, 1996; Raheim, 1997; Sullivan, Scannell, Wang, & Halbrendt, 1997) have proposed that self-employment is a means to exit poverty, or an alternative when nothing else is available (Dennis, 1996) or during times of transition due to immigration or a change in health status (Carroll & Mosakowski, 1987). Many of these reasons for self-employment do not indicate job stability, but rather mobility. In relation to home-based employment, Christensen (1988) found that some large companies used home-working options as a way to keep valuable employees with the company. In certain cases, self-employment might be better viewed as a dynamic process, perhaps a phase in one's employment history, than as a permanent job.

Defining and Counting Self-Employment

Problems in defining and in counting who is self-employed have been noted by many. This section considers some of these problems to highlight how the differences in defining this variable lead to difficulties in comparing studies, drawing conclusions about the breadth of self-employment, or accurately accounting for gender differences in self-employment participation.

Carr (1996) noted that self-employment as measured by the Current Population Survey (CPS) declined between 1920 and 1970. That trend reversed, and since 1972 the CPS numbers on self-employment have been increasing. However, changes in the classification systems that define who is counted as self-employed have led to decreased official numbers of self-employed. The CPS classifies employment by industry, occupation, and class of worker. A worker can be classified as working for wages or salary, as being an unpaid family worker, or as being self-employed. In the CPS since 1967, those persons responding affirmatively to being self-employed have been asked, "Is this business incorporated?" People with incorporated businesses are then counted as wage and salary workers because technically they are employed by their own business. Bregger (1996) noted that there were fewer self-employed persons in 1996 than there were in 1948, even with population growth. The change in the classification of workers over the years has shifted many incorporated business owners into the category of wage and salary workers, and thus they are not counted as self-employed. Bregger described the self-employed (excluding incorporated business owners) as more likely to be older, and possibly pursuing post-retirement careers.

Another problem with trying to count the number of the self-employed relates to the Internal Revenue Service (IRS) classifications of corporations for tax purposes. Incorporated businesses differ in the rate used to assess taxes based on characteristics of the business. If a corporation, as defined by the IRS, meets certain criteria such as having fewer than 35 shareholders, it can file taxes as an S Corporation, that is, a small corporation. These S Corporation businesses pay taxes at the owner's personal income tax rate or at a rate equivalent to the tax rate for self-employed unincorporated businesses. This practice might lead to corporations being taxed at a relatively low rate if the owner's income is reported as being relatively low. Additionally, incorporation allows for certain protection from losing personal property as a result of lawsuits that those with the self-employed classification do not enjoy. This tax code rule and related practices might inflate the number of incorporated businesses, and in turn explain Bregger's (1996) reported decline in the number of the self-employed. In reality, many S Corporations are self-employed persons who have incorporated.

Dennis (1996), in order to count the number of people who were self-employed, analyzed the number of filed tax returns indicating self-employment income. If a tax return included a Schedule C listing business income and expenses, then the taxpayer was counted as self-employed. He reported that the number of self-employed increased by 11 million from 1970 to 1993, with the largest increase among those operating very small businesses with little income. However, for the reason that all people reporting self-employment income might not be self-employed as their primary job, the importance of these results is that there was an increase in self-employment rather than in the magnitude of that increase.

In evaluating the advantages of self-employment compared to paid-work, Bernhardt (1994) used a representative sample of white Canadian men who either owned or partially owned an incorporated business on a full-time basis. He found workers in paid-work had higher potential earnings than those who were self-employed. Dennis (1996), in examining the motives behind self-employment, defined a self-employed worker as anyone in a profit making firm who claimed as a primary occupation working for himself or herself. Dennis included members of incorporated businesses as well as farmers and ranchers, who are often excluded in such studies because of their industry affiliation. He found that people who were self-employed preferred self-employment to other work arrangements.

In brief, the definition of self-employment can include or exclude those in incorporated businesses and farmers and ranchers. Because no definition is universally accepted, exact numerical counts are difficult if not impossible. The differences among official counts can be an important piece in the puzzle of explaining self-employment and should be considered in research on self-employment.

Women and Self-Employment

Women continue to enter the U.S. work force at an increasing rate. The participation rate for women in the labor force increased from 49% in 1970 to almost 72% of all women over age 18 years in 1995 (U.S. Bureau of Census, 1996). This is more than five percentage points higher than the forecast made by Bowen and Hisrich (1986) that 66% of women would participate in the labor force by the year 1995. Additionally, women are increasingly starting their own businesses (Devine, 1994; Fairlie & Meyer, 1996), reporting being self-employed and not owning an incorporated business (Bregger, 1996), or holding multiple jobs (Stinson, 1997).

Devine (1994) examined the changes in participation of women in self-employment and in wage and salary work during the 1980s. In trying to explain the large increase in the number of self-employed women, Devine examined the changes in self-employment as compared to wage/salary work for women by education and experience. She reported an increase in the number of self-employed women who had the highest education and the most experience. Those women who were less skilled were less likely to choose self-employment than were more skilled women. Often women who have the highest income potential in wage and salary work could earn more from self-employment. Those women with lower education and experience skills encountered a decrease in potential earnings from wage and salary jobs in the 1980s, but this change did not hasten a move to self-employment.

Comparing self-employed with wage and salary workers, using data from the 1980 census, Carr (1996) reported that self-employed men and women were older than were wage and salary workers. This is a similar finding to Bregger's 1996 analysis of more recent data from the CPS. Additionally, Carr's results showed that self-employed men worked longer hours than did men who worked for a wage or salary. Self-employed women worked fewer hours than men and might have selected self-employment for the flexibility it affords. Carr also reported that the presence of pre-school age children was a significant positive reason for women's choosing self-employment. Having pre-school age children did not increase the likelihood of men's choice of self-employment.

Stinson (1997) reported the redesign in 1994 of the CPS to obtain estimates of the number of multiple-job holders. He established some historical trends for multiple-job holders using a May supplement to the CPS. As expected, since 1970, men were more likely than were women to have more than one job. However, the proportion of multiple-job holding women grew faster than the proportion of men holding multiple jobs during the 1980s. In 1996, the incidence rate for multiple jobs for both men and women was the same. Among men, married men were the most likely to work multiple jobs in 1996. Single, widowed, divorced, and separated women were more likely than were married women to be working more than one job. Self-employment was the principal secondary job for about a quarter of the male moonlighters, and for about 18% of the women.

In summary, the literature indicates that classifying home-workers by occupation might not tell the whole gender story. In fact, the use of nine occupational groups by past researchers could have masked underlying gender differences. Grouping what workers do by industry can provide additional insight into gender differences or similarities. In addition, given that women might be looking for employment with greater flexibility and proximity to family responsibilities, the likelihood of self-employment by home-workers might provide new insights into the choice of specific home-based employment and into the relationship between gender and home-based employment.

METHODS

Data and Sample

The data for this study were from the Cooperative Regional Research Project, NE-167, a nine-state project focused on households in which at least one individual generated income by working at or from the home. In 1989, 30-minute telephone interviews were conducted with 899 household managers in households in which there was home-based employment (Stafford, Winter, Duncan, & Genalo, 1992).

Income was imputed for households that did not furnish that information. The data were weighted by the relative importance in the population of the respective states and the rural/urban areas in these states (Stafford et al., 1992). A household with home-based employment was defined for this study as a household with one or more members who work at or from the home for pay or profit. To qualify for the current study's sample, a respondent had to have worked a minimum of 312 hours per year at the home-based employment and had to have been working at home for a minimum of 12 months.

Industry Grouping

For the analysis in this chapter, each respondent's answer to the question "What does the home worker do?" was categorized by industry, using the Standard Industrial Classification (SIC) major division code as identified by the U.S. Department of Commerce (1987). The SIC manual provided a structure to code industries by major divisions. This structure code was a hierarchical classification by which companies were initially grouped by major industry, then further subdivided by product. The firm's annual sales volume for the primary product or activity was the basis for the classification (U.S. Bureau of Census, 1996). SIC provided means to classify each business by industry division and sublevel. For example, services (Code Number 8) was a major industrial division that included accounting service (Code 87) as one major subgroup. This subgroup could be broken down further into bookkeeping service (Code 8721).

Because 40% of the sample reported here was classified in the industrial division "services," it was decided to break the group into two subgroups so that the industrial groupings were more similar in size. The subgroups of services, "consumer services" and "health and education services," were used because all services fell in these categories.

Variables

Gender was a variable of interest in all analyses. Gender of the home-worker was the dependent variable in the first analysis, and business ownership status was the dependent variable in the second. Business ownership divided the sample into self-employed and wage workers. Ownership was determined by the response to the question "Do you own your business?" Those responding "yes" were classified as "self-employed" and the rest as "wage workers."

The independent variables, described in Table 7.1, included age and education of the home-worker, household size, rural or urban location, industry, home-based employment income, full-time and seasonal statuses, other full-time employment, number of years in home-based employment, and business ownership. If the variables were not normally distributed, they were divided at the median for the logistic regression analysis.

Interruptions such as telephone calls or clients' dropping in can influence the family either positively or negatively. Heck, Walker, and Furry (1995) described the four questions used in this study to measure the amount the home-based employment interferes with the family. These included items on answering telephone calls, seeing clients at home, experiencing employment-related interruptions, and sharing space. For the study reported in this chapter the responses to the four questions were summed to form a scale to measure the level of interruptions using the Fitzgerald and Winter (1995) format. The mean score for summed items on interruptions ranged from 0 to 5. A higher score indicated more interruptions to the family due to the home-based employment.

Analyses

For descriptive purposes, the data were organized and analyzed by gender using t-tests and chi-square analyses. Then, multivariate logistic regression analysis was performed, using gender of the home-worker as the dependent variable and the industry categories, based on the SIC system, as the independent variable of greatest interest. For the second analysis, business ownership status (self-employed or wage worker) was the dependent variable and gender was the main independent variable of interest. Other employment and worker characteristics were also included in these analyses as independent variables as described in Table 7.1.

The multivariate research models of gender and business ownership used the logistic regression procedure because the dependent variables were dichotomous with the value of either 0 or 1. The advantage of a multivariate analysis is to

Table 7.1
Description of Variables in Logistic Regression Analyses

Variables	Description
Worker characteristics	
Age	Continuous variable, the age in years of home-worker.
Education	Continuous variable, number of years of formal education completed by the home-worker.
Household size > 3	Dichotomous variable, dividing the sample by the median. Households with more than 3 persons were coded 1 and 0 otherwise.
Location (urban residence)	Dichotomous variable, 1 if living in an urban area, 0 otherwise.
Work characteristics	
Net home-based employment income (> $11,187.77)	Net income in 1988 from home-based employment. Dichotomous variable dividing the sample by the median, 1 if income > $11,187.77, 0 otherwise.
Full-time home-based employment (> 35 hours / week)	Working status computed from the number of hours of home-based employment per year divided by 50 weeks. Using the Department of Labor definition of full-time and part-time work, the sample was divided into two groups, 1 if working full-time (35 or more hours per week), 0 otherwise.
Seasonal work	Dichotomous variable, 1 if seasonal, 0 otherwise.
Other full-time employment	Dichotomous variable, 1 if respondent worked outside the home full-time in addition to home-based employment, 0 otherwise.
Years in home-based employment	Continuous variable measured by the number of years worked in home-based employment.
Business ownership (self-employed)	Dichotomous variable, 1 if self-employed, 0 otherwise.
Industry	Categorical variable classified by SIC with 9 categories of industry: Agriculture related; consumer services; construction; manufacturing; transportation; wholesale trade; retail trade; finance, insurance, and real estate; and health and education services. The category health and education services was used as a reference group because it was the largest.

show the effect of one variable while holding all other variables constant. Backward stepwise deletion of variables was used in both of the logistic regression analyses; see Hosmer and Lemeshow (1989) for additional information. With this technique, all of the predictor variables first entered the model together and were tested for significance. The process worked by removing the variable with the highest p-value above the criterion value (in this case, greater than .05 significance level). Then, the model was re-evaluated. This process was repeated in subsequent steps, except that after the first step, variables that had been removed were evaluated for possible re-entry into the model. This process continued until no more variables met the entry or removal criteria or until the last model was identical to the previous one.

The industry group health and education services was the reference group used in the multivariate analyses. In other words, the other eight industry groups were compared to health and education services to establish whether the industry effect was significant. When a categorical variable has more than two groups, one group is always omitted from a regression procedure for statistical reasons. The criterion for choosing the reference or omitting one is not precise. The three most common criteria are having an equal distribution on the dependent variable, having the greatest frequency, or having the lowest frequency. Health and education services was chosen because it included the greatest number of home-workers.

A t-test was used to evaluate differences on the interruption items by gender. An analysis of variance test was used to determine differences on the interruption items by industry.

FINDINGS

Descriptive Gender Comparisons

More than half of the sample were male home-workers (58%). Table 7.2 presents a comparison by gender on some variables of interest. Significant differences were found in age, household size, gross household and net home-based employment income, hours per week worked, number of years in home-based employment, other full-time employment, and industry. Women, on average, were younger (age 42.5 years) than the men (44.3 years). They also lived in larger households than the men in the sample. No differences by gender were reported related to other selected worker characteristics: years of education, marital status, home ownership, or residence in an urban area. The sample men and women were highly educated, having completed on average almost 14 years of education.

Men and women differed on many work characteristics. Men had significantly more average gross household income ($45,796) and average net home-based employment income ($24,603) than women ($37,373 and $8,466, respectively). Men had worked at home more years, were more likely to be full time home-workers, and more often had other full time employment than women. At least part of the difference in income could be explained by other work variables in the analyses. For instance, the higher family income could be related to working another job full-time or working more hours. The other full-time employment could not be classified by industry or earnings because specific questions were asked only about the first job.

Table 7.2
Descriptive Statistics and Chi-Square or *t*-Test Analysis of Worker and Work Characteristics by Gender of Home-Worker (*N* = 899)

Variable	Women n = 377	Men n = 522
Worker characteristics		
Age (mean years)	42.5	44.3*
Education (mean years)	13.9	13.9
Married (%)	83.7%	85.4%
Household size (mean)	3.5	3.3*
Own home (%)	85.1%	88.9%
Location (urban residence) (%)	71.8%	74.3%
Work characteristics		
Gross household income (mean)	$37,373	$45,796***
Net home-based employment income (mean)	$8,466	$24,603***
Full-time home-based employment > 35 hours (%)	84.3%	94.7%***
Seasonal work (%)	12.1%	14.6%
Other full-time employment (%)	46.2%	87.0%***
Years in home-based employment (mean)	7.7	10.3***
Business ownership (self-employed) (%)	42.7%	57.3%
Industry (%)***		
Agriculture	6.5%	5.2%
Consumer services	21.3%	18.1%
Construction	1.2%	25.3%
Manufacturing	13.0%	5.3%
Transportation	0.9%	4.4%
Wholesale trade	4.2%	9.7%
Retail trade	14.7%	10.3%
Finance, insurance, real estate	3.8%	5.5%
Health and education services	34.4%	16.1%

Note: Weighted numbers, percentages, and means.

*p < .05; ***p < .001 based on results of chi-square tests or t-tests

There were differences in the proportion of men and women who worked in all classifications of work by industry. Overall, most home-workers were concentrated in the health and education services and consumer services industries. When divided by gender, women were most likely to be in the health and education services (34.4%), consumer services (21.3%), retail trade (14.7%), and manufacturing (13.0%) industries. Men were most likely to be in the construction (25.3%), consumer services (18.1%), health and education services (16.1%), retail trade (10.3%), and wholesale trade (9.7%) industries. The largest difference was found for the construction industry, in which the largest percentage (25.3%) of men were employed but the second lowest percentage (1.2%) of women were employed. In contrast, about 34% of women worked in health and education services compared to about 16% of men.

Multivariate Model Based on Gender of Home-Worker

The multivariate logistic regression analysis shown in Table 7.3 uses a plus sign to indicate results that predict the likelihood of being a man and a minus sign to indicate the likelihood of being a woman. Home-workers who were men were older and had smaller families than home-workers who were women. Men earned higher net home-based employment incomes and were more likely to be employed full-time in addition to having home-based employment than women. Self-employment was not a significant predictor in this analysis. That is, men and women were equally likely to be self-employed or to be a wage worker. Men were more likely than were women to work in consumer services, construction, and transportation than in health and education services.

Multivariate Research Model of Business Ownership

A second analysis was done on the same home-worker sample to determine which work and worker characteristics, including gender, significantly predicted ownership status. Those who owned a business were classified as self-employed and non-owners were classified as wage workers. The model was arranged to predict the probability that each individual was self-employed, given his or her scores on the predictors.

In Table 7.4 a plus sign indicates results that predicted self-employment and a minus sign indicates results that predicted the likelihood of being a wage worker. Gender was not a predictor variable for being either self-employed or a wage worker. Age was the only significant worker characteristic that predicted self-employment for these home-workers. Self-employed home-workers were significantly older than wage-workers. In terms of work characteristics examined, the self-employed were less likely to work seasonally and more likely to have other full-time employment in addition to their home-based employment than wage workers. Self-employed home-workers were more likely to be in the construction industry, compared to the health and education services, than were wage workers. Home-workers in wholesale trade, retail trade, and the finance, insurance, or real estate industries, compared to those in health or education services, were more likely to be wage workers. No significant differences among home-based self-employed and wage workers were found for home-based employment income, number of years in home-based employment, or the industrial categories of agriculture related, consumer services, manufacturing, and transportation industries as compared to the health and education services.

Table 7.3
Logistic Regression Results Based on Gender of the Home-Worker

Variable	Significant Effects
Worker characteristics	
Age	+
Education	
Household size > 3	−
Location	
Work characteristics	
Net home-based employment income > \$11,187.77	+
Full-time home-based employment	
Seasonal work	
Other full-time employment	+
Years in home-based employment	
Business ownership (self-employed)	
Industry[a]	
Agriculture related	
Consumer services	+
Construction	+
Manufacturing	
Transportation	+
Wholesale trade	
Retail trade	
Finance, insurance, real estate	
Health and education services	Reference
Constant	

Chi-square (12, $N = 899$) = 392.8, significant at .001 level

Note: Effects considered statistically significant at the 0.05 level or less. Plus signs indicate the predictive factors related to the likelihood of being a man.
[a]Health and education services was chosen as the reference category because it was the largest group.

Table 7.4
Logistic Regression Results Based on the Home-Worker's Being Self-Employed or Working for Wages

Variable	Significant Effects
Worker characteristics	
Male	
Age	+
Education	
Household size > 3	
Location	
Work characteristics	
Net home-based employment income > $11,187.77	
Full-time home-based employment	
Seasonal work	−
Other full-time employment	+
Years in home-based employment	
Industry[a]	
Agriculture related	
Consumer services	
Construction	+
Manufacturing	
Transportation	
Wholesale trade	−
Retail trade	−
Finance, insurance, real estate	−
Health and education services	Reference
Constant	

Chi-square (12, N = 899) = 392.8, significant at .001 level

Note: Effects considered statistically significant at the 0.05 level or less. Plus signs indicate the predictive factors related to the likelihood of being self-employed.
[a]Health and education services was chosen as the reference category because it was the largest group.

Interruptions by Gender

Female home-workers reported significantly higher scores on employment-related interruptions to the family at home than male home-workers (t = 5.88, 780 df, p < .001). There were no differences for interruptions by type of ownership, that is between self-employed and wage workers.

An analysis of variance test was conducted to determine whether there were differences in interruptions at home based on the worker's industry. The respondents reported significantly different levels of employment-related interruptions to families by industry ($F = 4.89$, 898 df, $p < .001$). Scheffe's test for significant differences of means between groups indicated that those employed in retail trade (M = 2.23) and in health and education services (M = 2.16) reported significantly more interruptions than workers in wholesale trade (M = 1.48) and construction (M = 1.67). Note that these are industries in which significant difference in participation by gender was found for home-workers.

DISCUSSION

Gender differences based on type of work by industry are prevalent in this nine-state study sample. This finding is consistent with Walker and Heck's (1995) study of the same home-workers classified by occupation. However, in the present study the multivariate analysis indicates that men are more likely than women to work in the consumer services, construction, and transportation industries as compared to the likelihood of working in the health and education services industry. Considering this finding in the context of occupational segregation and average income, it is clear that women are less likely to choose home-based employment that is "from" home such as construction and transportation. One explanation is that women who seek home-based employment do so for proximity to family responsibilities rather than for maximum income or flexibility. The different responsibilities of particular home-based employment certainly are another factor in the choice. A large percentage of both men and women chose the consumer services industry for their home-based employment. However, when all other factors are held constant in the logistic model, men are more likely than women to work in consumer services. The lack of significant differences between men and women who are home-workers in the other five industries perhaps speaks to the breadth of configurations of these industries, such as "at" home or "from" home, product or service type, and flexible hours and responsibilities. The possibilities for family involvement in the home-based employment might also vary by industry. For example, agriculture related, retail trade, and real estate often prosper with multiple family members' involvement and would be sought out by families who want to work together.

Women are more likely to be both the household manager and the home-worker (Heck, Winter, & Stafford, 1992). This suggests a greater diversity of responsibilities for women and, perhaps, a greater need for flexibility. Both in type of home-based employment and in employment-related interruptions to their families, women are more likely to be involved in home-based employment that allows flexibility and accommodation of both family and income-earning roles.

The present study points out that home-based employment for men is often one of two full-time jobs—at home work and another full-time job. Less than one-half of the women, on the other hand, have other full-time employment besides their home-based employment. This finding supports the traditional gender expectations of men and women and the research on women in all types of employment that suggests women's second job is running the household for no pay. For women in home-based employment, the situation is no different from that of other women employees—they have a second job at home after they complete their work for pay. Men with home-based employment are more likely to have two paying jobs, one home-based.

Although the logistic regression analysis for self-employment shows no greater likelihood of men or women to participate in home-based business ownership, the confusion between business ownership and independent contractor status among home-workers that Boris (1985) describes might partially explain this result. Whether a home-worker is an independent contractor of labor or is employed by an organization is a distinction mainly important to the Labor Department. Home-workers, particularly women, might have incorrectly responded that they owned a business rather than independently contracting their labor as a result of a misunderstanding of or lack of interest in the distinction. The consequence can be a lower number of home-workers, particularly women, who are classified as self-employed in this study. Future research should address the reasons women pursue home-based business ownership, an accurate accounting of female ownership, and the interrelationships between business ownership and family responsibilities.

Other results from this study agree with earlier analyses using census data. Bregger (1996) found that male home-workers were older than female home-workers. Women often wait to participate in paid-work until their children are in school or older and more independent, and perhaps home-based women workers reflect this trend. Carr's (1996) finding that self-employed women had large households is consistent with this analyses. Therefore, explanations for why women with large households participate in home-based business ownership might include the need to be available to family members and the need for additional household income.

There appears to be a gender-related difference based on employment-related interruptions to families at home. Both in the analysis reported here and in the Heck, Walker, and Furry (1995) analysis using the same data, there are intrusion differences reported by industry or occupation, respectively. In this analysis, home-workers in retail trade and health and education services industries are more likely to have employment-related interruptions to their families. As both of these industries are more likely to be selected by women, one conclusion that can be drawn is that the environment of the industries themselves allows for paid-work to be conducted flexibly during other family activities and that women, therefore, gravitate to these industries. These results indicate that employment-related interruptions to families in home-based employment deserve more study.

IMPLICATIONS

This study establishes new insights into the gender influences involved in choosing the industry in which to pursue home-based employment, whether to choose to own a home-based business or work for wages, and the likelihood of employment-related interruptions to families due to the home-based employment. The basic question is whether gender differences are perpetuating inequities between genders or accommodating valid choices that are differentiated by gender.

If gender differences are perpetuating inequities, then further research should be conducted on, and people should be educated about, the gender stereotypes that have financial and family implications. Women should be encouraged to consider industries that traditionally employ men and reap higher average incomes. If gender differences are accommodating valid choices, then finding ways to enhance the value of products and services in the industries of choice by women is necessary for both wage work and self-employment. Both issues related to the level of pay and family interruptions should be pursued. Additional ways to understand the importance and impact of employment-related interruptions to families by home-based employment and the impact on family interactions must be sought. Further research needs to address the particulars of these interruptions by gender, such as the initiator of the interruption, the length of interruption, and the impact on work completion and family life. With understanding, interruptions might be organized to have less influence on the efficacy of home production and family enjoyment.

Educators, career counselors, and youth group leaders should emphasize the economic consequences of career choice to both men and women. Potential home-workers should be encouraged to look for wage-earning options, including multiple income sources, in which they are interested with full knowledge of each option's financial and family rewards and challenges. Gender differences that offer flexibility of location, work time, and format, as well as accommodation of employment-related interruptions on families, should be presented along with home-based employment types and self-employment options.

NOTE

This chapter reports results from the Cooperative Regional Research Project, NE-167, *At-Home Income Generation: Impact on Management, Productivity and Stability in Rural and Urban Families*, partially supported by Cooperative States Research Service, U.S. Department of Agriculture, and the Experiment Stations at the University of Hawaii, Iowa State University, Lincoln University (Missouri), Michigan State University, Cornell University (New York), The Ohio State University, The Pennsylvania State University, Utah State University, and University of Vermont.

REFERENCES

Amott, T., & Matthaei, J. (1996). *Race, gender and work: A multi-cultural economic history of women in the United States.* Boston: South End.

Beck, E. M., Horan, P. M., & Tolbert, C. M. (1980). Industrial segmentation and labor market discriminations. *Social Problems, 28,* 113–130.

Bernhardt, I. (1994). Comparative advantage in self-employment and paid work. *Canadian Journal of Economics, 27,* 273–289.

Boris, E. (1985). Regulating industrial homework: The triumph of "Sacred Motherhood." *The Journal of American History, 71,* 745–763.

Bowen, D. D., & Hisrich, R. D. (1986). The female entrepreneur: A career development perspective. *Academy of Management Review, 11,* 393–407.

Bregger, J. E. (1996, January-February). Measuring self-employment in the United States. *Monthly Labor Review, 119* (1 and 2), 3–9.

Carr, D. (1996, February). Two paths to self-employment? *Work and Occupations, 23,* 26–57.

Carroll, G. R., & Mosakowski, E. (1987). The career dynamics of self-employment. *Administrative Science Quarterly, 32,* 570–589.

Christensen, K. E. (1988). *Women and home-based work: The unspoken contract.* New York: Henry Holt.

Coleman, S., & Carsky, M. (1997). Women-owned businesses, access to capital, and family support. *IFBPA Family Business Annual, 3,* 63–75.

Dennis, W. J. (1996). Self-employment: When nothing else is available? *Journal of Labor Research, 17,* 645–661.

Devine, T. J. (1994). Changes in wage and salary returns to skill and the recent rise in female self employment. *The American Economic Review, 84,* 108–113.

Edwards, L. N., & Field-Hendrey, E. (1996, November). Home workers: Data from the 1990 census of population. *Monthly Labor Review, 119* (11), 26–34.

Fairlie, R. W., & Meyer, B. D. (1996). Ethnic and racial self-employment differences and possible explanations. *The Journal of Human Resources, 31,* 757–793.

Fitzgerald, M., & Winter, M. (1995, April 30–May 3). *Intrusiveness of home-based business work on family life.* Paper presented at Home-based Business Conference: Choices, Challenges, and Changes, Lincoln, NE.

Heck, R. K. Z., Owen, A. J., & Rowe, B. R. (Eds.). (1995). *Home-based employment and family life.* Westport, CT: Auburn House.

Heck, R. K. Z., Walker, R., & Furry, M. (1995). The workers at work at home. In R. K. Z. Heck, A. J. Owen, & B. R. Rowe (Eds.), *Home- based employment and family life* (pp. 41–74). Westport, CT: Auburn House.

Heck, R. K. Z., Winter, M., & Stafford, K. (1992). Managing work and family in home-based employment. *Journal of Family and Economic Issues, 13,* 187–212.

Hosmer, D. W., & Lemeshow, S. (1989). *Applied logistic regression.* New York: John Wiley & Sons.

Jacobsen, J. P. (1994). Trends in work force sex segregation, 1960–1990. *Social Science Quarterly, 75,* 204–211.

Loker, S., & Scannell, E. (1992). Characteristics and practices of home-based workers. *Journal of Family and Economic Issues, 13,* 173–186.

Olson, P. D., Fox, J. J., & Stafford, K. (1995). Are women installing their own glass ceilings? *Family Economics and Resource Management Biennial, 1,* 163–170.

Parr, J., & Neimeyer, G. J. (1994). Effects of gender, construct type, occupational information and career relevance on vocational differentiation. *Journal of Counseling Psychology, 41,* 27–33.

Raheim, S. (1997). Problems and prospects of self-employment as an economic independence option for welfare recipients. *Social Work, 42,* 44–53.

Reskin, B. F., & Padavic, I. (1994). *Women and men at work.* Thousand Oaks, CA: Pine Forge.

Stafford, K., Winter, M., Duncan, K. A., & Genalo, M. A. (1992). Studying at-home income generation: Issues and methods. *Journal of Family and Economic Issues, 13,* 139–158.

Stinson, J. F. (1997, March). New data on multiple job holding available from the CPS. *Monthly Labor Review, 120* (3), 3–6.

Sullivan, P., Scannell, E., Wang, Q., & Halbrendt, C. (1997, June). Small entrepreneurial business: A potential solution to female poverty in rural America. In *Entrepreneurship: The engine of global economic development.* Proceedings of the International Council for Small Business 42nd World Conference, San Francisco.

U.S. Bureau of Census. (1996). *Statistical abstract of the United States* (116th ed.). Washington, DC: U.S. Government Printing Office.

U.S. Department of Commerce, Office of Federal Statistical Policy and Standards. (1987). *Standard occupational classification manual.* Washington, DC: U.S. Government Printing Office.

Walker, R., & Heck, R. K. Z. (1995). The hidden hum of the home-based business. In R. K. Z. Heck, A. J. Owen, & B. R. Rowe (Eds.), *Home-based employment and family life* (pp. 75–105). Westport, CT: Auburn House.

Watkins, J. & Watkins, D. (1984). The female entrepreneurs: Background and determinants of business choice—some British data. *International Small Business Journal, 2* (4), 21–31.

Chapter 8

Interweaving Home and Work Spheres: Gender and the Vermont Knitters

Suzanne Loker

INTRODUCTION

One of the most well publicized and controversial public debates on home-based employment was the case of the Vermont knitters in 1981–1986 (Boris, 1987; Owen, Carsky, & Dolan, 1992). The debate occurred in two segments and was based on the 1942 Fair Labor Standards Act, which prohibited the home production of goods in seven apparel-related industries: knitted outerwear, women's apparel, jewelry, gloves and mittens, buttons and buckles, handkerchiefs, and embroideries. First, in 1981, employers were sued for the hiring of home-based knitters to produce hats and sweaters using a knitting machine (or handloom) and to be paid by the piece. This lawsuit and surrounding debate caused then Secretary of Labor Donovon to lift the home-work ban on all seven apparel-related industries. After a countersuit by the International Ladies Garment Workers Union (ILGWU), the issue arose again in 1984 and concluded with the implementation of a redesigned certification system. Home-based knitters were required to submit monthly paperwork listing their hours worked and products sold, and firms buying knitted products to resell (i.e., wholesalers) were required to register with the Department of Labor. The resolution and the extended debate over the employment status of home-based knitters drew attention to the growing phenomenon of home-based employment and its unique nature.

The home-based knitters controversy could be described as the Goliath—ILGWU—going after David—mostly rural women who had few other employment alternatives as a result of education and limits of the local economy (Boris, 1987). The legal issue hinged on whether the knitters were earning minimum wage, were working in acceptable conditions, and had control over when and how much they knitted. The ILGWU appeared to be interested in the knitters as a strategy to get at the still functioning and oppressive "sweatshop" conditions in large cities. The knitters were a manageable group—mostly female, unorganized, and located in diffuse rural areas—for developing legislation that could be imposed on all home-based workers in the seven banned industries. Boris (1987) argued that the case of the home-knitters successfully challenged the historical focus of industrial home-based employment legislation on the workplace. However, she emphasized the need for other research to challenge the place the home should have in the economy and the place women should have in the home. These two questions focus the research and public policy dialogue on gender issues in industrial home-work and home-based knitting.

PURPOSE OF THE STUDY

The study reported in this chapter explores the connections between the work and family spheres for home-based knitters and was directed by two broad research questions in the context of home-based knitting:

What role does gender play in the choice, structure, and satisfaction with home-based employment, particularly among women knitting at home for pay?

How does home-based employment affect the personal, family, and economic well-being of the household?

This study focuses on the ways women and their families constructed their lives around their need for both employment and family and the reasons they chose to locate both at home. The responsibilities that each of these respondents has to home and employment, to their roles as family members and income earners, are analyzed for social, cultural, and policy implications. Does home-based employment make women subordinates in the family or just help them juggle household activities while making money? Should home-based employment legislation protect the "right to work" and the "right" to healthy work environments and fair labor practices? Are flexibility and personal control of home-based employment real or illusory? Is home-based employment good for individual women and women as a group?

LITERATURE REVIEW

The literature is reviewed in three sections. The first section establishes the importance of studying women in the workplace and, specifically, women in the home-based workplace. Research describing the substantial numbers of women working for pay and working at home for pay is cited. The second section outlines a feminist perspective on occupational segregation and the trends of gender effects in both personal decisions and policies affecting occupational choice. As the home-based knitters in this study lived in rural areas, a rural development framework used to explain home-based employment is presented in a third section to lay a foundation for this study.

Women, Work, and Home-Based Employment

Since the mid-1970s, women have been entering the workplace in record numbers (Hayghe & Bianchi, 1994; Shank, 1988). Using 1992 data, Hayghe and Bianchi (1994) reported that about 40% of married mothers worked for pay year round full-time, and nearly 75% worked at some point during the 1992 calendar year. About 70% of the fathers and mothers in the 24.7 million two-parent families worked for pay some time during that year. Almost 72% of all women over 18 years of age were in the labor force in 1995 (U.S. Bureau of the Census, 1997).

Along with the increase in labor market participation, Shank (1988) demonstrated that the nature of the connection of women to their employment changed as well. During 1950 to 1970, women's labor force participation rates formed an "M" shaped pattern, reflecting the dip in employment during childbearing years. By 1987, the pattern became more like the bell-shaped curve of men's employment, indicating employment right through the childbearing years. Most women who were employed worked full-time as did men, but women tended to work fewer hours than men, averaging 36.8 hours per week in 1986 compared to 43.9 hours per week for men. Shank predicted a continuing, though slower, increase in women's labor force participation for the future.

On the home front, the Bureau of Labor Statistics reported that the number of people working at home for pay increased from 20 million in 1991 to 21.5 million in 1997. Women made up almost half (10.3 million) of these home-based workers; 4.4 million of these women had children under 18 years of age ("Americans Bring," March 9, 1998). Home-based employment, by definition, encompasses both the family and work spheres of today's families. Historically and today, the connections between the family and paid work spheres have dominated the home-based employment debate.

Home-based employment is situated within powerful economic and social trends that are affecting American families and workplaces. Any discussion of home-based employment rapidly becomes a discussion of paid-work and family issues, women's participation in the labor market, corporate trends toward a two-tiered work force of a core of salaried employees and rings of contingent workers, and a growing class of underprotected workers in terms of health and pension coverage (Christensen, 1988).

Boris (1985, 1996) pointed out that both those in favor of and those opposed to home-based employment for women use the same argument to support their position—that women belong in the home as caretakers and should be protected and supported by their husbands' paid-work. Those favoring home-based employment for women view women's paid-work as supplementary to a family's income and women's primary role as household manager. Home-based employment allows them to fill both roles. Those against home-based er iploy-ment for women argue that paid-work does not belong in the home and em-ployment and home should be kept separate (Boris, 1985, 1996).

For many, home-based employment continues to be a viable alternative to out of the home employment. The benefits of home-based employment have been identified as independence and autonomy, flexibility in balancing em-ployment and family responsibilities, and the right to work where and when one wants (Christensen, 1988; Loker & Scannell, 1992). The disadvantages of home-based employment include the exploitation of home-based workers, often women and minorities (Boris, 1987; Daneshvary, 1993); the lack of social bene-fits such as health and disability insurance; and masking of the need for a na-tional child-care policy by women's working in the home (Christensen, 1988).

Heck, Owen, and Rowe (1995) edited a series of papers based on an empiri-cal study of workers with home-based employment in nine states. One major conclusion the editors reached was that gender effects on the home-based work-ers and non-home-based workers were similar. "On average, women home work-ers earned less; gravitated toward traditionally female occupations such as hair-dressing, child care, clerical, and craft work; restructured their time more to meet family demands; and spent less time on income-producing work than did males" (p. 216). So, on the one hand, home-based employment has provided another income generating option potentially available to men and to women (Pratt, 1993). On the other hand, home-based employment has not overcome the gender ideology of the out-of-the home workplace where women continue to earn only 75 cents to every dollar earned by men doing comparable work (U.S. Bureau of the Census, 1997).

Feminist Perspective on Work Force Segregation

Boris and Prügl (1996) presented a historical discussion of the structural dimension of gender divisions in the workplace. Their feminist perspective de-scribed the social and economic policies in the workplace as based on concep-tions of womanhood and manhood, the power of men over women, and the power of the more privileged over the less privileged. In other words, the work-place since at least 1934 has been structured to take advantage of gender divi-sions under the guise of protection—arguing that women should be at home caring for home and family and men should earn a living wage to support the family. Therefore, men's wages needed to be higher than those of the only women who belonged in the workplace—young single women. Boris (1996) described the power of myths about womanhood and manhood to shape public policy. She noted that policymakers throughout this century have separated gen-ders into two spheres of activity using the basic assumption that women belong at home, being mothers, and men belong in the workplace, earning the family's living.

Hartmann (1976) argued that job segregation by gender developed over time as the societal institutions of capitalism and patriarchy set about controlling men's benefits (i.e., wages, certain jobs) by controlling women's place in the wage-labor system. She contended that men maintain superiority over women by enforcing lower wages for women and keeping them responsible for domestic chores. "The hierarchical domestic division of labor is perpetuated by the labor market, and vice versa" (p. 139). Hartmann supported her argument with historical anthropological examples. She cited several examples of home-based employment that eliminated opportunities for women, both "putting out" systems and the move of certain jobs "out of the home." Men's area of dominance, paid-work, increased in importance as men controlled technology, production, and marketing and as women were excluded from industry, education, and political organization. She concluded that labor unions, in particular, have organized to benefit men and to keep women under control in subordinate positions and non-competitive with the masculine work force.

Women and Home-Based Employment as a
Rural Development Strategy

Gringeri (1990, 1996) studied several midwestern communities that were using home-based employment opportunities as a rural development strategy to increase job options. Industrial home-based employment added local money to the economy in two ways: by increasing the workers' incomes and by contributing indirect support to the community through building and training grants. Communities targeted women for new jobs, and, in most cases, these jobs were viewed as supplementary or secondary income, not as a replacement for the primary income of the family earned by the male heads of households.

Gringeri interviewed 78 home-based employment households in two rural communities, focusing on working conditions, division of labor at home, and the worker's home-based production for pay. She found a blurring between the contracting and self-employment working conditions in the sample. The home-workers were paid by the piece, and yet contributed to making the production process more efficient and lowering the overhead costs. In other words, they acted as self-employed workers with responsibility for more than just piecework completion, but were paid by the piece. Although the female workers who had children reported that working at home for pay was advantageous, they also reported difficulty in completing their paid-work and watching their children at the same time. The men and women interviewed had different experiences of how others, including family members, perceived their home-based employment. Men felt that their home-based employment was viewed as another "real job," whereas women felt their home-based employment was something they could do while they were doing their household work. The women were given a more flexible way to complete their two responsibilities while the men were given a flexible way to complete their only job—to earn a living wage.

Gringeri (1990, 1996) concluded that in the cases of rural economic development that she studied, home-based employment actually perpetuated the traditional view of women belonging in the home and doing any and all kinds of work in the home. Adding home-based employment opportunities to a community did add to the local economy and did not disrupt the local wage structure, but it also added to the already heavy and unpaid household work expectations of those women choosing to add home-based employment to their role set. The gendered nature of paid and unpaid work in the home being done by women was perpetuated.

Christensen (1988) also considered whether the worker is an independent contractor or an employee, an important issue for women in home-based employment. She outlined five important characteristics, based on common law rules, that distinguish an independent contractor from an employee: control, opportunity for profit or loss, substantial investment, skill level, and permanency of relationship with employer. She also described the prevalence of the independent contractor designation by (a) employers who do not want to pay benefits and/or continue pay over slack periods and (b) workers who either think they are employees or do not think they would have any work if they demanded employee status.

Christensen went on to present the problem of independent contractor determination in terms of its voluntary or involuntary nature. The voluntary independent contractor would "self-consciously" make a decision to be self-employed, whereas the involuntary independent contractor's decision would be "forced by inadequate alternatives in the marketplace" (p. 83). Christensen pointed out the potential effect of the involuntary independent contractors' contributions to segregation in the workplace if women continue to be the most likely to take on this type of work. Female home-based paid workers, who often lack confidence and experience to recognize the alternatives and to view their work as highly skilled and demanding a high wage, are easy targets for oppression as involuntary independent contractors. On the other hand, some female and male home-workers might seek out the independent contractor arrangement for individual reasons advantageous to their circumstances.

Summary

It is clear that most women's role sets include both paid employment and family/household responsibilities. The case of home-based employment provides a special example in which paid-work and family/household responsibilities are most likely to be interwoven. The feminist work force segregation literature presents paid employment as a social structural phenomenon based on a traditional view of women as well as workplace policies developed by patriarchal societal leaders. Home-based employment as a rural development strategy also appears to depend on segregation by gender, as women are targeted for piecework employment to supplement the families' main incomes, earned by the male heads of households. The present study of a home-based employment type dominated by women offers the venue to study the role gender plays in women's choice, structure, and satisfaction with home-based employment as well as its influence on the personal, family, and economic well-being of the household.

METHODS

This study was conducted in 1986, during the middle of the controversy with the U.S. Department of Labor about the employment status of home-knitters. Two of the knitters interviewed and observed testified at the hearings held by the Department of Labor and the others were well aware of the controversy. All had considered their home-based employment and the relationship of home-based knitting to their family's well-being in a more public way than is usually necessary in U.S. society. Social and family discussion of the issues of home-based employment was common and community members held strong opinions about the controversy. The timing of the study is therefore significant; it documents the home-based knitters' experiences as they lived through the public policy changes that put their livelihood at risk. Moreover, the study documents the thoroughly analyzed feelings these knitters have about their paid-work, their families, and the interweaving of these spheres.

Prior to the interviews and observation that constituted the main study, a convenience sample of 29 home-knitters was surveyed to set the context for the study. Surveys were mailed to manufacturers who contracted labor from knitters, to knitting machine dealers, and to several knitters known to the researcher. The manufacturers and dealers distributed and collected the surveys and returned them to the researcher. The surveys provided data on demographic and knitting characteristics of the home-based knitters.

Then, two-hour interviews were conducted with five women in Vermont who were knitters and one knitting couple, followed by a two-day observation period with these knitters. The knitters were chosen for their full-time status over several years and as representatives of several geographical locations, business structures, and family types (one retired, one couple, a knitting mother and son, three with young children at home). The importance of work and social relationships in the context of the home-knitters' lives made the inclusion of socially connected or related knitters in the study important to its design. The study focused on the knitters' motivations and rewards surrounding their choice and perpetuation of home-based knitting for pay. Activities conducted on knitting days were identified as primary or interruption activities, and their relationships to family and employment were examined. The knitting husband and wife and mother and son and the involvement of other knitters' husbands in knitting at home for pay provided a special dimension to the gender analysis of the interviews. Interviews were recorded and transcribed. The transcripts were analyzed to identify emerging themes consistent among knitters, unique characteristics of individual knitters, and issues related to gender.

CONCEPTUAL MODEL

The knitters were observed and their actions recorded on a matrix developed from one section of Beutler and Owen's (1980) conceptual model of home production and Owen, Carsky, and Dolan's (1992) adaptation of the model to home-based employment (see Figure 8.1). The continuum of home-based activities of the knitters describes activities promoting economic livelihood and emotional life. This study focused on home-based employment, household production (such as child care and food preparation), and propinquous production defined as those activities with outcomes "important in the development of family members and in the social and spiritual vitality of families and communities" (Owen et al., 1992, p. 127). Propinquous production is often a by-product of home-based employment or household production, such as the benefits of conversation among family members while washing dishes or driving to a location to mail an order. Household production is studied only in relation to the other three activities.

The interview transcripts and records of daily activities were analyzed for overarching themes as well as unique idiosyncratic ideas and behavior. The ways home-based knitters constructed their family, household production, and knitting spheres to meet needs and promote personal and family growth and development led to the emergence of five themes as a means to organize and analyze the data. The five themes are circumstances surrounding home-based work; social relationships; household production, home-based work, and propinquous production; personal growth, satisfaction, and achievement; and economic benefits.

Figure 8.1
Conceptual Model

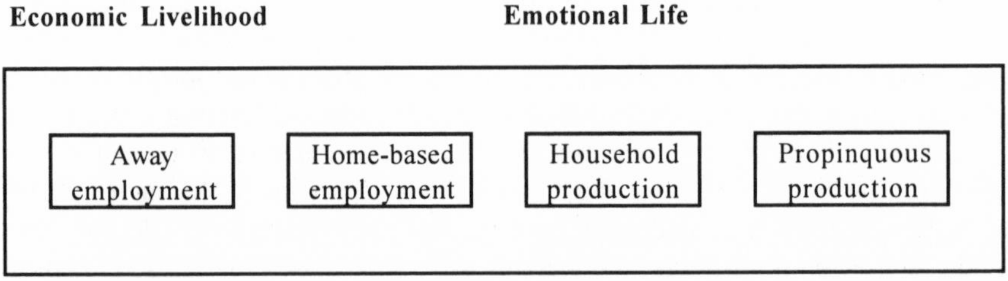

Economic Livelihood   **Emotional Life**

| Away employment | Home-based employment | Household production | Propinquous production |

LIMITATIONS

Limitations of the study include the small sample size, snapshot time period of the study, inclusion of only home-knitters who successfully knitted for pay for several years, and inclusion of several home-knitters who were friends or relatives and who sold knitted goods to the same firms. The qualitative method of the study and the nature of the home-knitting community with its sharing of expertise, coordinated shipping strategies, and overlapping social and work relationships allow for these limitations. Nonetheless, any conclusions drawn from the study should acknowledge these limitations.

RESULTS AND DISCUSSION

Survey Results

The 29 surveyed knitters were predominantly women (93%) and ranged in age from 18 to over 65 years with over 75% between 31 and 65 years of age; 86% were married. Twenty-one percent were college graduates and another 17% had completed some college. The mean household size was 2.97 and the knitters averaged 1.1 dependents, either children or dependent adults.

For the sample, the average years of knitting was 5.3 years. The respondents averaged 6.0 hours of knitting per day and knitted 5.1 days per week. Fifty-five percent of the sample worked every month, and 21 days was the average vacation taken each year, though the seasonal nature of some knitters' work affected some knitters' answer to this question. Only four knitted as the sole household income and a different four indicated that knitting was the largest household income. Insurance for 10 of the 20 knitters answering this question was paid for by another family member's employer, 5 knitters purchased their own health insurance, 11 knitters had their own life insurance, and 3 had set up their own retirement plan. Therefore, of 20 persons responding to the insurance question, 15 were covered by health insurance either by an employer (other than for knitting or from another family member's employment) or as an independent worker. Five knitters' spouses also knitted and two had a parent who knitted.

Knitters often chose to knit either hats or sweaters. Most knitters (64%) picked up supplies and delivered the finished knit products to contractees, and 23% used the mail. The average number of hours knitters spent on paperwork was 4.25 per week. Eighty-five percent of the knitters also knitted articles for their family and friends.

Interviews and Observation Results

The results and analysis of the interviews and observations are organized by the five themes emerging from the data. The knitters who were interviewed are labeled by numbers 1 through 7 in parentheses, with 6 and 7 the wife and husband, respectively, of the knitting couple and two the mother of this husband.

Circumstances Surrounding Home-Based Employment. Respondents all knitted full-time and ranged from 4 to 18 in total years knitting for income. They resided in rural areas without many job opportunities to provide alternative choices for employment. Work types pursued by the knitters before they turned to knitting in their home full-time included waitress, carpenter, factory worker, factory sewer, Amway salesperson, custodian, gas station attendant, hardware and grocery store clerk, and hairdresser. Several had knitted part-time before becoming full-time knitters, either for extra income or as an addition to their social security benefits. Each had a story about when she or he started, the circumstances that led to home-based knitting, and people who had influenced the decision.

One night there was a path just wide enough for the truck to get going through and the snow was right to the top of your car. So I put it in second and put it to the floor and made it through. And then I heard about this knitting where I could work at home and would not have to drive that road every day. And that's why I wanted to work at my home. (1)

It was 1969 and I saw an ad in the paper for home knitters to knit ski hats. And [he] would purchase the machine for you and allow you to pay him back monthly or weekly or however you wished by using some of the hat money as payment for your machine. So, I thought this would be a good way to get a machine, and this was my primary objective when I started knitting hats, was to get a machine and so I started knitting for him. They taught me how to use the machine and provided me with one and then I just continued to do it because I enjoyed it so much and while knitting hats, I also used the machine to create my own sweaters and, you know, different patterns and things. So basically when I started, the reason wasn't economical, it was more or less as a chance to be creative and obtain the machine I wanted so that I could use it to create things. (2)

We needed the extra income. I could stay at home and knit and not have to worry about running another car, quite honestly the pay scale in Vermont is not that great. Knitting has given us financial security because I knit year round. When my husband is laid off, it's been no problem. I can make as many sweaters as I want. (3)

Young children sometimes influenced the choice to combine knitting with respondents' roles as child-care provider and household manager.

When you have young kids you have a lot of school activities you have to go to and different things along that line. I can work when I want to. If I want to take the morning to do something, I can knit this evening if I want to. I know basically how much I accomplish every day to get everything done by the end of the week and hopefully get myself the whole weekend. (3)

I used to leave her with my mother-in-law and, you know, say, "If she starts to creep today, you're not to let her 'til I get home to see her." And I got to where I says, I can't stand this. I've got to be with them. I've got to be there when they take that first step and get their first teeth. And so, I just started knitting at home. (4)

Both the flexibility around children's schedules and transportation, for example, only one car or distance to job sites set the context for choosing home-based employment.

It worked out so well for her [my neighbor] and I could see that. You know, she had time to do things that I wasn't going to have time to do if I had to work out of the home. (4)

Three knitters had special family needs that initially drew them toward knitting at home or kept them knitting. One had an elderly parent living with the family sometimes (1). Another had a paraplegic child who needed at home attention. She also had bad eyesight that prevented her from getting a driver's license, thus limiting her ability to get work away from home (2). A third had injured his leg, restricting his employability, and thus began knitting (7). He used state funding from vocational rehabilitation to learn how to knit and to buy his first equipment. Home-based employment was the best option for several knitters in terms of family circumstances; for example, two knitters mentioned the lack of job alternatives in the geographic location (2 and 3).

In sum, there were a variety of motivations and precipitating events that led knitters to home-based employment. Several were influenced by family and health considerations, others by logistical problems and economic situations. Circumstances within both family and paid-work spheres motivated the decision to knit at home for pay.

Social Relationships. Social relationships seemed to influence the choice of knitting at home, learning new knitting techniques and ongoing problem solving about knitting projects, solicitation strategies used to get orders, and socializing activities. Mothers, sons, daughters, husbands, and friends enabled others to choose the work option of home-knitting.

My sister-in-law was knitting at the time. (3)

Well, my mother got me started. She decided that she was going to start doing it. So I happened to go up with her when she ordered her machine, so then I kinda decided well, this looks like fun. So I just decided to do it. (5)

Well, I think it was pretty much Mom. Mom and I have always been able to talk, and I brought it out that I was worried about not being able to do anything and she brought up the knitting then. Sure, willing to try anything. So she taught me. She taught me how to knit and it just went on from there. (7)

Home-knitters who did not have relatives knitting generally seemed to hear about it by word-of-mouth, though one answered an ad in the paper for knitters. Perhaps the connectedness of knitting to the home made it a more likely topic of conversation in the family, increased the influence of social relationships on its existence, and separated it from the organized manner in which out-of-the home employment is identified and sought. The husband and wife knitters in the sample (6 and 7) and the knitter whose husband knits seasonally (3) indicated that this connection was an added benefit. The spouses encouraged each other, both to start knitting and to continue when they were not motivated to do so. The knitting couples described the growth of their relationship through their home-based employment.

We have always been able to work together. I think it's kind of fun to work with—seems like the only time we have together is when we're knitting. (6)

[We] find we work better together. More and more every day since he's gotten involved in [knitting], he's much more conscientious of where things are going and what is happening. It does work a lot easier when you both know exactly what is going on and why this week we can't afford to do that and next week we can. (3)

However, knitter 7 mentioned that some think of knitting as "women's work":

How many men do you run across that knit? You know, run into town and someone says, "Well, what do you do for a living?" I'm a knitter. They'd say, "What a pansy."

Nonetheless, three other husbands of knitters interviewed in this study knitted part-time. One knitter describes how her husband started.

I never thought he would 'til he got on Social Security. I don't think he ever went to my room a dozen times. But after he got on Social Security, he'd be setting there, I'd be knitting and I'd bought another machine 'cause I got a good deal on it. I didn't really have to. He began to do the plain knitting in that week and now he can knit any sweater just as much as I can. He really likes it. He really does. (1)

Knitting has given us financial security because I knit year round. When George is laid off it's been no problem; you got to wait five or six weeks before the unemployment checks are coming in. We set up the budget so everything is covered between that time. (3)

Knitters or their husbands (1, 2, and 3) also were wholesale distributors for knitting machines or repaired machines for themselves and others. The interwoven connections made economic as well as strategic sense. As machines break, they have to be fixed. Distributors can either repair them on site or send them to the manufacturer. It was quicker to fix the machines locally and even quicker when a family member did the repair. The employment and family interface for these families goes well beyond the location issues of doing paid-work in the home to an interweaving of family and employment lives for many hours of each day.

Knitters recognized the family contributions the home location of their paid job permitted. During the two-day observations, knitting and child care overlapped extensively. Sometimes knitting continued as a child's question was answered or directions for children were called to them in the next room. Other times, knitting was interrupted to listen or talk with a spouse, handle a dispute between children, or give assistance.

Some children were taught how to knit, providing a shared family activity. But, more importantly, knitters felt that they were teaching their children self-sufficiency, independence, security, and cooperation. Knitters said that children learned to respect the meaning of work time and to help parents get free for a family event by both letting the knitter work and helping with some household chores. Knitters were clear about their time. They needed some time for knitting—both time for undivided attention and time when they could do two things at once. They also needed time for family. All had a structured schedule that established for them and their children work time and play time. Although all said that they had the option of not knitting when they did not feel like it, they described very specific schedules of good times for them to knit and good times for them to spend with their families.

Learning how to knit also depended upon social relationships. Although shops selling knitting machines provided lessons as part of the purchase price, both the long-term skill development needs and the connection of the sale, repair, and production functions of home-knitters established social relationships. Knitters expressed their belief that teaching others to knit was their responsibility, but with limits. One (1) taught with the understanding that the new knitter would have the responsibility of passing on her skills to another new knitter. One (2) charged for instruction when the client was not buying a machine from her. Knitters described a tremendous turnover in home-based knitters. According to the respondents, many prospective knitters dropped out before they became proficient enough to knit for income and, if part-time, some dropped out as a result of personal income or time needs. These drop out knitters were not represented in the study.

Home-knitters described a social network among knitters for problem solving and cooperation in their work, rather than a competition for orders. Help often was needed in figuring out the easiest way to approach, knit, or finish a new design. Knitters shared equipment when machinery was being repaired and when orders required certain types of machines or yarn. Groups of knitters delivered their orders to one location for UPS pickup each week. Here discussions ensued about the orders, knitting, or family and community social events, and friendships grew.

Knitters tended to segregate into hat knitters and sweater knitters. There seemed to be a preference for one or the other based on level of difficulty, creativity, and ability to do other things at the same time. These characteristics of the knitting could explain the migration to social relationships with knitters producing the same products. Knitters seemed to seek out and enjoy one another's company during leisure times as well. In the summer the local lake provided a place for the children to swim and play while several knitters shared both work related and family information.

Some knitters did the sewing to complete the hats and sweaters but some paid others to sew their hats and sweaters, make pom poms, or inspect the products, creating another, more invisible layer to these microenterprises and more social connections. The sewers were likely to be relatives, friends, or acquaintances, further establishing the importance of social relationships in the structure of this home-based employment type.

Social relationships were important to the three knitters in the sample (2, 6, and 7) who established their own businesses. Sales were often concluded by word of mouth and marketing and production contracts for labor were often established through social relationships.

As I say, it's all been word of mouth. Someone wanted some hats and called someone and they didn't have time to do them so they give them my name, this kind of thing. (2)

Household Production, Home-Based Employment, and Propinquous Production. In households with home-workers, the home-based employment, household production, and propinquous production are interwoven, sometimes seamlessly. This can be advantageous to the household and personal health of household members, giving them flexibility and peace of mind while fulfilling their multiple roles. But the lack of division between roles made knitters responsible for defining their days into schedules that functioned effectively for their families and their income generating needs. Most were quite structured in developing schedules that allowed for work, family, and leisure.

Monday is my day off. I usually catch up on the housework, the laundry, go to the beach. We bowl on Monday nights. I have to do my banking and the kids both have jobs, the older kids. So, Mondays I take off. I start knitting on Tuesday morning 'til eleven o'clock. Then I go to the beach. I usually take two weeks off a year, vacation. (4)

[I] can go off and do laundry or anything like that. You just do it. If we want to take a week off, we can. We work four hard weeks before that so we can do it, but we can do it. (7)

I prefer knitting to doing housework, any day, because I don't like housework. But I also, I could be sitting in there knowing that the dishes haven't gotten put in the dishwasher or there's pots and pans piled up and I begin feeling guilty. And so, then I'll come out and I'll take, you know, 45 minutes to an hour and pick up and then go back in. (5)

Saturdays usually, I might knit until noon. And then after that, I don't, no. Not unless I'm on like a three week order. I can because that will mean I can take the last week off, you know, can have a week off if I'd like to get my rug shampooed and all that stuff. Like right now, that's what I'm aiming for. . . . And I don't like having, knowing that I've got work to do in there and be out here doing something. I'd rather have all that done first and then get all my big things out here done. (5)

Propinquous production, such as sharing moments of success with their children or spouse with a particularly difficult knitting pattern, was found by knitters to be a by-product of the household and home-based employment. Working in the home and juggling employment and family responsibilities had additional benefits to the families. But the structured schedules described by the knitters belie the continuous interruptions that usually accompanied propinquous production. Figure 8.2 illustrates the actual schedule of two knitters (4 and 5) for one day, as documented through observations of the knitters' activities during their knitting time.

Knitters described some of the propinquous products they have encountered.

It's, you know, even your health and everything else is better 'cause I'm always at ease. If it's a bad time, I'll do something else. I'll go and figure out new designs for sweaters or something. (1)

Well, he [husband] just went into business for himself in November and he's getting a lot more business than he anticipated. So, I have to give up a lot of my time to do his book work. No, [it doesn't infringe on my knitting] we usually do it on Sunday evenings. And, in fact, I've got my oldest daughter balancing our checkbooks now. (4)

Randy [daughter] knit a piece on the bulky machine. She just knit this strip and I showed her how to latch tool it off and then she took it off and I showed her how to put it together into a little pocketbook. (3)

On the other hand, a down side of working at home for pay is that there is not a division between wage-earning work, household production, propinquous production, and leisure time that is visible to others. Several knitters complained that people did not think they were working if they were at home. Knitters described intrusion by neighbors into their workday.

One of the things that really upsets me about working in your home is the fact that people don't think you work. He'll say, "Can you run me into Rutland?" And I'll say, I'm sorry, but I'm working. He hemmed and hawed and sat around here and watched us for a while and then went back home and called down 10 minutes later and asked if I was still busy. (7)

You couldn't ask for a better friend and I used to stop knitting every time she came. And I just couldn't keep up. I mean, she was coming every single day, right in my knitting time. And finally, I just said, this is the way it is. If you want to come to visit, fine, make yourself a cup of coffee on your way through and come downstairs and visit. So that's what she does now. It's okay. I'd prefer that she wasn't there during my knitting time, but rather than hurt her feelings, I just try to do two things at once. (4)

Personal Growth, Satisfaction, and Achievement. All knitters, men and women, expressed personal satisfaction about their knitting. Not only were they

Figure 8.2 Family and Work Interactions – Two Sample Days
Knitter 4

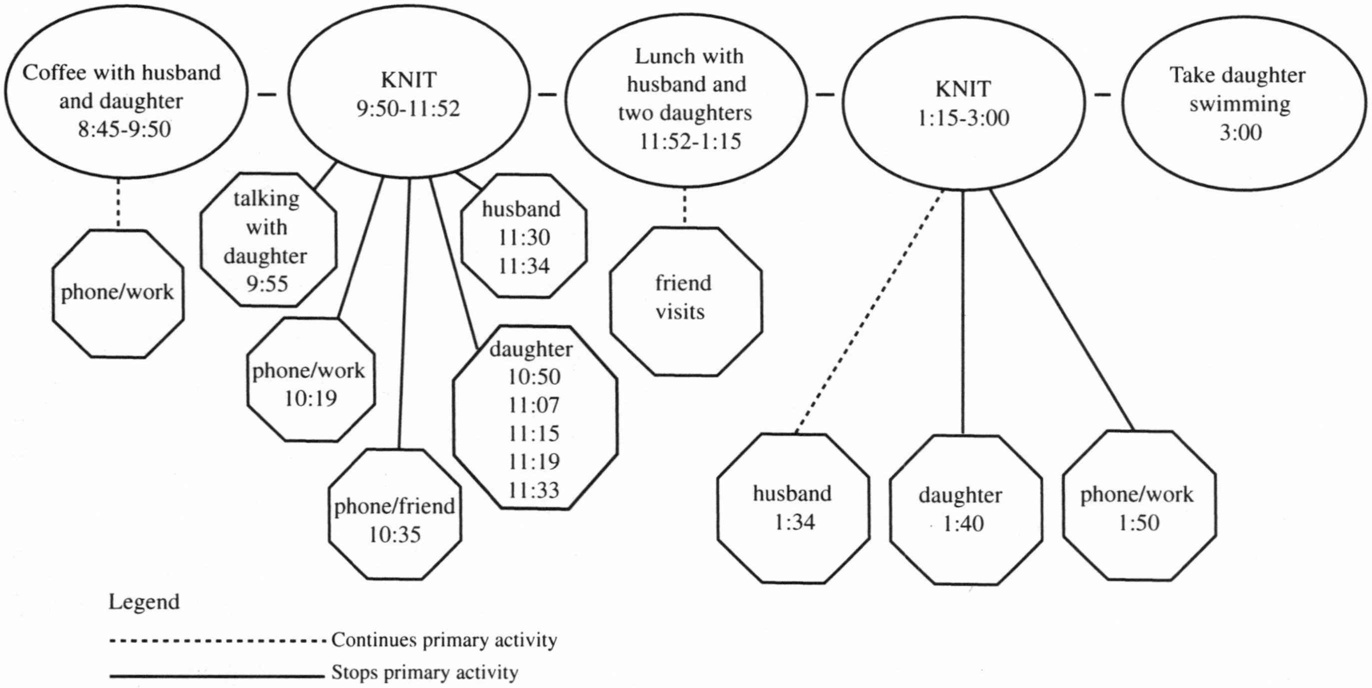

Take daughter swimming
3:00

KNIT
1:15-3:00

phone/work
1:50

daughter
1:40

husband
1:34

Lunch with husband and two daughters
11:52-1:15

friend visits

KNIT
9:50-11:52

husband
11:30
11:34

daughter
10:50
11:07
11:15
11:19
11:33

phone/friend
10:35

phone/work
10:19

talking with daughter
9:55

Coffee with husband and daughter
8:45-9:50

phone/work

Legend

-------- Continues primary activity

———— Stops primary activity

204

Figure 8.2 (continued)
Knitter 5

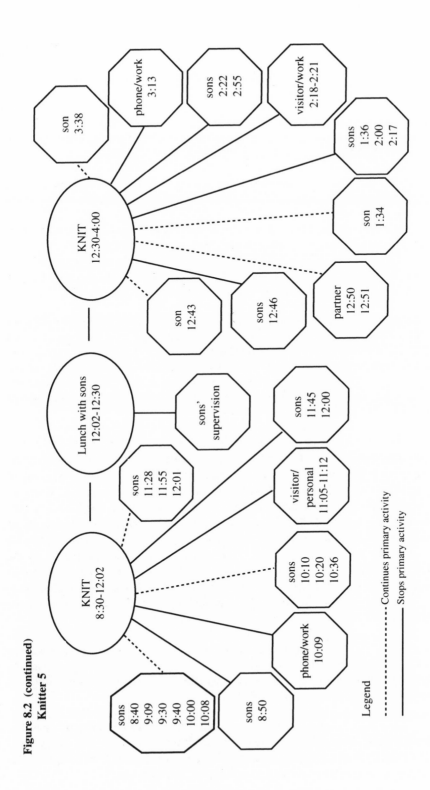

Legend

.... Continues primary activity

————— Stops primary activity

205

making money, but they were also proud of the resulting garment as a design and as a high-quality product.

I like to make my own designs. I just make them up in my head. I think this is a knack I happen to have. I just love to knit. That's it. I just love it. To use my machines. I think I'm contented knitting everything. (1)

In production, you don't make the whole product. In knitting you do, so you can control the quality. (6 and 7)

Knitters expressed their connection to their work in positive terms, such as self-motivation, reliability, and constant learning of new things.

Yeah, it's just a good job. You know, you're your own boss and you do what you want to and, but yet you've got an income coming in all the time. (1)

I'd worked in factories and that was kind of, factories are really boring. It's the same thing over and over again which is basically the same thing here. But, somehow it's different when you do it in your own home than if you go in and punch a clock. You are so independent, make your own schedule. At the same time you have to be reliable. They aren't going to keep on using you if your work isn't up to par and they want to be able to know they can count on you for "X" amount of things done during the course of a week. (3)

Perhaps because of the small initial investment and the culture of home-knitting, there seemed to be potential for growth and change, a type of career ladder, as knitters worked at their trade through the years. One knitter (3) knitted part of the time and then coordinated the work of other knitters for the manufacturers who purchased the home-knitted sweaters. Another (4) tested the first patterns before the rest of the knitters received knitting instructions and helped set the knitting price on the basis of completion time. And two became dealers for knitting machines (2 and 3) to get wholesale prices for their own machines and to help their husbands to get into machine repair and their fellow knitters to have a local repair alternative. These changes in their home-based employment responsibilities gave rise to an intrinsic independence that they did not have before.

Well, we're kind of building towards different things. We've just started a dealership which will open up another thing. I'm at the point where I'd like to get away from the knitting a little bit and teach girls, let them take over some of my responsibilities instead of doing quite so much knitting. (3)

Economic Benefits and Problems. All knitters reaped economic benefits from knitting. They felt they were getting a fair wage for their work. They indicated that knitting gave them economic freedom, whether for extra things for the family, a personal line of credit, or a home of their own.

Something that made me feel like I was contributing, you know, a little something here, you know, for income and stuff. 'Cause I have my own money now and nobody can tell me "no" now! Things that I've always wanted [vacations and trips to see family and a water bed]. (5)

The knitters were responsible for their mistakes but felt that was the right way to do business and it did not take long to correct the mistakes. Knitters varied in the ways they took orders, but had a choice in what they knitted. They could choose to complete orders every week or on a different schedule. They could choose to knit a particular pattern or not.

And if I don't like them, I don't make 'em. I just say, you know, I'm not making that sweater. (4)

Knitters were aware of the differences among potential work contracts and were somewhat perplexed by the fuss about minimum wage and protection of their "rights." (The interviews were conducted in 1985 after the lawsuit and before the final ruling that certification of employers would allow home-knitters the right to work.)

I can make more here than any place I worked. Best paying job I had in Vermont was $8.40 an hour as a mechanic and I had to travel. We can make that right here and more here. (3's husband)

[The Labor Department representative is] telling me that I have to claim my sewers' time in my sweaters and I say why? It doesn't make sense, actually it's written off as an expense. He finally agreed. (4)

Knitters either sought orders from a number of organizations and firms or worked consistently with only a few firms. The price per sweater or hat varied according to the organization or firm as well as the difficulty of the design and the yarn. When knitters sold directly to consumers, they could charge full retail value.

Some knitters used their skill for family and gift giving, birthday and Christmas presents. One knitter knitted hats and sweaters as school and community contributions and for kids to sell for college savings. These in-kind contributions to the family economy were another example of the uncounted benefits of home-based employment. On the other hand, another knitter said that she never knitted for the family.

One knitter, especially with the added responsibilities of teaching and machine repair, saw the economic benefit of selling machines as a trade-off.

There's not much profit in selling a machine. And once you sell it, then you have to give them lessons and you've got to keep their machine repaired, and I don't really like it. But it's one way to be able to get my own machines and accessories and whatever I need at wholesale prices. (2)

Even so, the husband of this knitter became involved with knitting and machine sales and repair. One other husband of these knitters (3), in addition to the man interviewed as part of a couple, was also involved in knitting and machine sales. As is true in many home-based employment situations, the proximity of the work to the family makes family members more aware and, perhaps, directly involved in the work.

Economic disadvantages included the seasonal nature of the work, paying of one's own taxes, lack of health and unemployment benefits, and upkeep and expense of machines. Knitting orders were seasonal, as most were made in the summer and fall. Sometimes knitters had to turn down orders because of the short order time or other orders. Knitters indicated that they were trying to work with some of their repeat customers to get orders earlier or in two or three stages, rather than all at one time exactly when the customers needed the hats and sweaters. Others were working to develop products that would be desired in the off season.

We're also trying to develop something that we can sell in the summer. We'll have a more consistent paycheck coming in every week, instead of having a consistent pay-check for the last six months of the year. (7)

The paperwork for the Labor Department and tax records took several hours per week for each knitter. But most did not consider this a burden. Paperwork seemed to be a symbol of independence and self worth.

I keep my own paper work. I have my own, ah, accountant that does my taxes for me. You know, I, I work for myself. We pay taxes quarterly. We're set up like a business. I have a tax number and I pay my taxes quarterly. Every legal deduction I can take out of my taxes, I'm gonna do it. (7)

I got my health insurance, and I got my own retirement plan set up and everything. Being self employed, I pay my estimated income tax, social security and everything. Long as I'm working for myself, I just set everything right up like that so I've got everything. (1)

GENDER IMPLICATIONS

Home-based employment and household production are forever interwoven for women. The family reality is that women with home-based employment work two jobs in the home, one paid and one unpaid but assumed. The knitters in this study have made a conscious choice to do paid-work in the home, often in order to accomplish their two jobs. Vermont knitters were predominantly women, though spouses and partners sometimes became involved in knitting or machine sales and repair. The knitters indicated some gender biases to their employment—knitting—and to the belief that knitting is women's work. These expressions of bias could be reflections of societal beliefs or internalized values of the individuals. In either case, the comments support the literature on work force segregation and the feminist conceptual approach to home-based employment presented earlier (Heck et al., 1995; Prügl & Boris, 1996). The literature suggests that the employment of women and men in the home differs in type and importance (Gringeri, 1996; Loker & Scannell, 1992). Men should make a living wage for their families; women should complete household responsibilities first, and, if there is time, work based in the home close to their household chores (such as knitting) can be conducted for pay. The interviewed female knitters in this study and the one man also completed household chores, including child care. Exploration of home-based employment within this context should continue in order to describe more fully the differences for women and men, both perceptual and behavioral, based on societal expectations of gender.

The knitters in this study met their needs and were satisfied, growing personally and managing their families through their home-based employment and its propinquous activities. They are in control of both the family and employment spheres of their lives, making more than a minimum hourly wage and feeling positive about their family roles. Their story is not only about increasing their household income. It is about constructing their lives around what is important to them—meeting their families' needs and growing in their multiple family and paid and unpaid work roles. The individual stories presented by the knitters indicate the importance of their family lives and their abilities to strengthen the bonds among family members by working for pay in the home while earning enough to be financially independent. The knitters feel confident and feel fulfilled by their knitting. They express, some with delight, the positive effects that knitting has on their self-esteem and economic lives. Future research should focus on the emotional benefits of home-based employment as well as the economic. Enhanced connections with family, positive self-esteem, and control over one's life are concepts identified in this study that are appropriate for further study.

However, the question proposed by Boris (1987) is still valid: although the choice of home-based employment is good for individual workers, is home-based employment good for all home-workers? An additional question is whether the trade-off to the individual worker is greater in both economic and personal sacrifices than it should be.

This study was the result of a public policy debate on home-based employment with a focus on protective legislation for workers employed by someone to produce knit or sewn products at home. Knitters argued that they were independent contractors of labor rather than employees. Christensen (1988) broadened the debate by suggesting that an independent contractor designation was determined by whether one's work is voluntary or involuntary. She suggested that an involuntary designation means that there are few or no other choices of employment. But is this the right definition? Perhaps a more appropriate definition, at least for home-knitters, is whether they "feel" in control of their work. The knitters in this study feel in control of their work, are being paid more than minimum wage for their work, and gain flexibility and independence in their lives by working at home.

Should home-knitters and others with home-based employment be protected or left to their own responsible choices? It seems that there are arguments for both. On the one hand, home-based employment perpetuates the segregation that exists in the out of the home labor force. Women in home-based employment earn less, are more likely to work in female-dominated job types, adjust their time around family responsibilities, and spend less time on income generation than men in home-based employment (Heck et al., 1995). Industrial home-work, less idyllic than that examined here, exists in apparel production and other assembly operations. Protective legislation and regulatory services for child labor, minimum wage violations, and other unfair labor practices are still necessary. Conversely, home-based employment can be a deliberate choice and can help some women achieve an independence and self-confidence not available to them in the out-of-the home labor force because of educational level, job availability, health care concerns, transportation, family responsibilities, self-confidence, or skill challenge.

More research is necessary on the invisibility of the work force—in this case, both the predominantly female knitters and the sewers they hire as well as the families that support them in economically uncalculated ways. If invisibility indicates "under the table" pay for work that is illegal, changes are needed. But invisibility could indicate a place on the continuum from economic livelihood to emotional life for these workers different from that of workers who work away from home and even others in home-based employment. Those who choose more invisible work, often women, might value a sound emotional life more than a grand economic livelihood that receives recognition outside of their immediate family and community. Research and dialogue can address the role public policy can play to support healthy home-based employment environments for both women and men without hindering individuals and families from constructing their particular balance between paid-work and family.

The knitters won the right to work at home. But their stories are not complete. They can continue to knit at home, give it up for a job out-of-the home, or opt for retirement. Whatever the future brings, the time that these knitters spent working at home for pay was a good choice for them. They were doing something that gave them time with their families, satisfaction in creativity and accomplishment, and economic independence. They constructed a family and employment life-style that matched their values and needs. Just as others continually adjust their work and family priorities throughout the life cycle, so will these knitters adjust theirs.

Although this study focused on only one type of home-based employment, it begins to describe the qualitative advantages that could be present in all home-based employment types. Satisfaction in home-based employment might be the result of a complex mix of fulfillment from emotional and economic satisfaction and work and family roles as the model of Owen et al. (1992) suggests. The study reported here places home-based employment in the appropriate context, the home, and begins to conceptualize the family "interruptions" of home-based employment as propinquous production, a positive by-product of family interactions and home-based employment that is especially important to families. Future research can build on the results of this study, addressing the economic and emotional benefits of home-based employment in the context of women's family roles and the interconnected home-based employment, household production, and propinquous production. Studying the economic benefits of home-based employment paints only part of the picture for women and the families of home-workers.

NOTE

This research was funded by the Vermont Agricultural Experiment Station. Special thanks to Mary Pierce, for her assistance in gathering data, and Rebecca Saxton, for her transcription of the audio tapes. .

REFERENCES

Americans bring work home for pay. (1998, March 9). *Ithaca Journal*, p.1.

Beutler, I., & Owen, A. J. (1980). A home production activity model. *Home Economics Research Journal, 9*, 16–26.

Boris, E. (1985). Regulating industrial homework: The triumph of "Sacred Motherhood." *The Journal of American History, 71*, 645–763.

Boris, E. (1987). Homework and women's rights: The case of the Vermont knitters, 1980–1985. *Signs, 13*, 98–120.

Boris, E. (1996). Sexual divisions, gender constructions: The historical meaning of homework in Western Europe and the United States. In E. Boris & E. Prügl (Eds.), *Homeworkers in global perspective: Invisible no more* (pp. 19–37). New York: Routledge.

Boris, E., & Prügl, E. (Eds.). (1996). *Homeworkers in global perspective: Invisible no more.* New York: Routledge.

Christensen, K. E. (Ed.). (1988). *The new era of home-based work: Directions and policies.* Boulder, CO: Westview Press.

Daneshvary, R. (1993). Homework in apparel-related industries. *Journal of Home Economics, 85*(1), 57–63.

Gringeri, C. E. (1990, May 17–18). The nuts and bolts of subsidized development; industrial homeworkers in the heartland. In *Proceedings of the National Rural Studies Committee* (pp. 81–88). Cedar Falls, IA: Western Rural Development Center.

Gringeri, C. E. (1996). Making Cadillacs and Buicks for General Motors. In E. Boris & E. Prügl (Eds.), *Homeworkers in global perspective: Invisible no more* (pp. 179–201). New York: Routledge.

Hartmann, H. (1976). Capitalism, patriarchy, and job segregation by sex. *Signs, 1* (3, Suppl. part 2), 137–169.

Hayghe, H. V., & Bianchi, S. M. (1994, June). Married mothers' work patterns: The job-family compromise. *Monthly Labor Review*, 24–30.

Heck, R. K. Z., Owen, A. J., & Rowe, B. R. (Eds.). (1995). *Home-based employment and family life.* Westport, CT: Auburn House.

Loker, S., & Scannell, E. (1992). Characteristics and practices of home-based workers. *Journal of Family and Economic Issues, 13,* 173–186.

Owen, A. J., Carsky, M. L, & Dolan, E. M. (1992). Home-based employment: Historical and current considerations. *Journal of Family and Economic Issues, 13,* 121–138.

Pratt, J. H. (1993). *Myths and realities of working at home: Characteristics of home-based business owners and telecommuters.* (Research Summary No. 134). Washington, DC: United States Small Business Administration.

Prügl, E., & Boris, E. (1996). Introduction. In E. Boris & E. Prügl (Eds.), *Homeworkers in global perspective: Invisible no more* (pp. 3–17). New York: Routledge.

Shank, S. (1988, March). Women's link to labor market grows stronger. *Monthly Labor Review,* 3–8.

U.S. Bureau of the Census. (1997). *Statistical abstract of the United States* (117th ed). Washington, DC: U.S. Government Printing Office.

Index

About the Contributors

D. JILL AMYOT is a Client Services Manager with the Workers Compensation Board of British Columbia. Her thesis research for her M.Sc. degree in Family Studies from The University of Manitoba provides the basis for the chapter in this book "Home-Based Employment and Work-Family Conflict: A Canadian Study." Ms. Amyot has held a variety of positions with government agencies and private firms including the Manitoba Workers Compensation Board and Manitoba Department of Labour and Manpower.

JEANETTE ARBUTHNOT is an Assistant Professor and Coordinator of the Apparel Merchandising program in the Department of Human Environments at Utah State University. Her research interests include entrepreneurship, women-owned businesses, gender-related issues in the workplace, and domestic and international retailing issues. Her work is published in the *Journal of Small Business Management, Journal of Business Ethics, Clothing and Textiles Research Journal, Utah Family Journal*, and *Utah Journal of Research in Home Economies* as well as *Specialty Store Services*, an industry publication. Ms. Arbuthnot has served as a reviewer for *Clothing and Textiles Research Journal* and *Themis: Journal of Theory in Home Economics* and for various publishers including Delmar, Macmillan, and Fairchild.

SHARON M. DANES is a Professor and Family Economist in the Department of Family Social Science at the University of Minnesota. Her research interests lie at the intersection of social and economic decision making in families; in family businesses this means her focus is the issues that occur in the overlap of the family and business systems. Ms. Danes has published in the *Journal of Family and Economic Issues, Journal of Comparative Family Studies, Journal of Marriage and the Family, Family and Consumer Sciences Research Journal,*

Family Business Review, Financial Counseling and Planning, Social Indicators, Human Services in the Rural Environment, Family Perspective, and *Journal of Consumer Affairs.* She currently is on the editorial board of the *Journal of Family and Economic Issues.*

KAREN A. DUNCAN is Assistant Professor in the Department of Family Studies, Faculty of Human Ecology, at The University of Manitoba. Her research interests include the value of time, time in household work, balancing of work and family, and the management of families engaged in family businesses. Ms. Duncan has published in the *Canadian Home Economics Journal, Journal of Family and Economic Issues, Journal of Consumer Studies and Home Economics, Family Business Review,* and *Housing and Society.* She serves on the overseas advisory board of the *Journal of Consumer Studies and Home Economics* and on the boards of directors of the American Council on Consumer Interests and the Community Financial Counselling Services, Winnipeg.

KAREN P. GOEBEL is a Professor and Extension Specialist in Family and Consumer Economics at the University of Wisconsin–Madison. Her past research has examined time use patterns of Wisconsin families; her current research examines family management of family-owned businesses. She completed her doctorate in family ecology at Michigan State University. Ms. Goebel has published in *The Consumer Interests Annual, Family Economics and Resource Management Biennial, The Journal of Home Economics, Home Economics Research Journal, Proceedings of Western Region Home Management and Family Economics Educators, Journal of Consumer Studies and Home Economics, Extension Review, ACCI Proceedings, National Agricultural Outlook Proceedings,* and *WI International Year of the Family Proceedings.* Ms. Goebel has served on the policy board of the *Journal of Consumer Research* and served on the editorial board of *Journal of Extension,* and as reviewer for *Lifestyles: Family and Economic Issues, Family Relations, Advancing the Consumer Interest,* and *Journal of Consumer Affairs.* She is past President of the Wisconsin Home Economics Association and past national President of the American Council on Consumer Interests and recipient of their Distinguished Fellow Award.

DEBORAH C. HAYNES is an Assistant Professor in the Department of Health and Human Development at Montana State University. Her research interests are in work and family issues, especially child-care. Ms. Haynes has published in the *Journal of Family and Consumer Sciences* and the *Journal of Small Business Management* and has presented papers at the American Council on Consumer Interests annual meeting as well as at the annual meeting of the American Association of Family and Consumer Sciences. Ms. Haynes was employed in a large business and was involved in owning and managing a small business for over ten years before working in academia.

GEORGE W. HAYNES is an Assistant Professor in the Department of Health and Human Development at Montana State University. He has been actively involved in small business finance and substance abuse treatment demand issues. The small business finance research track has been supported by competitive grants from the Small Business Administration and the United States Department of Agriculture's National Research Competitive Grants Program to study several debt structure issues, the intermingling of family and business financial resources, and the impact of public support programs on Native American business development. Mr. Haynes has recently published articles in *Small Business Economics, Journal of Small Business Management, Economic Development Quarterly*, and *Family Business Review.*

RAMONA K. Z. HECK is Professor and the J. Thomas Clark Fellow of Entrepreneurship and Personal Enterprise at Cornell University. She leads the Family Business Research Institute, involving a multidisciplinary group of faculty, positioned on the Cornell University campus as a major institute within the Bronfenbrenner Life Course Center. Ms. Heck conducts research related to family businesses and the owning family's internal social and economic dynamics, the effects of the family on the family business viability over time, and gender issues within family firms. She has published numerous articles on family management and decision making theory and public and private policy related to families and has recently edited two books, *Home-Based Employment and Family Life* and *The Entrepreneurial Family.*

CHARLES B. HENNON is Professor and Associate Director of the Family and Child Studies Center at Miami University. His research interest includes rural families as well as family-centric policy and family-centered practices. Mr. Hennon has published over fifty articles and book chapters and is co-editor of *Diversity in Families: A Global Perspective* (Wadsworth, forthcoming); *Lifestyles of the Elderly: Diversity in Relationships, Health, and Caregiving* (Human Sciences); and *Families in Rural America: Stress, Adaptation and Revitalization* (National Council on Family Relations). He is co-author of *Family supportive policy practice: International implications* (Columbia University Press) and is the founding editor of the *Journal of Family and Economic Issues.*

HOLLY HUNTS is Assistant Professor at Montana State University. Her research interests are in the balance of work and family issues, particularly how families cope with young children. Ms. Hunts has published in the *Journal of Family and Economic Issues* and the *Family Business Review.* She has given several national presentations on the topic of child-care and employment issues and serves as an ad hoc reviewer for the *Journal of Family and Economic Issues.*

CYNTHIA R. JASPER is Professor and Chair of the Department of Consumer Science at the University of Wisconsin–Madison. Her research interests include consumer behavior issues as applied to retailing and family businesses. Ms.

Jasper has published in *Journal of Consumer Affairs, Journal of Direct Marketing, Journal of Advertising Research, Clothing and Textiles Research Journal, Journal of Small Business Management, Psychology and Marketing,* and *Journal of the Community Development Society.*

SUZANNE LOKER is Professor in the Department of Textiles and Apparel at Cornell University. Her research interests are home-based employment and apparel industry studies, including management of technology in apparel manufacturing, work skills standards, and privatization and market development in the Czech apparel industry. Ms. Loker has published in the *Clothing and Textiles Research Journal, Home Economics Research Journal, The Journal of Home Economics, International Marketing Review, Journal of Retailing and Consumer Sciences,* and *Journal of Family and Economic Issues.* She co-authored two chapters in the book *Home-Based Employment and Family Life* (Heck, Owen, & Rowe, 1995) and co-edited the monograph *Softgoods to the World* (Loker, Good, & Huddleston, 1998). She currently serves as Associate Editor for the *Clothing and Textiles Research Journal* for business, industry, and international research.

ROSEMARY S. L. MILLS is Associate Professor of Family Studies at the University of Manitoba. Her research interests include parenting and its consequences for the social and emotional adjustment of children. Ms. Mills is currently investigating links between hurtful communication in the family and adjustment problems in children. She co-edited the book *Developmental Psychology of Personal Relationships* (Mills & Duck, 1999).

BARBARA R. ROWE is Associate Professor and Extension Specialist in the Department of Consumer Sciences and Retailing at Purdue University. Her current research interests include the interaction between employment and family, especially in minority and women-owned family businesses; the economics of divorce; evaluation of child support guideline legislation; and the economic well-being of women and children. Ms. Rowe's published work has appeared in numerous texts and journals, including *Family Business Review, Willamette Law Review Journal of Contemporary Law, Journal of Divorce & Remarriage, Conciliation Courts Review,* and *The Encyclopedia of Marriage and Family.* She is co-editor of the book *Home-Based Employment and Family Life,* published by Auburn House (1995), and is co-editor of the *Journal of Family and Economic Issues.*

KATHRYN STAFFORD is Associate Professor in the Department of Consumer and Textile Sciences at The Ohio State University. Her current research work includes such topics as divorce settlements, at-home income generation, and management practices of families engaged in home-based employment.

ELIZABETH S. TRENT is Extension Associate Professor in the Department of Community Development and Applied Economics at the University of Vermont. She has written numerous Extension publications on financial management for limited resource and divorced families. Ms. Scannell's research is published in numerous journals and proceedings. Currently she is working on research related to women entrepreneurs, gender and industry affiliations, and prevalence of family owned businesses.

ROSEMARY WALKER is a Professor in the Department of Family and Child Ecology at Michigan State University. Her research interests include home-based businesses and family businesses, particularly the gender effects on employment and economic outcomes. Ms. Walker has published in *Family Business Review, Journal of Family and Economic Issues, Journal of Consumer Affairs*, and *Journal of Home Economics*. She co-authored two chapters in the edited book *Home-Based Employment and Family Life* (Heck, Owen, & Rowe, 1995).